MISSION
IN
PALESTINE
1948-1952

Mission

in

Palestine
1948-1952

by

PABLO DE AZCÁRATE

THE MIDDLE EAST INSTITUTE
Washington, D. C.
1966

Publisher's Preface

It is a pleasure for the Middle East Institute to be the publisher of the work of Dr. Pablo de Azcárate, distinguished diplomat and international civil servant, on a significant, Middle Eastern, portion of his career. The subject with which he has to deal here, the Arab-Israeli dispute in general and the work of the United Nations Palestine Conciliation Commission in particular, is one of great and continuing controversy. Dr. de Azcárate, as one of the principals during an important period of this controversy, has given both objective facts and his own opinions fully and frankly. This Institute, which takes no stand on the issues, does not necessarily share the opinions, but finds it a rewarding obligation to help to make an important record available to the reading public.

Dr. de Azcárate particularly wishes to thank Miss Teener Hall, the translator of the body of the work, and Mr. William Hovey, the translator of the Epilogue. The text was written in Spanish.

The Institute is also grateful to the Carnegie Endowment for International Peace for assistance in making the publication possible.

Contents

CHAPTER I

Partition: The Palestine Commission and its "Advance Group"

THE FIRST WORLD WAR unleashed in the Middle East two powerful political forces whose inevitable clash is taking place before our eyes under that convenient label "Palestine question." On the one hand, Zionism, doubly stimulated by its messianic spirit and its considerable financial resources, was already openly on the march with banners unfurled towards what constituted its very *raison d'être*—the creation of a Jewish state in Palestine. On the other, Arab nationalism—violent, incoherent, a perpetual prey to internal strife, born or reborn of the ruins of the Ottoman Empire—was launching itself with equal ardor and enthusiasm towards the liberation of all the Arab peoples and the establishment in all their lands of political régimes directed and controlled by Arabs. The clash between these two forces was inevitable, due to a circumstance which has not always received the attention it deserves and that is, that Palestine, for the purpose of determining the concrete and immediate responsibilities of our generation, must be regarded as an Arab country. Neither the wise and erudite arguments of the rabbis concerning the reign of David in Palestine three thousand years ago, nor the controversy surrounding the correspondence between Sharīf Ḥusayn, Amīr of Mecca, and British diplomatists and agents, as to whether Palestine was, or was not, excluded from the territories where the right of the Arabs to establish sovereign states was recognized, have amounted or can amount to much in the face of the basic, fundamental and indestructible fact that from the time of Muḥammad the population of Palestine has been Arabized and the Arabs cannot reasonably be expected to stop thinking of it as an Arab country. Thus occurred what was bound to occur: Zionism, in its efforts to further the realization of its ideal, clashed with Arab nationalism in its task of establishing in Palestine a political régime which, in conformity with the Arab ideal, would be directed and controlled by its Arab population.

1

Such is, so to speak, the skeleton of the so-called "Palestine question"; and it would be a good thing if moralists refrained from interfering with their hard and fast distinctions and their mania for dealing out rewards and punishments. There is nothing more senseless than to speak of good or evil, of just or unjust, of lawful or unlawful, when dealing with political trends like Zionism or Arab nationalism with their deep human and historical roots. Considered in themselves, both the aspiration of the Jews to see a Jewish state established in Palestine and the reluctance of the Arabs to see that Jewish state established in what they rightly regard as an Arab country, are worthy of respect. This is what gives the Palestine question that dramatic tone and that appearance of "insolubility," according to the rigid standards that separate the just from the unjust. The fact is that it is not, nor can it be a question of saying that the Jews are right and the Arabs are wrong, or that the Arabs are right and the Jews are wrong. Faced with a situation like that created by an historical contradiction of this nature, the only possible and reasonable thing to do is to help both sides to surmount with the least possible damage the difficult and painful crisis provoked by the clash of their respective ideals, until time, combined with good advice, friendly pressure and, if the circumstances warrant it, threats and even sanctions have opened the road to an honorable and constructive compromise in which both would find reasonable satisfaction for their aspirations.

This should have been the historical sense and the supreme aim of the mandate over Palestine conferred on Great Britain by the Great Powers at the end of the First World War. But if the British authorities and those elements in the League of Nations whose business it was to see that the mandate was properly carried out understood it in this sense, it must be admitted that the practical means employed were notoriously inadequate. The mission of helping two great peoples rich in ancient traditions, inspired almost to frenzy by their anxiety to see the realization of their respective and contradictory ideals, was entrusted by the British government to the Colonial Office—a department which was admirably suited and trained to ensure the domination of the white race over primitive peoples through the old and well-tried maxim of "divide and rule." Unfortunately, the Arabs and Jews were very far from being primitive peoples, and what was required in Palestine was a maxim diametrically opposed to the panacea employed by the British Colonial Office, and indeed by all colonial offices everywhere, for the solution of all their difficulties. It is not strange, therefore, that the British mandate failed in the task of finding a compromise between the Zionist ideal of the Jews and the nationalist ideal of the Arabs, which would enable a political régime to be established in Palestine such as would make peaceful coexistence possible.

However, as everything in life is relative and there is no success without its drawbacks and no failure without its advantages, the failure of the British Colonial Office had at least the advantage that it proved beyond a doubt that territorial division was the only foundation on which it would be possible to construct a political régime enabling Arabs and Jews to live together peaceably in Palestine. The idea of partitioning Palestine had already been the subject of prolonged and exhaustive consideration by the British during the mandate. One of the commissions sent out by the British government to study the question on the spot and to make recommendations, the Peel Commission of 1937, included in its report a plan of partition because it considered that partition was the only effective method of attacking the root of the difficulty. The following year another commission, this time under the chairmanship of Sir John Woodhead, was sent to Palestine in order to study and submit to the government concrete recommendations for the application of the plan of partition embodied in the report of the Peel Commission. For reasons which need not be discussed here, the British government did not think fit to adopt the reports of these Commissions and the policy therein recommended, and the idea of partition remained in abeyance until, in 1947, the Special Palestine Committee set up by the United Nations on inheriting the British mandate, revived it as the basic and fundamental principle of its majority report—the report which served as the basis for the resolution adopted by the Assembly of the United Nations on November 29, 1947, when it was decided that Palestine should be divided into two zones, each of which should serve as the territorial seat, respectively, of an Arab state and a Jewish state.

*   *   *   *

The plan for the partition of Palestine recommended by the majority of the Special Committee (UNSCOP) can be summarized under the three following headings: the creation of two independent states; the establishment of an international régime for the zone of Jerusalem; economic union among the three entities. As a result of a stormy and confused debate, followed by a vote which the Arab states and their "anti-partitionist" adherents have always stigmatized as irregular, if not actually invalid, this partition plan was incorporated in the resolution adopted by the Assembly on November 29, 1947.

From that time, the partition of Palestine was virtually accomplished and the road left clear for the establishment of a Jewish state in Palestine. Right from the outset, the Arab states showed an unyielding opposition: first, during the discussion in the Assembly, with arguments; later, in Palestine, with armed force. But they lost both battles—the battle of arguments and the battle between the armed forces. The idea of the partition of Palestine was already too deeply ingrained in the international conscience for it to be destroyed either by good polemicists or by good generals; and besides, the Arabs had neither the one nor the other. In the interests of truth I must add that, while polemicists and generals floundered in the insuperable difficulties of their struggle against partition, eminent and responsible Arab personalities recognized in private that partition was already an accomplished fact and concentrated their criticisms not so much on partition itself as on the concrete modalities of the plan of partition established by the resolution of November 29.

In this field, the struggle against partition offered far fewer difficulties. The truth is that the plan of partition of November 29 was full of defects: some could and should have been foreseen by its authors; others were of the kind which are clearly labelled *"ex post facto,"* but which no one could have foreseen. As if this were not enough, the discussion in the Assembly went on, as I have said, in a deplorable atmosphere of passion, frivolity and confusion, crowned by a vote which the Arabs still regard as irregular, if not null and void. It is difficult to say how far all these unfortunate circumstances helped to aggravate a crisis which was already delicate and dangerous. In any case, it is clear that the 1947 Assembly did not succeed in imparting to its examination of the Palestine question the elevation, serenity and repose which were indispensable if the United Nations were to shoulder with unimpeachable moral authority the heavy responsibilities devolving upon them as a result of accepting the inheritance of the British mandate.

*　　*　　*　　*

However, if the plan of partition of November 29 was defective, and if its adoption by the Assembly took place in conditions that were far from ideal, what barred the last hope of seeing it executed was the Palestine Commission, the organ specially created by the Assembly to prepare and initiate its implementation. With this Commission, my personal participation in the Palestine question began. When in December 1947 this ill-fated Commission was preparing to embark on its task, the Secretary General of the United Nations wired me in Mexico, where I was staying for a time with my elder brother, asking me if I would accept a post in the Commission's secretariat. I accepted in principle; and when I passed through New York on my return journey to Europe and in London, a few days later, everything was decided and arranged during a conversation I had with Mr. Lie. I was appointed assistant Principal Secretary of the Commission (Ralph Bunche was the Principal Secretary) and it was proposed to send me immediately to Jerusalem at the head of a group of experts whose function it was to arrange on the spot the transfer of powers to the Commission at the expiry of the British mandate, already fixed for May 15, 1948.

On February 4, I left London to take over my new functions at Lake Success. This was my first flight over the Atlantic and the "take-off" from Shannon on a night of wind and rain was not exactly an auspicious initiation. After a bumpy and uncomfortable flight, I arrived at New York on the afternoon of the following day in somewhat poor physical condition, but with excellent morale and ready to embark on my new mission with the greatest enthusiasm. To be quite candid, this early enthusiasm did not last long. The work of the Commission and its Secretariat seemed to me disorganized, incoherent and without team spirit, with the possible exception of Bunche and the small group of his immediate personal collaborators. I very soon realized that I was going to find myself pushed into acting as a kind of *franc-tireur,* isolated from the Principal Secretary and the Secretariat and in direct relations with the members of the Commission, especially the three Spanish-speaking members.[1] But this was by no means pleasing to me, first, for reasons of principle and secondly, because I was not particularly attracted by the thought of cultivating personal relations either with the three persons in question or with the Chairman of the Commission, Mr. Liscinski, my former colleague in the Secretariat of the League of Nations, whom I had met again in London during the war as Secretary of the Czechoslovak Legation.

1. The Commission was composed of a Czechoslovak (Chairman), a Bolivian, a Dane, a Filipino and a Panamanian.

This equivocal situation lasted about three weeks; but just as its continuation was beginning to worry me seriously, the clouds lifted with the decision to put into practice the project which the Secretary General had discussed with me on the occasion of my appointment—the creation and immediate dispatch to Jerusalem of what was called the "advance group," formed, under my leadership, of a soldier (Colonel Roscher Lund of the Norwegian army), an economist (Professor Ghosh of India), a political and legal adviser (Mr. Stavropoulos, Greek member of the Secretariat's Legal Department) and two secretaries, Miss Audrey Owen (Australia) and Mrs. Tobin (United Kingdom). The preparations for the constitution of the group, its terms of reference and the practical arrangements for its arrival, installation and conditions of work in Jerusalem were difficult and laborious. Everything had to be done in agreement with the British authorities, whose chief preoccupation lay in impeding by every possible method the presence in Palestine of anybody or anything remotely connected with the United Nations, and particularly with the Palestine Commission, which the two factions rightly regarded as the author of the partition plan and the organ specially responsible for putting it into practice. Not without reason did the British authorities think that the arrival in Palestine of elements of the United Nations in connection with the partition plan would inevitably exacerbate the irritation of the Arabs and delight the Jews, thus increasing the almost insuperable difficulties they already had to contend with in maintaining, during the last months of the mandate, the appearance of a public order which was daily becoming more precarious and costly.

This British opposition won an easy success in preventing the Commission from going to Palestine; and I use the word "easy" advisedly, because in spite of their declarations about the convenience of the Commission functioning in or near Palestine, most of its members were firmly resolved not to stir from New York. But the British were not so successful in preventing the departure of the "advance group," having to content themselves with making them the object, even before they left New York, of a policy of regular intimidation. The picture that some members of the permanent British delegation to the United Nations painted for me, during our conversations, of what was awaiting us in Palestine was truly somber and alarming. And though they could not refuse to accept full responsibility for our personal safety, they insisted that, for our part, we should undertake to respect and observe in the strictest and most scrupulous manner whatever regulations the British authorities in Palestine thought fit to adopt in relation to our residence and, above all, our movements. We were not slow in realizing, as soon as we set foot in Palestine, that the warnings uttered in New York had not been intended merely to make our flesh creep, but were going to have a very real and positive significance in Jerusalem.

*   *   *   *

On February 22 the "advance group" left New York. We were seen off at the airport with all the honors, including the presence of Mr. Cordier. My ignorance of that complicated machine, the Secretariat of the United Nations, did not allow me to appreciate at its full value the presence of the Executive Assistant to the Secretary General, for whom my admiration steadily grew during the four years of my service at the United Nations. With a patience and an ability that are far from common, Mr. Cordier introduced into the functioning of the Secretariat a minimum of regularity, to which no one who knows the inner working of the administration of the United Nations could fail to pay tribute. On the following day we arrived in London, where we spent two days which I devoted to conversations at the Colonial Office and the Foreign Office—conversations in which my interlocutors sounded the same gloomy and sinister note as their colleagues in New York. I also saw Sir Stafford Cripps, with whom I had been on terms of friendship ever since my embassy in London, and who gave me a letter of introduction to Sir Alan Cunningham, then British High Commissioner in Palestine.

After two days' delay, at the last moment on March 2, with the first light of dawn, we left Cointrin airport at Geneva and landed at Lydda at three o'clock in the afternoon. This was my first experience of this itinerary which, in the four years that followed, was to become, with slight variations, one of the most familiar routes for me: flight over the Alps and northern Italy; over the Adriatic and various Greek islands; finally across the eastern Mediterranean until the coast of Palestine appeared on the horizon, this time in the latitude of Tel Aviv.

At Lydda we were surprised to find no one waiting to meet the airplane and no special arrangements for seeing us through the customs and inspecting our passports, which would have been natural and almost obligatory seeing that our group represented an official mission of the United Nations to which the British authorities had offered their protection. A few minutes sufficed to clear up the mystery; in view of the danger of hostile demonstrations by the Arabs, the authorities had thought it better not to call attention to our presence at the airport. Hardly had we set foot on the soil of Palestine than the policy of "intimidation" was brought into play! Also for reasons of security, but in this case with better justification, the British authorities had decided that we should make the journey to Jerusalem by air. We spent the night, therefore, at Lydda airport and the following morning a British military airplane conveyed us in a few minutes to Kalandia, which was then a small R.A.F. station north of Jerusalem.

Here I must interrupt our narrative for a moment to refer to our visit to Wilhelma colony, near Lydda, which took place before we left for Jerusalem. Although, as I have said, most of the members of the Palestine Commission were firmly resolved, in their inmost being, not to leave New York, officially the Commission insisted on their desire to go to Palestine and carried their "zeal" so far as to criticize harshly the reluctance of the British to facilitate the accomplishment of their desire. This meant that one of our practical tasks was to discuss with the British authorities on the spot the possibilities of installing the Palestine Commission in conditions which would make its normal functioning feasible. The German colony "Wilhelma" near Lydda, whose inhabitants were about to be transported to Australia or New Zealand, was the only site the British authorities were able to propose (they were not, however, ironical enough to recommend it) as suitable for the headquarters of the Palestine Commission and, taking advantage of its proximity to Lydda, they had arranged for us to pay it a visit before continuing our journey to Jerusalem. Wilhelma colony, on the eve of being abandoned by its inhabitants, was in such a state of dilapidation and ruin that it was obviously uninhabitable without a great deal of work being expended on it, for which neither the time nor the labor were available. The offer of it as the *only* site for the Commission could have no other intention than to demonstrate in a manner at once graphic and expressive the impossibility of the Commission transferring itself to Palestine. The result was that the desire of the British government, which was intimately shared by most of the members of the Commission, was fulfilled: the Commission did not go to Palestine and ended its lamentable existence, without pains and without glory, in New York. It is enough to add that British opposition to the transference of the Commission to Palestine was more than justified. The presence in Palestine of the body which was called upon to put into practice the plan of partition could, in itself, reasonably be regarded as a source of possible disturbances and confusion. But the presence in Palestine of the Commission as it was actually composed, with the peculiar characteristics of its members, its internal quarrels and its arbitrary and unjustifiable hostility towards anything that could be considered of British origin or initiative, would have been really catastrophic for the prestige and moral authority of the United Nations in the Middle East.

On our arrival at Kalandia we found the familiar policy of intimidation already awaiting us as we stepped out of the airplane, symbolized this time by a military truck which, escorted by an armored car, was intended for our transport. We made the journey to our lodging in this, seated on the floor, not only in discomfort but with the added torture of being able to see absolutely nothing either of the countryside or of the city of Jerusalem, since the canopy was fastened down and the side curtains drawn. Moreover, the Palestine police sergeant who accompanied us made us bend our heads from time to time, which meant literally putting them between our knees, as a precaution against stray bullets. But what finally dispelled our last illusions as to what lay in store for us was our arrival at the quarters the British authorities had prepared for us, which consisted of a few rooms on the ground floor (some of them actually in the basement) of one of the houses south of the Y.M.C.A. and opposite the King David Hotel. And to say that the rooms were prepared is an exaggeration, for when we arrived the preparations were still in full swing; walls were being whitewashed, electric light and sanitary conveniences installed and, above all, a kind of hole was being made in one of the walls to provide communication among all the rooms. This hole, which did not allow even persons of medium height to pass without stooping, ended by becoming famous in Jerusalem for, during the following weeks, all our visitors had to pass through it, however exalted their rank and however high their stature. The furniture was on a par with the rest, as miserable in quantity as it was in quality, which gave the rooms the appearance of cells, either convent or prison, according to taste.

At first I hesitated whether to allow the "group" to install itself in such surroundings; but I soon changed my mind, realizing that the best policy was to show unconcern and good will, and thanks to the magnificent spirit of my colleagues it was only a matter of a few hours before we had organized a family life in which the cordiality of our relations supplied the deficiencies of our physical surroundings and we were ready to begin our work. I should add that this result was due, not only to the good will and excellent morale of all my companions, but in great part to the consistently admirable way in which Miss Audrey Owen carried out the many functions she so generously took upon herself to perform: helping to draft important political communications, coding, the administrative side of the mission, and what was probably the most difficult and meritorious part of her task, the management and control of the group's domestic life. We succeeded, after some trouble, in obtaining two Jewish servants, who had to be taken to and fro by taxi across the Arab zone surrounding our house. Food and drink proved to be one of the most difficult problems. For the first few weeks the Palestine police secured our supplies, at the same time as their own, in the Arab zone; this was the golden age of our table. But one fine day the British authorities informed us that the police had received orders to stop our food supply in order (so it was explained) to prevent possible incidents with the Arabs, among whom a rumor had apparently begun to circulate that part of the provisions the police were acquiring were destined for us. Whether this was merely a pretext or not, the fact was that from that moment we entered upon a régime of austerity. The Jewish Agency lent us great support in the person of one of its most distinguished officials, Dr. Biran (then Bergman), who was to become Governor of Jerusalem. Moreover, the story began at once to spread round Jerusalem that the British had "cut off our food supplies," a story which was cleverly exploited by the Jews; and friends, taking pity on our hapless plight, hastened to our assistance, one with a joint of meat, another with a few pounds of sugar, another with a pot of jam or a box of biscuits. It was a lamentable episode; and apart from the disagreeable consequences to us, did great harm to the prestige of the British in Jerusalem.

Our quarters were situated in security zone "C," which was the most strictly guarded and a kind of British "holy of holies," access to which was reserved for British officials and a very limited number of persons who were not officials. This zone "C" comprised the King David Hotel, which was entirely occupied by the central services of the British administration, the Y.M.C.A. with its grounds as far as King George's Avenue, and the three houses in one of which we had our living quarters and offices. The zone was surrounded by barbed wire with two entrances strongly guarded by machine-gun posts. Our house was further protected by a supplementary post mounted on the roof of a garage at the entrance. We enjoyed freedom of movement inside the zone, which meant in practice that we could cross the road to go to the King David Hotel where, as I have said, the central offices of the British administration were installed. If we wanted to leave the zone we had to give twenty-four hours' notice to our liaison officer with the British authorities, notifying the hour of our departure, the place or places where we proposed to go and the approximate hour of our return. Then the police would send a car for us, escorted by one or two armored cars, according to the circumstances. After a time the car began to fail to turn up, and it was the armored car itself which had to serve us for transport. My friendly remonstrances were in vain; my refusal to return the official visit of the Dutch Consul in an armored car led to a letter of apology, but the armored car continued to arrive alone and the automobile was conspicuous by its absence. The Belgian Consul, who was an enthusiastic amateur photographer, regretted later that he had not taken a snapshot of a respectable United Nations official struggling with his years and his lumbago to perform the hazardous operation of climbing in and out of a British armored car!

The order not to allow us to leave zone "C" without authorization and without an escort was very strictly observed. I remember one day when I had been invited to lunch with the Greek Consul and, owing to some muddle, the famous armored car did not arrive. After much insistence on my part and much consultation over the telephone, the Palestine police sergeant who was responsible for our personal safety allowed me to make the journey on foot, escorted by two policemen who kept their fingers all the time on the triggers of their Sten guns. Fortunately, the streets of Jerusalem were not particularly crowded at that time, especially in the districts which were exposed to fire from the walls of the Old City; but the few people we encountered gazed at us in astonishment, wondering whether I was a dangerous terrorist from the Irgun or the Stern gang who had just been taken into custody by the police.

It will readily be understood that in these circumstances our sorties from the zone were practically confined to official visits to consuls, leaders of the Jewish Agency and the British High Commissioner at Government House.

Sir Alan Cunningham, the last High Commissioner in Palestine, was a man with a typically British shyness of manner, a gift for conciliation, and a great love of nature and wild flowers. Taking compassion on us for the kind of concentration camp existence he was forced, no doubt much against his will, to condemn us to, he used to send a car for us once or twice a week so that we could spend a few hours at Government House. On most of these occasions he himself accompanied us on our rambles through the park, pointing out the various wild plants that grew there with much more gusto than when he was describing to me in his office his fruitless endeavors to bring about a suspension of the hostilities which were by then already raging, more or less sporadically, in the greater part of Palestine. Obviously, the strong man during those last months of the mandate was the Chief Secretary, Sir Henry Gurney,[2] a man with a long colonial career behind him, energetic, intelligent, an excellent organizer, who yet had never succeeded in assimilating the peculiar characteristics of the problem which had to be confronted in Palestine, so different from the problems posed by colonial administration. Among the high officials of the British administration whom I had occasion to deal with personally, there were two who made a particular impression on me, as much by their character as by their intelligence. One was Mr. Eric Mills, one of the oldest and most brilliant officials of the mandate, who was immediately responsible during those last weeks for what might be called the liquidation of his administrative apparatus. The other was Sir William Fitzgerald, the Chief Justice, who enjoyed universal respect and was a great partisan of the internationalization of Jerusalem.

Apart from the British official element and a group of Jewish personalities in Jerusalem, our social life was restricted to the consular corps, where far and away the most interesting and attractive person was the French Consul, M. René Neuville. The fact that he was half Spanish was apparent in his ardent temperament and in the vigor with which he defended his opinions. Well-informed, constantly endeavoring to clarify his knowledge in the light of the experience gained during his numerous years of service in the Middle East, with a lively and quick wit, he was always ready to share his ideas, his impressions, his hopes and his disillusionments.

*   *   *   *

2. Assassinated some years later in an ambush when he was High Commissioner for Malaya.

As we had foreseen, our mission was cordially received by the Jews and ignored by the Arabs.

The Palestinian Arabs were represented by the Arab Higher Committee, which was officially recognized by the United Nations as their representative organ, and whose delegate was present, in company with the Jewish Agency delegate, at meetings of the Security Council and of the various committees whenever the Palestine question was discussed. The Arab Higher Committee had its headquarters at Jerusalem; following the precedent established with other international missions and in strict harmony with the attitude it had adopted towards the Palestine Commission itself, it scrupulously avoided every opportunity of official or personal contact with us during the two months our mission lasted. My only contact during that period with any outstanding Arab personality was with Farraj Bey, the Egyptian Consul in Jerusalem, and that was due to the intervention of the Belgian Consul. Farraj Bey was an open-minded man, with broad and moderate views; but those views were obviously at variance with what was then the prevailing mood of Arab politicians. The conversations I had with him at the Belgian Consulate were the beginning of a cordial friendship which was later renewed in Cairo and New York.

The Arab boycott placed us in an awkward situation, owing to the contrast between Arab hostility and Jewish cordiality. Hardly were we installed in Jerusalem than the Jewish Agency officially appointed two liaison officers to the "group"; one a civilian, Walter Eytan, soon to be Secretary General of the Israeli Ministry of Foreign Affairs, and the other a soldier, Major Vivyan Hertzog, later military attaché at the Israeli Embassy in Washington. Both these men, each in his own sphere, carried out their mission in a really admirable manner. In almost daily conversations, in spite of the difficulty they had in gaining access to zone "C" and our residence (during the first weeks, and until we were able to move the offices to a neighboring house, we had to receive our visitors in our own bedrooms and the bed was the only moderately comfortable seat we were able to offer them), they continued to expound to us the Jewish point of view on all aspects of the question. And what I particularly appreciated was the moderation they displayed in refusing to exploit unduly the manifest advantage which the vacuum created by the Arab boycott gave them to influence our opinion. All the same, our objectivity was subjected during that period to a severe test, from which it fortunately emerged not only intact but with redoubled vigor to survive any further tests that the future might hold.

*   *   *   *

The mission entrusted to our "group" was purely informative in character. We had to study on the spot, with the help of the British authorities, the appropriate means for ensuring the transfer of powers from the Mandatory Power to the Commission when the mandate expired on May 15, 1948. We soon realized that the transfer of powers was an expression of very relative practical significance, for the simple reason that the "powers" which the Mandatory Power was exercising in Palestine were already, at the time of our arrival, somewhat corroded, and the process of corrosion was progressing steadily with every day that passed. Moreover, it must not be forgotten that the mandate had only two more months to run, which made it imperative for the Commission to concentrate its efforts on what was essential and urgent and not waste time and attention on problems which were irrelevant to the rapidly deteriorating situation in Palestine. To us it was evident that, apart from the maintenance of a minimum of order and security (which I shall deal with in the following chapter), the essential thing was to ensure as far as possible the continuance, however precarious, of those public services whose interruption involves the immediate collapse of the entire administrative structure, such as communications (railways, postal services, telegraphs, etc.), health, the administration of justice, collection of taxes, and so forth. Guided by these considerations, the "group" concentrated its efforts on studying this aspect of the problem and in its frequent communications to the Commission not only kept it informed of the result of its work, but submitted a series of concrete measures, the adoption of which would, in my opinion, have facilitated the putting into practice of constructive solutions before it was too late. Having first secured the assent of the British authorities, we repeatedly recommended, *inter alia,* the immediate dispatch to Jerusalem of a director of posts and telegraphs, a railway manager and a health expert who, with the assistance of the heads of those departments in the mandatory administration, would have been able to take the necessary measures to prevent the respective services from at least coming to a dead stop when the mandate expired. Equally concrete and precise recommendations were submitted to the Commission about other public services and the maintenance of courts of law, as well as statistics about the possible number of officials in the mandatory administration (British, Arab and Jewish) who would be willing to continue serving under the Commission. But everything broke on the rock of the Commission's inertia; capable of spending entire afternoons in interminable discussions, they were smitten with deadly paralysis whenever it was a question of taking decisions and carrying them out.

But important though it was to ensure that the basic public services should continue to function, however precariously, it was obvious that everything, including those same public services, depended on how far it was possible to restore to Palestine a minimum of order and security. But this deserves a separate chapter.

CHAPTER II

War: The Siege of Jerusalem

WHEN I ARRIVED in Jerusalem at the beginning of March 1948, the British mandate over Palestine was already in full process of disintegration. A state of war between Arabs and Jews already openly existed, though in a sporadic form, and no one attempted to pretend otherwise. Arab attacks on Jewish agricultural settlements and Jewish attacks on Arab villages during the months of March and April formed part of normal daily life. As time went on, these attacks took place more frequently and with ever-increasing bloodshed, as the forces on either side became better armed and organized. Nevertheless, until the end of the mandate, the struggle never developed beyond guerilla warfare and isolated attacks. In Jerusalem the situation was the same: relative calm during the day, save for scattered shots or bursts of machine-gun fire from some Jewish or Arab post. But as night fell, rifles and machine-guns opened fire and kept up a more or less intense but incessant barrage, principally around the Jewish suburb of Montefiore, which was situated under the very walls of the Old City and constituted a veritable "enclave" in what was then an exclusively Arab zone—without counting occasional mortar fire and explosions caused by the blowing up of houses which enemy groups had converted into strongholds. This miniature nocturnal battle was of considerable consequence to us owing to the situation of our house. On the south side, on a level with our rooms, there lay a great expanse of waste land, full of rocks and thickets, which made an excellent shooting ground, so that the firing positions were frequently in a line with our windows; and on more than one occasion a bullet (whether stray or not, there was no means of telling) penetrated one or other of our windows, fortunately without hitting any of the occupants of the house. The regularity of the event helped us, no doubt, to accustom ourselves rapidly to the situation, disagreeable though it was. The firing began between seven and eight in the evening when we were preparing for dinner and while Colonel Roscher Lund and I were having our game of "casino" (with what admirable patience did the Colonel succeed in overcoming my natural lethargy to card games!); it lasted two or three hours and generally died down towards ten or eleven o'clock to the scattered shots which were considered part of a normal situation.

Though disagreeable, this was not the worst part of the struggle in Jerusalem. The attacks of a really terroristic nature were a thousand times more dangerous and compared with these, and the violent aggressiveness they revealed, the nocturnal pseudo-battles seemed almost like a game played by boys who, instead of passing the time at the movies or in a café, took their rifles or machine-guns (there was no youth but had some weapon at his disposal) and spent the evening behind a rock or bush firing a few rounds at the Jews of Montefiore. The blowing up of a wing of the King David Hotel, in which a great number of British officials lost their lives, and the destruction of an entire house in Ben Yehuda Street, the most central and crowded of the Jewish zone of Jerusalem, where a great many Jews were killed or wounded, had taken place some months before our arrival. During March and April there were three serious outrages, without counting others of lesser importance.

The first was the blowing up of a wing of the great building of the Jewish Agency in King George's Avenue. This occurred during the morning of March 11 and claimed several victims, among them the wife of Major Hertzog, our military liaison officer, who received a head wound which fortunately was not serious. The explosion was tremendous; at the moment when it occurred I was talking to Mr. Mills in his office at the King David Hotel and the whole building shook to its foundations. It is significant that neither of us made any comment and the conversation continued, each of us reflecting to himself that, this time, the charge of explosive was a little too big. But what most revealed the semi-chaotic conditions to which life in Jerusalem had already been reduced was the fact that the authors of the outrage accomplished their purpose by making use of the American Consul General's own car. Thanks to its official appearance, this car was admitted to the central court of the Jewish Agency and the chauffeur, an Arab, after drawing up by the curb opposite that part of the building it was intended to blow up, got out and walked off under the pretext of buying a newspaper. A few moments later the car exploded, destroying the building and killing many people inside it. This incident gave rise to a delicate situation with the American Consulate, and indeed it was difficult to explain satisfactorily why the consulate had not employed an American chauffeur, but had entrusted such a responsible and confidential post to an Arab.

The second terroristic outrage occurred on April 8. Jewish irregular troops infiltrated the Arab village of Deir Yasin, some miles to the east of Jerusalem. During the night they set fire to the village and massacred a great part of the population—men, women, children and old people. This is the outrage which the Arab governments have continually made use of during discussions on the Palestine question at the United Nations in order to show that the Jews, even before the end of the mandate, had tried to spread terror among the Arab population, thus provoking an exodus which, in their opinion, was the true origin of the Arab refugees. Whether the massacre of Deir Yasin was part of a premeditated plan, as the Arabs assert, is difficult to affirm, much less to prove. The truth is that in its dreadful proportions it was an isolated event; and, as was to be expected, both the Jewish Agency and its regular military defense forces (Haganah) not only denied any participation in or responsibility for it, but officially condemned it (even sending a telegram to King 'Abdullāh), attributing it to terrorist elements outside their control. I can truthfully say that nothing that came to my ears in Jerusalem at the time when the incident occurred, or subsequently in the course of private conversations or official discussions, led me to doubt the truth of the explanation given by the Jewish Agency and the Haganah. My conviction is that, whatever its effects on the morale of the Arab population, the Deir Yasin outrage was the work of uncontrollable terrorist groups and that the leaders of the Jewish Agency and the Haganah were not only distressed by it but, in the depths of their consciences, condemned it as much on humanitarian grounds as because they thought it highly prejudicial to the Zionist cause.

There can be no doubt that the massacre of Deir Yasin provoked a wave of panic among the Arab population and led to the abandonment of many neighboring Arab villages by their inhabitants. This renders all the more noteworthy the case of the little hamlet of Abugos, some miles to the west of Deir Yasin on the Tel Aviv main road, which has kept its Arab population—a small island in a region now populated solely and exclusively by Jews. Perhaps this curious phenomenon is due to the personality of a French monk, Father Alexander, who for the last forty years has been parish priest of the ancient and romantic church built by the Crusaders on the site where, according to tradition, St. John the Baptist was born. The universal respect in which Father Alexander was held was no doubt considered by the Arab peasants residing there sufficient protection against the peril which, with the events at Deir Yasin, they had reason to believe was imminent. And it is encouraging to find that either the danger was not in reality so great as they had reason to fear, or that Father Alexander's moral authority and prestige were sufficient protection against it.

The third case occurred on April 13. A convoy of ambulances carrying wounded and medical staff to Hadassah hospital on Mt. Scopus was attacked at Shaykh Jarrak by bands of Arab irregulars. The ambulances were immediately immobilized and for several hours were under fire from Arab rifles and machine-guns. The result was about seventy dead and twenty wounded. Among the dead were Dr. Yassky, Director of Hadassah hospital, Professor Bonaventurea, professor of psychology, and nine members of the university staff; the rest were nurses, wounded and sick. Some days later the *Palestine Post* published a dramatic account of the attack by one of the survivors who had been in the same ambulance where Dr. Yassky died. According to this account, the intervention of British troops, seven hours after the attack had begun, prevented the total extermination of the convoy by the Arab bands who at that moment were already surrounding the ambulances in a state of tremendous excitement. Public opinion was profoundly shocked by the outrage. The Arab Higher Committee issued a communiqué alleging that the convoy was transporting arms for the military garrison on Mt. Scopus. This was never cleared up; but in any case it would not have justified the barbarous attack on the convoy. Why did the British troops wait seven hours before intervening, when the attack took place in full daylight, while the convoy was still in the outskirts of Jerusalem and only a short distance away from a Palestine police post? Nobody, so far as I know, had a satisfactory explanation for this; and when next afternoon I visited Dr. Magnes, then Chancellor of the University, I realized that this incomprehensible passivity on the part of the British troops was one of the reasons for his justifiable depression and bitterness.

* * * *

The truth is that during the last months of the mandate the British authorities had, for all practical purposes, given up trying to maintain in Palestine that equilibrium of forces which is commonly called public order and security. The contrast between the actual situation and the statements made by the British government either in the House of Commons or through its representatives at Lake Success, repeating the assurance that until the mandate finally expired the government would fulfill its obligations and responsibilities with regard to the maintenance of public order in Palestine, inspired Mr. R. M. Graves, the last British mayor of Jerusalem, to utter this bitter comment: "The statement that we are not only responsible for security but that we are effectively preserving it has been made so often recently at Westminster and Lake Success that truth-loving Britons in Palestine—of whom there are more than a handful—have become absolutely disgusted with the discrepancy between the claim and the facts."[1]

This policy of abstention was so general that it is difficult to point to concrete cases in which it was clearly manifest. The struggle between Arabs and Jews, the dominant factor in the entire life of Palestine during that period, went on amid the indifference of the British authorities and the British troops, who intervened only when they thought that the result of a battle might affect their own security; which meant, in the majority of cases, supporting the Arab forces to prevent the occupation of their positions by the Jews.

The British authorities had completely disclaimed responsibility for any measures that might help to guarantee a minimum of safety to traffic on the roads, except, of course, when it was a question of their own transports. Here is what I wrote in my diary on March 25 with regard to this:

> Luncheon at the house of Caminada, the *Times* correspondent, with the Belgian Consul and the Inspector General of the Palestine Police. During luncheon the Consul describes the most incredible adventures he had experienced during a journey he had just made to Haifa, that is, on one of the most important high roads in Palestine. Hold-ups along the road by Arab patrols armed to the teeth, who check and recheck his papers, subject him to interrogations, bring him before the local mayor where he is again interrogated etc.; and all this accompanied by threats and often thrusting their

1. *Experiment in Anarchy.* Gollancz: 1949. p. 183.

rifles at his breast. He describes all this as if it was a great jest and the Inspector of Police listens as if he, too, thinks it a diverting story which has nothing to do with public order and security in Palestine, for which he is chiefly and directly responsible. And after the journey to Haifa the Consul describes another journey, this time to Tel Aviv, when he met with more or less the same adventures with armed Jewish patrols and bands; and the Inspector listens to the joke with the same indifference.

When I arrived in Jerusalem at the beginning of March, the various consulates had already, in actual practice, established relations with, on the one hand, the Arab Higher Committee and, on the other, the Jewish Agency in place of their former relations with the British authorities. Whenever incidents arose which involved citizens of European countries (a frequent occurrence), the respective consul took up the case not with the British authorities, but with the Jewish Agency or the Arab Higher Committee, according to whether the incident occurred in the Jewish or the Arab zone. The same thing happened when the consular corps, represented by its doyen the French Consul, thought it necessary to protest against the restrictions placed on the admission of consuls to the Jewish zone after the attack on the Jewish Agency, which was carried out, as we have seen, by means of the American Consul's car. The laborious negotiations to which this incident gave rise were conducted by the French Consul, in the name of the consular corps, and the Jewish Agency, without the British authorities having any knowledge of, or share in the matter; and this occurred two months before the termination of the mandate!

*　　*　　*　　*

This policy of "abstention" in matters connected with public order and security had a kind of complement in the policy followed by the British government in respect to the progressive partition of Palestine and Jerusalem into two zones—Arab and Jewish. My opinion is that after the Jews themselves and, perhaps, the United States government, no one contributed more to the partition of Palestine and hence to the establishment of the State of Israel than Great Britain—and this was due not only to the Balfour Declaration of 1917, but also to the British government's policy in Palestine during the last six months of the mandate. Under cover of official assurances that the authorities would fulfill their obligations and responsibilities until the end of the mandate, the British government lent passive, and at times active aid to the progressive transfer of powers and responsibilities from its own organisms in Palestine to Arab or Jewish institutions. This operation took place in a form which was incomparably more complete, regular and ordered when the transfer was to Jewish organizations than when it was a question of handing over the administration of public services to the Arabs. The latter, mainly because of their eternal domestic quarrels, never succeeded in setting up administrative organs capable of assuring the efficient working of public services of a general character. The transfer was made, therefore, in an irregular and precarious form, to the traditional municipal authorities.

In contrast, the handing over of powers and services to the Jews was accomplished in particularly favorable circumstances. The Jewish Agency, directed by men of great political and administrative experience, with the collaboration of a carefully chosen staff who had specialized in all branches of administration, and with inexhaustible financial resources, was already at the beginning of March, 1948, a state in embryo, capable of undertaking the administration of the most technically complicated public services (including, naturally, the police and the maintenance of public order) with as much, if not more efficiency than the same organs of the Mandatory Power.

This policy led inevitably to the creation of distinct and separate territorial zones where, under nominal British authority, the real authority lay in the majority of cases in the hands of Arab or Jewish bodies. This applied rather to the Jewish than to the Arab zone, since while the British authorities withdrew, in principle, from the territories under Jewish control, they continued to live side by side with the Arab population in the rest of Palestine, taking a more or less effective share in its government and administration. Jerusalem offered a fair sample of this. Apart from the British security zones where almost all the British, civilian and military, lived under the direct protection of the Palestine police and the British army, the city was then already divided into two zones, one Arab and the other Jewish, quite distinct and separate. This separation was effective in two senses: first, because, with the sole exception of the Jewish quarter inside the Old City, the populations of each zone were already exclusively Arab or Jewish; and secondly, because all communication between them was already completely and absolutely cut off. As in the rest of Palestine, the British circulated freely in the

Arab zone, while access to the Jewish zone was forbidden them by the British authorities themselves. During my visits to the Jewish zone of Jerusalem, the British car or armored truck did not go beyond the barrier marking the limits of British security zone "C" in King George's Avenue, more or less opposite Terra Santa; from there I had to walk about a hundred yards to the entrance to the Jewish zone where a car from the Jewish Agency awaited me, with the corresponding escort of Jewish police, impeccably uniformed and armed and differing from their British counterparts only in the use of a jeep instead of an armored car.

As we have seen, the Jewish quarter in the Old City provided the only exception to the racial purity of each zone—a purity which should nevertheless be interpreted not in its positive sense, signifying that *all* the inhabitants of each zone were exclusively Arabs or Jews, but in its negative sense, implying the absence, respectively, of Arabs or Jews in each zone. This quarter formed, in effect, a veritable Jewish island in the Old City which, for our purposes, must be regarded as the most compact and basic nucleus of the Arab population of Jerusalem. In it had lived from time immemorial about a thousand families of the purest and strictest rabbinical orthodoxy and in the labyrinth of its filthy and malodorous alleyways were to be found two of the most sacred and revered Jewish "holy places"—the Wailing Wall and the Hurve Synagogue. When I arrived in Jerusalem, the suburb was already practically in a state of siege under the protection of a small garrison of the Haganah, and it continued thus until May 28 when it surrendered to the Arab Legion and the civilian population was evacuated.[2] Nevertheless, until the end of the mandate on May 14, the Jewish quarter endured a siege which was, so to speak, passive; it suffered no military attacks worthy of the name, but it was so completely isolated that the British, for lack of a better arrangement, undertook to send in supplies by military convoy which made its way every Wednesday across the Old City, bringing to the unfortunate inhabitants the means of subsistence until the following Wednesday.

Even before the termination of the mandate, the boundaries of the two zones in Palestine varied according to the vicissitudes of the struggle. At the beginning of March, the Jewish zone was limited to Tel Aviv and its environs, the Jewish part of Jerusalem and the numerous agricultural settlements *(kibbutzim)*

2. *Vide* Chapter VI.

scattered throughout Palestine and at that time already organized as military posts able to defend themselves against the attacks of the surrounding Arab population or, if the occasion presented itself, to attack Arab villages in the vicinity. The first important modification in this territorial situation was introduced on April 22 with the capture of Haifa by the Jews. When the British evacuated the city and concentrated on a zone around the port which they held until the evacuation of the British army from Palestine was completed, the Jews who were occupying the up-per part of the city on the slopes of Mt. Carmel seized the rest almost without firing a shot, owing to the panic and general dis-array of the Arab population, which neither attempted to defend itself nor, probably, was in a position to do so. With the capture of Haifa the Jews took over control of the coastal plain as far as Tel Aviv. Some weeks later and immediately following the with-drawal of the British troops, the Jews made themselves masters of Jaffa; later, between the two truces, Lydda, Ramleh, Tiberias, Nazareth and Safed fell into their hands. In broad outline, they had only to occupy the Negev and western Galilee to complete what today forms the territory of the State of Israel, and this they did as a result of their two offensives in the autumn of 1948, during the second truce.

The Jewish zone of Jerusalem in March 1948 (apart from the Jewish quarter of the Old City) was considerably smaller than it is at present but, unlike the rest of Palestine, no change took place in its boundaries until the evacuation of Jerusalem by the British on May 14. On that day and the following two or three days the Haganah occupied with lightning speed and without much fighting the southern districts (Katamo, the German col-ony, etc.), a purely residential quarter where the rich Arabs of Jerusalem had their villas and estates, which had been abandoned during the last weeks or months by almost the whole of its pop-ulation. Again, a few minutes after their evacuation by the Brit-ish armed forces on the same day (May 14), the Haganah occu-pied the block of buildings formed by the Central Post Office, the Anglo-Palestine Bank and the Italian Insurance Company, thus securing not only control over the telephone system and tele-graphic communications but, what was yet more important, mili-tary domination of all the central part of modern Jerusalem, forc-ing the Arabs immediately to withdraw their lines which, until then, had run close to these same buildings. With the exception of the Jewish attacks on the Old City during the following weeks and the fighting in the Jewish quarter within its walls, what gave rise to the bitterest struggle in Jerusalem during the days immediately following the end of the mandate and in the period between the two truces was the supreme effort of the Jews to seize the rest of the modern districts north of the Old City and ensure their communications with Hadassah hospital and the Hebrew University on Mt. Scopus. Unfortunately, the same road that leads to Mt. Scopus also leads to Ramalah, Nablus and the region, further to the north, which a few weeks later came to be known under the name of the "triangle" (Nablus-Jenin-Tulkram) as the strategic center of the Arab campaign against the State of Israel. Its possession was, therefore, equally important to the Arabs as to the Jews, if not more so; and as a result of the fierce resistance offered by the Arabs to the Jewish attacks, the line of demarcation established by the second truce and confirmed by the armistice, though some yards away from the coveted high road, left it in the hands of the Arabs, so that while the latter kept open their line of communications with the "triangle," the Jews have remained since that time isolated from Mt. Scopus.

*　　*　　*　　*

All this is enough to understand that the maintenance of public order at the termination of the mandate was one of the themes on which the "advance group" of the Palestine Commission concentrated its attention with the greatest intensity. I mean maintenance of public order in the widest sense: it was not a question of ensuring the continuation of a normal police service capable of protecting the inhabitants of Palestine against criminals and malefactors, but of bringing about an immediate cessation of a latent state of general violence and of guerilla warfare and sudden attacks which daily increased in volume. Above all, the aim was to prevent this guerilla warfare and these *coups de main* from degenerating, at the end of the mandate and as the British troops withdrew, into a real war ("major war" was the expression we used in our cables)—an unavoidable tragedy if a way were not found to induce the Arab states to forego putting into practice their plan to prevent the creation of the State of Israel by force of arms now that they had been unable to achieve their object by discussion in the Assembly of the United Nations. To sum up, however important the preparation for the transfer of powers to the Palestine Commission (and we have already seen that this transfer was being carried out at an ever-quickening tempo, not to the Commission but to Jews and Arabs), everything was subordinate to the primordial question of whether it would be possible to put an end to the guerilla warfare now raging and to prevent it from degenerating into a "major" war when the mandate expired.

Almost immediately we began, with monotonous insistence, to present this aspect of the question to the Palestine Commission. Colonel Roscher Lund sent memorandum after memorandum, not only explaining the actual situation, but indicating what measures ought to be adopted to remedy it or to prevent its constant deterioration. From the end of March onwards we began to insist on the necessity for a truce. We were obsessed by the idea of averting the danger of "major" war, which would inevitably occur if international effort and, in particular, the effort of the United Nations and its Palestine Commission continued to concentrate exclusively (according to the sacred formula) on carrying out partition when partition was already an accomplished fact, and the problem consisted in consolidating it by peaceful means and not as the result of armed conflict. And there was only one method of bringing this about: the immediate conclusion of a truce. This seemed to me so vitally important that early in April I proposed that the Secretary General should broadcast an appeal to the population of Palestine, Arab and Jew alike, in favor of an immediate truce. However, as usual, I never discovered the fate of my proposal or even whether it ever came to the notice of the Secretary General. And it should be observed that, at that moment, the imposition of a truce would have virtually barred the way to a group of states which were then publicly announcing their intention of preventing by armed force the execution of the resolution adopted by the Assembly on November 29, 1947.

It is worth pointing out, as a curious precedent, that the idea of using neutral officers as observers to guarantee that the truce was respected—the cornerstone of the system which the armistices established a year later—can be found already explicitly mentioned in a memorandum which I sent to the Commission on April 9, where the use of "neutral military observers" is textually recommended as one of the means of ensuring observance of the truce.

CHAPTER III

Interlude at Lake Success:
The Special Assembly

O N APRIL 6 the news reached Jerusalem of what can now be
called the United States government's first change of front
in its policy towards Palestine. The *Palestine Post* published that
day under huge headlines the text of the proposals submitted the
previous day by the American representative on the Security
Council to an official meeting of its members. These proposals
recommended the establishment of a temporary trusteeship, to
be intrusted to the United Nations, until the Arab and Jewish
communities of Palestine should agree on the future government
of their country. During the following days, the State Department
took two further steps which were the natural sequels to the
previous initiative. In the first place, it proposed that the Security
Council should invite the contesting parties to agree upon a
truce. In the second place, it set in motion the necessary measures
for immediately convening a Special Assembly where the new
proposals could be discussed and eventually adopted.

This radical change of front in American policy made, as was
to be expected, a profound impression in Palestine, both among
Arabs and Jews. The latter saw in it nothing less than a betrayal
of the cause of the partition of Palestine and the creation of the
State of Israel; and their disillusionment was all the more bitter
since the chorus of almost lyrical praise recently directed towards
the United States for her decisive intervention to ensure the
adoption by the Assembly of the resolution of November 29,
1947, sanctioning both partition and the creation of the Jewish
state, was still ringing in the ears of all Jews. Among the Arabs
the reaction was less intense. They regarded with indifference
and scepticism the American change and continued their preparations which, with ingenuous optimism, they regarded as a
much more effective medium than any change of American policy

for radically and finally destroying any prospect of partitioning Palestine and creating a Jewish state.

Today, in the knowledge of what has since occurred, it is easy to criticize the new American proposals. But for those who were living in Palestine with the anguish of seeing how day by day the struggle between Arab and Jew was becoming more envenomed and blood-stained and a real war more and more inevitable as the end of the mandate drew near, the new American policy with its proposal for a truce and its attempt to explore the question anew on different bases, could not but present certain attractions. And, in fact, not only neutral elements, but moderate and conciliatory Jewish elements like the group that drew its inspiration from Dr. Magnes, showed interest and even entertained the hope that the new American policy would open the way to a solution not based exclusively on the result of a war. Even certain leading elements of the Jewish Agency did not refuse to recognize, in private conversation, the advantages of avoiding a war whose result neither they nor anyone else could then predict—even at the cost of deferring for a time the official proclamation of the State of Israel, then already intended for the 15th of May, the last day of the mandate. On the other hand, however, they affirmed that the idea of the immediate proclamation of the Jewish state had created such an outburst of enthusiasm, especially among the Jewish youth, that anyone who mentioned the mere possibility of deferring it would immediately be branded as a traitor and treated as such—one more case of politicians becoming prisoners of the very ideas they themselves have created! The truth is that however meritorious the intention of the United States government in trying to alter the course of events in Palestine, which must inevitably lead to a real war in which the Jews would be confronted not only with the Palestinian Arabs but also with the Arab states, its proposals of April 5 were doomed to failure. Not even by passing a sponge over the question of "partition" did they succeed in arousing among the Arabs sufficient interest to induce them to abandon the warlike plans and preparations in which they placed all their trust. The result was that the Arab leaders, ruled by their profound distrust of American policy, shrugged their shoulders at the new proposals and went on with their military preparations as urgently as before.

On the other hand, the attempt to wipe out "partition" with a stroke of the pen presented an unsurmountable obstacle to Jewish acceptance and it had, moreover, the serious disadvantage of forgetting that "partition" had ceased to be the mere text of an Assembly resolution, which could be replaced by another, and had become a reality incorporated into the very life of Palestine which no pen could strike out or efface, however powerful the hand that wielded the pen.

I thought then, and I still think, that it would have been worth while trying the formula of a temporary United Nations trusteeship, and I indicated as much in my communications to the Palestine Commission and the Secretary General. But the concrete modalities of this formula as I conceived it were markedly different from those of the formula contained in the American proposals. The temporary character of the mandate ought to have been vigorously and unequivocally emphasized and the term of its duration fixed. The maintenance of "partition," already existing in Palestine, and its consolidation should have appeared as one of the mandate's concrete objectives. At the same time, the mandate should have been presented in such a way as to show that it was intended to place at the disposal of the Arab and Jewish authorities the necessary technical and financial assistance to ensure the continuance of public services. Above all, the mandate should have undertaken to conclude an immediate truce and to guarantee its observance. Finally, the mandate should have appeared as the instrument destined to bring to both Arabs and Jews the soothing and conciliatory action which they so much needed, either in the form of counsel, of friendly pressure, of admonition and even, if circumstances warranted it, the application of sanctions. All this, however, without forgetting for a moment that, whatever the method employed, the essential aim of the mandate was to help both Arabs and Jews to surmount the crisis—a bitter crisis for the Arabs, a joyful one for the Jews —which the official acceptance of the establishment of the Jews in Palestine as an integral part of its future political and economic status was bound to provoke. A mandate of this description might perhaps have succeeded by dint of patience, energy, tenacity and good will in preventing war, thus freeing the new State of Israel and the Arab population of Palestine from many of the difficulties and misfortunes which they have to face today.

The truth is that when the Special Assembly met the die had already been cast and the psychological conditions were certainly not the most appropriate for constructive and conciliatory formulas of compromise to prosper. As might have been expected, one of the results of the fall of Haifa had been to strengthen that body of opinion, already predominating among the Jews, which favored the proclamation of the State of Israel on May 15, whatever the consequences. The minority which felt attracted by a policy of compromise found itself more and more reduced to silence, as events followed their headlong course. For their part, the Arabs were becoming more deeply entangled every day in the meshes of their own propaganda in favor of what they officially called a war of "liberation," but what in private conversation with them became a war of "extermination"; though their propaganda was not paralleled by an effort to overcome their disorganization and their constant quarrels and internal divisions. In any case, it was evident that the center of gravity of Arab policy in Palestine was shifting from the Palestinian Arabs under the Mufti of Jerusalem to the Arab states, grouped rather loosely in the "League of Arab States" under the notable and attractive personality of 'Azzām Pasha, its Secretary General. The real danger for the Arabs, as a distinguished French diplomat said to me shortly after my arrival in Jerusalem, was that Palestine might become the apple of discord among the Arab states. With great ability 'Azzām Pasha averted this danger. In fact, he succeeded in making the question of Palestine and of the military, diplomatic and economic war against the Jews the most effective cement to stop up the cracks which were continually appearing in the structure of the Arab League.

All this helped to create an atmosphere of such confusion that, as we shall see, the Assembly, very soon lost in so complicated a labyrinth, proved as impotent to force through the November 1947 plan of partition as it was incapable of drawing up a substitute plan; and the action of the United Nations was confined, for the time being, to the valuable and fruitful step of appointing a "mediator" and, through his intervention, ensuring the conclusion of a truce.

*   *   *   *

On April 22, I received the cable with the Secretary General's instructions to return immediately to New York. These instructions were contrary to what I had been recommending for the last two weeks, namely: immediate dissolution of the "advance group," which had lost its *raison d'être* now that the Special Assembly had been convened to examine the new American proposals, leaving me to stay in Jerusalem as the representative of the Secretary General to ensure the physical presence of the

United Nations during the gathering storm. Already the profound conviction had taken root in my mind that the presence of the United Nations in Jerusalem, even though represented, as would have been the case, by a mere official of its Secretariat, was the keystone of the plan to discharge the responsibilities which, for good or ill, the United Nations had contracted with regard to Palestine. How far I was then from thinking that my fidelity to this idea was to be, four years later, one of the factors that contributed to my falling into disfavor with the Secretary General!

I decided in the end to comply with the instructions without further insistence on my own opinion and, on April 24, I left Jerusalem in company with a British official who was going to London. As we could not enter the Jewish zone, it was impossible to take the direct road to Lydda and we were obliged to pass through Ramallah in order to make the journey without leaving the Arab zone. The country was ostensibly "on a war footing," in its own fashion. Not that there was any sign of organization or discipline, but there was not a man, young or old, who was not armed in a more or less picturesque manner. Moreover—and this was most significant—at the entrance and exit of each village there were control points consisting of armed groups whose aspect was far from reassuring and who were manifestly acting on their own account and their own responsibility. Thanks to the armored car which preceded us, we passed through all this warlike display without the slightest difficulty. At the airport of Lydda there was an air of tension and nervousness. The British officer commanding the detachment of Palestine police guarding the airport was visibly disturbed by the anger and animosity which the Arabs showed to the British as the result of the events at Haifa; he was afraid that the airport would be destroyed in the struggle for its possession. As it happened, his fears proved to be groundless; some days later the Haganah seized the airport almost without a struggle and in a short time Lydda resumed the prominent place it had occupied in the network of international aerial communications.

We took off in a B.O.A.C. airplane, one of the last to leave Lydda while it was still under British control. A brief landing at El Adem, British military airport near Tobruk; a night and part of the following day at Malta, due to a defect in one of the engines and, late on the night of the 25th, we arrived in London. There I found awaiting me fresh instructions from the Secretary

General, which had arrived at Jerusalem after my departure, telling me to defer my journey. This delay annoyed me considerably, but as communications with Lydda had been cut during the last twenty-four hours, the Secretary General confirmed his instructions to proceed to New York. The flight was not without unexpected incidents, for when we were already in the air we were told that, because of the bad weather, instead of following the normal route Shannon-Gander, we were making for Iceland where, in fact, we landed at dawn. From there we took off for New York where I arrived without further surprises towards noon on the 28th.

*   *   *   *

During the Special Assembly the Palestine question was examined on three distinct and, in fact, independent levels. The first committee of the Assembly and its two sub-committees had under discussion, on the one hand, the report of the Palestine Commission and on the other, the American proposals for an international temporary trusteeship. The Trusteeship Council, at the Assembly's request, discussed with a great wealth of argument the specific problem of Jerusalem. Lastly, the Security Council concentrated its efforts on bringing about a truce, the only suggestion which, at the time, had any practical significance for the situation in Palestine.

The Assembly had the good judgment to ignore the report of the Palestine Commission and without discussion decided on its immediate dissolution. In contrast, the American proposals and the numerous counter-proposals, amendments and suggestions to which they gave rise were the subject of prolonged discussions not only in the plenary Assembly and its first committee, but in the two sub-committees which were set up to facilitate its work. As was to be expected, the discussions were somewhat confused and, one might almost say, chaotic. Proposals, counter-proposals, amendments and arguments went on day after day, losing all contact with the palpitating and painful reality in Palestine. The following extract from my diary for May 8 will serve to show the growing distance that was separating the conference rooms of the Assembly from the streets of Jerusalem and the fields of Palestine—and I mean distance not in the geographical, but in the psychological sense:

> There is one more week before the end of the mandate and the sub-committee has spent the entire morning hearing and

discussing a report from Lisicky which is almost entirely
devoted to comments on the public services (railways, bus
and coach services, electricity, telegraphs, etc.); but does one
have to shout at them to make them understand here that in
Palestine there is already a war raging and that if they don't
take steps to stop it within a week the whole of Palestine,
including Jerusalem, will become a real battlefield? What
sense is there, what object can there be in discussing things
like motorbus services and telegraphs? And the worst of it
was that at one o'clock the Committee decided to suspend its
sessions until Monday, after having charged the rapporteur
with the preparation of a memorandum summarizing the various proposals. And when an official of the Secretariat with
wide experience and extensive knowledge of the subject offered to draw up a draft, the rapporteur refused the offer,
saying that he preferred to do the work alone. The rapporteur's grasp of the situation was shown by the fact that the
two questions in which he displayed a special interest during
the discussion were the distribution of food and the position
of minorities. No comment!

At the very last moment, faced with the obvious impossibility
that the Assembly would approve in time the American plan or
any other similar plan, the American delegation itself put forward the idea of appointing a "mediator," a straw at which the
Assembly eagerly snatched, enabling it to avoid the shameful
spectacle of its own impotence either to put into practice the
plan of partition which it itself had approved six months previously or to devise some other formula which might open a way
out of the impasse into which the Palestine question had fallen.

In my two oral reports, one to the Palestine Commission on my
arrival and the other to one of the sub-committees of the Assembly's first committee, I had made every effort to persuade my
hearers that the immediate and pressing mission of the United
Nations ought not to consist in the elaboration of more or less
perfect formulas to replace the British mandate, but in preventing the guerilla warfare which had been raging in Palestine during the last few months from merging into open and declared
warfare as soon as the British troops disappeared from the scene
at the end of the mandate. Whenever I had the opportunity I repeated with monotonous insistence that partition was already an
"accomplished fact" and that the transfer of public services to
the new Arab and Jewish organizations and authorities would
continue without great difficulty so long as war was avoided. If

war was not avoided, there was no sense at all in discussing the future political and administrative organizations of Palestine, since everything would depend on the result of the armed struggle. However, I soon realized, not without bitterness, that I was a voice crying in the wilderness and during the rest of my stay in New York I had to stand by unhappily while the debates went on in the same atmosphere of indifference to the real situation in Palestine.

It was significant, in this respect, that, with few exceptions, no delegate had the curiosity to make himself acquainted, by private and personal contact, with the impressions of a man who had recently arrived from Jerusalem, where he had spent three months taking a direct and personal part in recent events about which, whatever the opinion of his capabilities, he might be expected to have something interesting to say.

The outcome of all these debates, translated into resolutions, was as follows:

1) On April 17, the Security Council appealed to the combatants to conclude a truce and six days later, on the 23rd of the same month, appointed the Consular Truce Commission, composed of representatives of those members of the Security Council who had career consular officers in Jerusalem. In accordance with this criterion and in view of the fact that Syria declined to be represented, the Commission consisted finally of the Belgian, American and French Consuls. In the following chapter there will be occasion to discuss in more detail this Commission, the veritable "Cinderella" of the United Nations in Palestine.

2) On May 6, the Assembly, on the proposal of the Trusteeship Council, recommended to the Mandatory Power the appointment of a special Municipal Commissioner for Jerusalem. As with the Consular Truce Commission, fate willed that I should become personally involved in the vicissitudes that followed this strange resolution and I shall have more to say about it later on.

3) On May 14, the eve of the expiry of the mandate, the Assembly adopted the important resolution appointing a United Nations "mediator" in Palestine and fixing the terms of his mandate. The appointment of Count Bernadotte took place a few days later and from that time until the conclusion of the armistices a year later, the Mediator, either in the person of Count Bernadotte until his death or in that of his successor, Dr. Bunche, as temporary mediator, filled the international stage of Palestine.

The Security Council's resolutions appealing to the combatants to conclude a truce and creating the Consular Truce Commission were in harmony with what the Palestine situation called for and, in principle, met its requirements. Whether the appeal was launched in conditions which would ensure its success and whether the Consular Commission had at its disposal the necessary means to fulfill its mission, was another matter. But this we shall deal with later. The appointment of a special Municipal Commissioner for Jerusalem will also be the subject of comment in a later chapter; seen from Jerusalem, with its streets and squares converted into a battlefield, both the appointment of a Commissioner and his mission to "carry out the functions hitherto performed by the Municipal Commission" were not far from having the appearance of a cruel farce.

The Assembly's resolution appointing the United Nations Mediator was naturally on a completely different level. The creation of this post and the appointment of the holder of it figured as two of the United Nations' greatest successes and remain as memorable dates in the annals of its intervention in Palestine. All of this does not detract from the fact that the terms of the mandate conferred on him by the Assembly were somewhat out of keeping with the realities of the situation which had then to be confronted. To use his good offices with the local authorities in order to ensure the functioning of public services necessary to the "safety and well-being" of the population of Palestine and the protection of the Holy Places was, manifestly, an impossibility unless war were averted and indeed the Mediator himself came to recognize this in his report to the Assembly. The promotion of a peaceful adjustment of the future situation of Palestine would require much more calm and time for reflection than the then anxious circumstances allowed, when every effort and every attention was not enough to bring about what could not be delayed, the *sine qua non* of all the rest, namely, the conclusion and observance of a truce. And whatever may have been the merits of the substantive proposals that Count Bernadotte submitted first to the contesting parties and later to the Assembly, it was certainly not these that have assured him a place in the contemporary history of international relations. This place he owes to the ability, the energy and the inexhaustible tenacity thanks to which he accomplished what at that time even the most optimistic thought already unrealizable—the conclusion and observance of a truce between the Arabs and the Jews; an enterprise which his successor, Dr. Bunche, completed the following year by substituting for a truce, armistices agreed upon under his presidency between the State of Israel and the four neighboring Arab states. It is noteworthy that this part of the Mediator's mission, the part that related to the avoidance of war and that, through the very force of events, became not only the principal but the only one to give positive results, appears in the text of the Assembly's resolution as entirely secondary and accessory. The resolution confines itself, in fact, to laying down that the Mediator shall "cooperate with the Truce Commission appointed by the Security Council," words in which, in the light of the future relations between the two parties, we can only find an ironic flavor. It was only one more sign of the false perspective in which the Assembly was viewing the Palestine question.

*   *   *   *

An incident that occurred during the afternoon session of May 14, when the resolutions we have just been discussing were adopted, served not only to break the solemn monotony of the debate but to throw into relief the manner in which the Assembly allowed itself to be outdistanced by events. A rumor began to circulate among the delegations to the effect that the State of Israel had been proclaimed in Tel Aviv and recognized immediately by the United States government. The Colombian delegate put a question to the United States delegation which, not without embarrassment, had to confine itself to replying that it had learnt of the rumor from the press but that up to the present moment it had had no official information on the subject. In reality, the proclamation of the State of Israel, intended for May 15, had been put forward twenty-four hours because the 15th fell on the Sabbath.

*   *   *   *

Every day that passed impressed on me more clearly the uselessness of my presence at Lake Success and the importance of the United Nations being present in Jerusalem at the moment when the British mandate came to an end. The Secretary General, yielding to my importunities, decided that I should return to Jerusalem as Secretary of the Truce Commission. When four years later this same idea of the presence of the United Nations in Jerusalem was to cost me vexation and disappointment, I could not help recalling the words of encouragement spoken by Mr.

Lie when he drank a toast to me at the conclusion of a dinner to which I was invited at his house on the eve of my departure!

At noon on May 9, I left New York with Mr. Macabe and a secretary, Mr. Burns; this time the mission was considered too dangerous and uncertain for it to include a feminine element. Breaking our flight only at the usual landing-places, Prestwick, Amsterdam and Rome, we arrived at Cairo on the following day, the 10th, at eight o'clock in the evening. On the following morning a British military airplane arrived to pick us up and after an unforgettable flight over the Pyramids, we landed at Kalandia shortly before noon. The die was cast. No retreat was possible; and the thought of what the future might hold filled us with foreboding.

CHAPTER IV

The British Leave Jerusalem

O N OUR ARRIVAL at Kalandia airport we met with an
unpleasant surprise—there was no means of transport to
Jerusalem and no one had been advised of our arrival. We telephoned to Jerusalem and after a couple of hours an armored car
appeared, which solved the problem. Kalandia was still occupied
by the British Air Force, but signs of immediate evacuation were
visible.

We reached Jerusalem at about one o'clock and I confess that
it was with emotion that I saw again those bare, gloomy rooms
where we had had to overcome so many difficulties, if not to ensure the success of our first mission, at least to avoid complete
failure. Circumstances had changed; when we arrived in Jerusalem for the first time in February, it looked as if we were in
for an exciting and perilous adventure, and yet that first period
seemed to us a bed of roses compared with what we were expecting now. After luncheon I went to the French Consulate
where the Truce Commission was holding its meetings. The three
consuls were already there and I found them in a deplorable state
of mind—irritated, indignant and complaining bitterly that Lake
Success had left them in the lurch. I tried to calm them down as
best I could, assuring them that the Security Council had full
confidence in the Commission and would lend them every support; and at four o'clock I went off to see Sir Alan Cunningham, the British High Commissioner.

The High Commissioner received me with his usual courtesy
and I think he was pleased that I had returned. He told me that
he had succeeded in arranging a precarious cease-fire in Jerusalem, but he was very disturbed over the difficulties of bringing
about a real truce. Moreover, he was much upset over a telegram
he had just received from the British delegation at Lake Success referring to friction between him and the Truce Commission
over their respective functions. His proposal, in view of these

complications, was to summon the Truce Commission and hand over to them all his functions as far as the preparations for a truce in Jerusalem were concerned. Towards the end of our conversation he showed me how he was storing the furniture in the large ballroom and pronounced himself highly satisfied with the arrangement whereby Government House was to remain under the protection of the Red Cross. I accepted an invitation to have luncheon with him the following day.

There was no doubt that between the Commission and the High Commissioner a most lamentable state of tension had arisen. On both sides there were misgivings and suspicions as to what the other's intentions were. And as if this were not enough, the Red Cross had stirred up more trouble by its proposal to make Jerusalem an "open city" under the protection of its flag. It is only just to recognize that the Commission's ill-humor was not entirely without justification, since it is hard to imagine anything more likely to stultify all efforts to achieve a truce than to entrust them to three separate elements each working on its own account.

Luncheon with the High Commissioner on the following day, the 12th, was certainly not a cheerful affair. I forget if we were alone or if one of his aides was also present. The High Commissioner could not conceal his deep chagrin and anxiety at finding himself in the position of abandoning Palestine in a state which might well be called chaotic. He, more than anyone, could realize what it meant for his country to end a mandate which had lasted for twenty-five years, in such catastrophic conditions. It was not surprising that our conversation should have languished; the same ideas and fears perturbed us, but no one wanted to make them the theme of our conversation.

After luncheon I went to the premises of what had been the British information bureau, where a press conference was to be held. It was perhaps the last time that the group of international journalists still remaining in Jerusalem were going to meet. Two days later those who belonged to the British group went over to the Arab zone and set up their headquarters in the precincts of the Cathedral of St. George, while the rest remained in the Jewish zone, more or less concentrated in the Hotel Salvia. The press conference took place in an atmosphere charged with anxiety and incertitude. We all knew that in a matter of hours our personal situation was going to be not only difficult but dangerous, though no one could have foretold with moderate accuracy what fate had in store for us during the next few days. In my statement I confined myself to explaining my new mission as Secretary of the Consular Truce Commission, emphasizing that it was now completely detached from the "partition" plan and that my efforts would be concentrated on preventing war. At bottom, no one was much interested in all this and if my presence aroused a certain amount of interest and even sympathy it was, more than anything, because of the originality of our gesture in walking into the "rat-trap" of Jerusalem a few hours before the exit was finally closed.

I brought the press conference to an end just in time to hurry to my appointment that same afternoon with Sir Henry Gurney at the King David Hotel. During the course of our conversation, Sir Henry referred to certain suggestions he had made to the Truce Commission to the effect that the flag of the United Nations should be hoisted over the offices of the Government Press, which should be then intrusted to the protection of the Arab Legion. This suggestion filled me with dismay and I pointed out to him the impossibility of putting it into practice. It was, as a matter of principle, quite inadmissible to intrust to one of the contending parties the protection of places or establishments under the flag of the United Nations. The latter's neutrality would have been instantly nullified, and the opposing faction morally justified in attacking. If what was intended was to create an obstacle to the occupation of that part of the city (where the railway station was) by the Jews, the calculation was obviously mistaken. With or without the United Nations flag, no one could have prevented the Haganah from occupying all that zone of the city; and placing the United Nations flag under the protection of Arab forces would merely have served to provoke a conflict between the Jewish authorities and the United Nations, in which right would have been all on the side of the former. In the course of our interview, Sir Henry also informed me that the formal termination of the mandate would take place at midnight on May 14, which I interpreted, with what I later found to be excessive optimism, as meaning that neither the British administration nor the British army would leave Jerusalem before that hour.

The Truce Commission's official farewell to the High Commissioner took place that same afternoon (May 12). The High Commissioner received us at his office with his customary shyness and a rather forced smile. Hesitating and almost stammering, he informed us that if the Commission agreed, he proposed to relinquish to us his functions with regard to the truce in Jerusalem, so that we could combine our efforts in this direction with what we were doing to bring about a truce throughout Palestine as a whole. He also referred to the communication he had received from Lake Success regarding the difficulties that had arisen in his relations with the Commission. The ensuing discussion took place in a tense and disagreeable atmosphere. Both sides brought forward charges and recriminations, all naturally with the greatest correctitude and with the courtesy which was incumbent on the kind of personalities taking part in the conversation. The scene ended as all such scenes usually do end, with mutual smiles and more or less formal courtesies. Looking back, I marvel that the relations between the three most important consuls in Jerusalem and the British High Commissioner should have ended thus, a few hours before the historic moment when the British mandate over Palestine was about to expire. My leave-taking was, I think, more cordial and sincere; perhaps because, being more detached from local events, I had a clearer perception of the significance of the moment and realized better what the exit of the British High Commissioner from Jerusalem and the abandonment of Palestine by England meant. The fact is that, for one reason or another, the only note of cordiality in that glacial atmosphere was my handshake with the High Commissioner.

* * * *

About eight o'clock in the morning of May 14, the Belgian Consul and I were returning to Jerusalem from our visit to King 'Abdallāh at Amman. Hardly had we passed through the Damascus Gate and turned in the direction of the King David Hotel than we realized that something strange was happening in the city. The streets were deserted and a profound silence reigned. But before we had time to comment on it, we discovered the reason for this extraordinary sensation: the city was occupied by British troops—machine-gun posts at each corner, troops stationed in the streets, and strict control of all non-military traffic. When I arrived at our offices I found the explanation for all this display of military force. The High Commissioner and the Chief Secretary had left Jerusalem that morning, after a brief ceremony in front of the King David Hotel, when the High Commissioner reviewed the troops drawn up there before going on to Kalandia airport, where an airplane was waiting to take him to Haifa.

I was annoyed over this because, relying on what Sir Henry Gurney had told me two days previously about the official end of the mandate, I had thought to have a final interview with them during the course of the day. Moreover, I confess that it made a painful impression on me to see the High Commissioner and the Chief Secretary leave Jerusalem in this almost clandestine manner twenty hours before the official expiry of the mandate. This was bad enough, but it was not the worst. Though the British had never been willing to give us any indication of the date when the troops would evacuate Jerusalem, I had formed the idea (founded, as it turned out, more on wishful thinking than on sound reasons) that it would be towards the end of the period envisaged for the total evacuation of Palestine by the British, which did not expire until the first of August. In my ingenuous optimism I had always counted on the British trying to hold off as long as possible (especially in Jerusalem) the chaos which must inevitably follow their departure since the United Nations had been unable to establish a régime which, if nothing else, would have maintained a minimum of order and security; but it seemed that nothing was farther from their intentions than this reasonable and laudable project. The troops we had seen drawn up in the streets were not there as a safety measure; they were, purely and simply, drawn up ready to march and, in fact, one detachment after another moved off until, at about two o'clock in the afternoon, not a single British soldier remained in Jerusalem. The time had come for the plunge into the unknown.

Since there was now nothing more to be done with the British, I went to the French Consulate where the Belgian Consul was also thinking of going in order to render an account to the Commission of our mission to King 'Abdallāh. There we spent the morning in rather confused discussion, while the situation in the city rapidly deteriorated. The cease-fire arranged by the High Commissioner had passed into the realms of history and the firing around the French Consulate was becoming so intense that we decided to stay to lunch at the consulate; there we passed the afternoon until as darkness fell we were able to go out in conditions that I shall describe later. That afternoon shut up in the French Consulate comes back to me like a nightmare. In reality it was no different from many subsequent afternoons and mornings, but perhaps because it was the first, it remains more vivid in my memory.

Since the middle of the morning the firing had become more

general and was spreading in a truly alarming manner. The cross-fire between the walls of the Old City and the Jewish suburb of Yemen Moshe was already very lively by the beginning of the afternoon and as the consulate, being situated opposite the walls, was directly in the line of fire, all movement in the vicinity was particularly hazardous. And not only outside, but inside too, since in spite of the sandbags protecting the doors and windows of the main façade, bullets frequently found their way into the house and that very same day two or three of the consulate guards were wounded, one of them while crossing the great entrance hall.

In the rest of the city, hardly had the last English soldier disappeared than the Jews launched their offensive, consolidating their possession of Katamon and seizing the German colony and the other southern districts of Jerusalem. The last remaining Arabs there were liquidated, and from henceforth, the Jews were absolute masters of the southern part of the city. The struggle in this sector cut off the Belgian Consul from his consulate, due to his chauffeur being wounded while returning from one of his journeys to the French Consulate. The unfortunate man had to remain an hour without succor before a Jewish armored car was able to reach the spot where he fell and remove him to the hospital. I have already mentioned elsewhere how, in the early hours following the evacuation of the British army, the Jews seized the group of buildings housing the Central Post Office, the Anglo-Palestine Bank, and the building of the General Italian Insurance Company, thereby gaining control of all the central part of the modern city. During the last weeks of the mandate the Jewish authorities had been greatly perturbed over what would happen to these buildings when they were evacuated by the British and on more than one occasion I had, at their pressing request, mentioned the subject either to the High Commissioner or to the Chief Secretary. Though I could get no definite reply, my impression was that the British authorities were prepared to do what was necessary so that at the moment of their departure the buildings could be occupied by the Jews; a reasonable course if it is borne in mind that the offices occupied by the Bank and the Italian Company belonged to Jewish owners and that, forming a single block with the Post Office, it was inconceivable that the three should not remain in the same hands.

We spent the afternoon in the midst of a growing crossfire from rifles, machine-guns and an occasional mortar, doing all we could to bring about a suspension of hostilities. For this our sole medium of action was the telephone—an uninterrupted succession of calls to the Jewish Agency and to the headquarters of the Arab irregular forces in the Old City, proposing all manner of formulas and suggestions which might enable hostilities to be suspended if only for a few hours, during which something more permanent might be negotiated.[1] During the course of the afternoon and insofar as it is possible to reconstruct the rapid sequence of events, more than once it seemed as if we had succeeded in persuading both sides to send to the consulate delegates with whom we could parley; the Jews sent, first, Mr. Eytan and later Major Hertzog, the Jewish Agency's civil and military liaison officers with the Commission; but the Arabs never sent their representatives though they several times announced their immediate departure, alleging as their reason or pretext that to reach the consulate they would have to cross zones swept by Jewish fire and that the Jews, in spite of their promises of safe conduct, had never ceased fire so as to permit their passage. One way or another, the fact remains that we did not succeed in bringing about a suspension of hostilities. Nevertheless I am convinced that, thanks to the pressure of those incessant telephone calls, we prevented the struggle from degenerating at once into open warfare. And at that time, and with the means at the disposal of the Commission, this was no small thing. I remarked jokingly to the Chairman that he was saving Jerusalem with telephone calls; and there was a grain of truth in the jest.[2]

In these strenuous endeavors the afternoon wore on—believing at every moment that we were within an inch of seeing Arab and Jewish delegates arrive at the consulate ready to reach an agreement, only to find, a few minutes later, our hopes dashed to the ground by a telephone call from one or the other side. Today, after six months of similar efforts with means and resources incomparably greater than those at the Commission's disposal, our illusions will, perhaps, be condemned as too ingenuous; and this is true. But what else could we do? And, moreover, how could we help putting our faith in anything that might have checked, if only for a few hours, the avalanche that was sweeping us all to destruction? It is easy now to realize the extent of our naïveté.

1. These activities are described in more detail in Chapter VII.

2. A memorandum, written no doubt by Mr. Eytan about that meeting in the French Consulate, has been published by Koestler in his book *Promise and Fulfilment,* pp. 234-235.

The Jews, already perfectly organized, were carrying out methodically their plan to seize the whole of modern Jerusalem and were naturally very far from thinking of suspending, far less abandoning, the execution of this plan in deference to our telephone calls; and I do not think it would be very wide of the mark to say that with their passive resistance to a cease-fire in the zone which the Arab delegates would have to cross in order to reach the French Consulate, they rendered all negotiation impossible without incurring the responsibility for a blank refusal. As for the Arabs, it is not easy to say what their real attitude was, for the simple reason that probably they themselves would not have been able to say what it was. The so-called Arab forces were then "irregulars," indifferently controlled by improvised leaders under the nominal authority of the Arab Higher Committee. Possibly, at that moment they would have been glad of a suspension of hostilities and their explanation that the Jewish forces, by their fire, were preventing their delegate from reaching the French Consulate was sincere. Should this be so, one can but pay a tribute of admiration to the ingenuity of the Jewish leaders who appeared to be giving the greatest facilities for a settlement in which they were not interested and which they themselves rendered impossible.

Night fell without any apparent improvement in the situation; on the contrary, the firing between the walls and the Yemen Moshe quarter became more and more intense, so much so that we found ourselves obliged to accept once more the generous hospitality of the French Consul and Mme. Neuville and remain to dinner in the consulate, hoping that in the darkness it would be possible to traverse without being seen or heard the three hundred yards or so of road which was visible from the walls, and reach the corner of the King David Hotel. And here I must pay a well-deserved tribute of gratitude and admiration to M. and Mme. Neuville for the inexhaustible patience and magnificent spirit with which they faced all the risks, complications and difficulties attendant upon the situation of the consulate, augmented as they were by our daily and constant presence. With the consulate full of people, struggling with all kinds of obstacles to obtain the necessary provisions, with five members of the staff wounded, almost all inside the building by bullets that penetrated in spite of the sandbags protecting the doors and windows, with their five children taking shelter day and night in the cellars, we always found a welcome full of cordiality and a hospitality that manifested itself not only in words but in deeds, making us share excellent improvised meals when the firing was too intense to be able to leave the consulate without grave risk.

After dinner, when it was completely dark, we slipped out silently one by one to where Major Hertzog was waiting for us in the garden with his car and then, without lights and as quickly as possible, we passed, not without risk, through the consulate gates and drove at full speed round the corner of the King David Hotel, where we were at least out of the line of fire from the walls of the Old City. Taking every precaution, with Colonel Roscher Lund in the lead, his revolver in his hand, we entered our quarters and collected what we needed to spend the night in one of the hotels in the Jewish zone, since to sleep in our own rooms was out of the question. The building was, as I have said, in the reserved zone under British protection and after the departure of the British troops, had remained quite unprotected, becoming a kind of "no man's land" at the mercy of anyone who chose to occupy it—regular troops, *francs tireurs,* or simply hooligans and thieves. We gathered together what we could, which was not much since we were working in the dark and counting the minutes until the Arabs or Jews discovered the car and opened fire on it. Carrying what we had been able to collect under our arms and with the unpleasant feeling that what we were leaving behind we were leaving for good, we went out with the same precautions as when we had come in, got hurriedly into the car and drove off as silently as possible towards that part of the city which was under Jewish control, where we passed the night comparatively peacefully at the Salvia Hotel.

Just outside the hotel there was a kind of recruiting and training center and when I got up the following morning I spent some time watching the arrival of boys and girls hurrying to begin or complete their military training—lively and enthusiastic groups which brought me bitter and nostalgic memories of similar scenes I had witnessed in Madrid in the early days of the Spanish civil war. I spent the whole day with the Belgian Consul in the house he was occupying near the Salvia Hotel. We kept in touch by telephone with the Jewish Agency, the Arab high command and the American and French Consuls. But the rifle, machine-gun and mortar fire was too intense for it to be possible to think of moving outside the Jewish zone, still less of approaching the French or American Consulate.

After luncheon Colonel Roscher Lund appeared, returning

from the Jewish Agency where he had had a long conversation with the officer commanding the Jewish troops in Jerusalem; he was buoyed up with hope over a formula for a cease-fire which he had agreed upon with the Jewish high command. The question now was to obtain the agreement of the Arabs and this, as usual, could only be done by telephone. The entire afternoon and a good part of the evening were spent in consultations and negotiations over the telephone, orders that were not carried out, postponements, etc., until when the night was already far advanced we had to resign ourselves to the thought that this attempt also had failed. The only result was a sharp protest from the Red Cross which, I can't quite remember why, thought that Colonel Roscher Lund's interference had disturbed the favorable course of its own negotiations for the neutralization of Jerusalem.

The delicate and difficult problem of finding new headquarters did not admit of further delay. No doubt the ideal thing would have been to continue living independently in our old offices; but, as I have said, all that zone had become since the departure of the British troops a "no man's land," without any possibility of protection not only against military attack (for this could have been solved by an undertaking on both sides to respect the headquarters of the United Nations) but against the danger of assault by common thieves and hooligans. Moreover, the building was without running water and it was physically impossible to think of organizing either food supplies or the most rudimentary domestic service. This solution was, therefore, discarded from the very beginning. Bearing in mind that the Jewish zone (modern) and the Arab zone (Old City with a suburb north of the modern city) were separated by what had become within the last twenty-four hours a real battlefront, to set up our headquarters in one particular zone would have left us physically isolated from the other, obliging us to live, moreover, in an atmosphere saturated with Arab or Jewish propaganda. In any case, it was obvious that either solution would have destroyed any appearance of impartiality on our part and in our present circumstances the appearance of impartiality was almost as important as impartiality itself.

I therefore decided to accept the offer of M. de Regnier, Head of the Delegation of the International Red Cross Committee in Jerusalem, to install ourselves in the Y.M.C.A. building which, with the King David Hotel, formed one of the security zones under the protection of the Red Cross. In order to comply with the regulations which strictly forbade the Red Cross to admit any kind of political activity in places under its protection, it was agreed that it was not the United Nations mission which was installing itself in the Y.M.C.A., but its members as private persons; the mission kept its official domicile in our old headquarters where the archives remained and where we worked during the daytime. This arrangement was possible thanks to the fact that our old headquarters were situated alongside the grounds of the Y.M.C.A., from which they were separated only by a street. It should not, however, be forgotten that to cross a road in full view of snipers or of more or less regular military posts could entail perils more grave than to traverse half the city well out of their range or sight. And this applied in some measure to the street we had to cross to get from the Y.M.C.A. to our offices; not only was the street directly in line with the walls of the Old City, but to get to it we had to climb rather acrobatically up and down a ladder—an operation unpleasant enough in normal conditions and much more so in those we were actually faced with.

Life in the Y.M.C.A. was very comfortable, given the circumstances. The domestic service, even including washing and ironing, functioned with complete regularity; food was abundant and good; and, what was a great blessing, thanks to the enormous cisterns, we had drinking water and, though rationed, enough water to wash in and even a weekly bath. Being built of blocks of solid masonry, the thickness of the walls afforded ample protection against even artillery bombardment. There was, of course, always the danger of a stray bullet finding its way through a window, and this in fact happened several times, our secretary, Mr. Burns, being slightly wounded on one occasion. On the other hand, it was dangerous to walk about the recreation grounds or even the terrace, since the neighboring houses were infested with snipers and to leave the building at all involved a risk.

Everything was arranged by telephone during the course of the afternoon. Unfortunately, when I prepared towards nightfall to set out for our new residence, it was impossible to find a car to take me and it would have been rash to make the journey on foot, at night, through zones exposed to the fire of one side or the other. In the end, I had to give up the idea and accept the Belgian Consul's kind invitation to spend the night at his house.

CHAPTER V

Temporary Municipal Commissioner of Jerusalem

THE FIRST NOTICE I received of the appointment of Mr. Harold Evans as Municipal Commissioner for Jerusalem and of my own appointment as temporary Commissioner until his arrival was a telephone call from the British Consul on the morning of May 15. The Consul had just received a message from the President of the Assembly and the Secretary General, instructing the British High Commissioner to appoint Mr. Evans, a distinguished Quaker from Philadelphia, Municipal Commissioner for Jerusalem; the message specified that Mr. Evans had been accepted by the Arab Higher Committee and by the Jewish Agency. Since it would be some time before Mr. Evans could reach Jerusalem, the High Commissioner was asked to inform me that I had been appointed "temporary" Municipal Commissioner until his arrival. When this message reached Jerusalem, the High Commissioner was already at Haifa on board the cruiser *Devonshire,* which was to take him back to England and it was, I think, on board ship that the decision was taken whereby Mr. Evans was invested, in Philadelphia, with his high functions as Municipal Commissioner for Jerusalem and I with the more modest, but more immediate, function of *ad interim* Commissioner in Jerusalem until his arrival.

Before going on to describe the events arising out of this episode, I should like to mention the impression that these decisions by the Assembly made on all of us in Jerusalem. As I have said elsewhere, they seemed almost a cruel farce and the expression does not appear to me exaggerated. For a city which was physically divided into two enemy camps by a real battlefront, it was proposed to appoint a Municipal Commissioner, whose mission was to "carry out the functions hitherto performed by the Municipal Commission," and this with the cooperation of the "community committees already existing in Jerusalem." This did not worry

Mr. Evans much because, as he himself informed me in one of his early telegrams, the terms of his appointment expressly provided for the impossibility of his assuming his functions until peace was restored in Jerusalem. But then, what sense was there in appointing me temporary Commissioner? To throw on me obligations and responsibilities which, temporary though they were, knowingly could not be carried out? All the more so as Mr. Evans had let me know in his telegram that I could not count on his presence in Jerusalem until the fighting had ceased, for the curious reason that, being a Quaker, he was not sure he could accept the protection of a military escort. I tried to overcome the painful impression all these contradictions and illogicalities had made on me and set about, without loss of time, finding out what could be done in the circumstances.

The creation of the post of Municipal Commissioner and my appointment as temporary Commissioner until Mr. Evans' arrival were very favorably received by the Jews of Jerusalem, who immediately prepared to give me every facility in the zone under their control. This welcoming attitude obliged me to be on my guard against the danger that the little or much that it was possible to do in municipal affairs would be limited to the Jewish zone. The danger was very real for two reasons. First, the difference between the relative facility of communication with the Jewish district and the fact that it was almost impossible for me to communicate with the Arab part of the city.

Our office was within walking distance of the Jewish zone, a walk that was not without danger, due mostly to snipers, but feasible at any hour of the day without the need for special preparations. In contrast, the journey to the Old City, where the Arab municipality had its seat, meant crossing the lines of what, as I have so often said, was a real battlefront; and this required elaborate and detailed preparation, since all the military posts, both Arab and Jewish, of the sector we had to cross, had to be informed of the exact hour of our passing, given our personal descriptions and warned not to fire on us. But in addition to this reason, which was due to the actual circumstances surrounding us, there was another more substantial one. For some months before the departure of the British, the Jewish part of the city had actually been organized as a municipality, in which the basic municipal services functioned regularly with exclusively Jewish personnel and funds. Collaboration with it was, therefore, not only possible, but relatively easy; bearing in mind, also, that the

Jews from the first moment were prepared to cooperate with the Municipal Commissioner. The situation in the Arab zone was entirely different; there a municipality properly so-called did not exist, the municipal services were rudimentary or nonexistent, and the only effective authority was the very precarious authority of the military leaders over their bands of "irregulars." Only when, some days later, the Arab Legion arrived in Jerusalem was a real and effective authority established, and then its exclusively military character did not do much to change the situation as far as the possibility of collaboration with more or less well defined municipal institutions was concerned. For both these reasons, there was undoubtedly a real danger that for the Municipal Commissioner to base his activities, as he could not help but do, on collaboration with municipal organisms would result, in practice, in these activities being limited to the Jewish sector, however great the objectivity and impartiality he would have liked theoretically to impart to them. And I might add that the leaders of the Jewish Agency, with whom I discussed this problem of mine, were unreservedly of the same mind and entirely agreed that it would be prejudicial to allow collaboration with Jewish municipal institutions to assume disproportionate dimensions in relation to what circumstances made possible on the Arab side. It was, therefore, imperative and urgent for me to establish contact with the Arab municipal authorities and find out exactly what possibilities existed for cooperating with them. The chance occurred on May 17, on my return from my second mission to Amman when I was accompanying the Belgian Consul as Chairman of the Truce Commission.[1]

On May 17 the Arab Legion was about to make its entry into Jerusalem, but had not yet taken over its government or administration. Authority was still in the hands of rather loosely defined committees and, above all, of the leaders of the "irregulars," volunteer troops who were defending the Arab city. In this welter of civil and military personalities, engaged with varying titles in the exercise of authority, circumstances brought me into contact with Dr. Mūsā Ḥusaynī, a distant cousin of the Mufti of Jerusalem (though on bad terms with him), a man of Western education and intellectually much attached to German culture. Our relations during the following years were always very cordial and his execution at Amman, in August 1951, for alleged com-

1. *Vide* Chapter VII.

plicity in the assassination of King 'Abdallāh moved me profoundly.

I recall that that same evening of May 17, Dr. Mūsā Ḥusaynī accompanied us on a visit to the military hospital which had been installed in the ancient and venerable buildings of the Austrian Hospice, where we were invited to dine, after our visit, with the Director. And we did not spare our compliments to the Director and his colleagues for the surprising results they had obtained in adapting those austere and gloomy premises to the needs of a modern hospital. There, too, we met Father Ayad, a man who was then held in high esteem by the Arab Christians of Jerusalem and who had undertaken to find us a lodging for the night in the Latin Patriarchate. Under a brilliant full moon we traversed the deserted and silent streets of Jerusalem on our way to the Patriarchate. Patrols of "irregulars," who challenged us from time to time in a somewhat alarming manner, allowed us to pass on recognizing Father Ayad or Dr. Mūsā Ḥusaynī in the light of their torches. At the Patriarchate we found cells prepared for each of us where we spent the night. I cannot say that we slept, because the Jewish troops chose that night for one of their most violent attacks on the Jaffa Gate, some hundreds of yards from the Patriarchate; so that it was quite impossible to sleep a wink, either because of the rattle of Arab machine-guns firing from the walls a few paces from our windows, or because of the shells from Jewish mortars which were falling quite thickly in the neighborhood. I am, of course, referring only to the noise, because as far as danger was concerned, we ran absolutely no risk; protected by the city walls and the thick stone walls of the Patriarchate, we were quite out of range of machine-gun or mortar. Much of the same sort of thing must have happened to the combatants themselves, for the following morning I learned to my great satisfaction and not without surprise that the number of casualties suffered by the Arab forces during the attack mounted to not more than half a dozen slightly wounded.

A preliminary conversation with Dr. Mūsā Ḥusaynī had convinced me that there was no possibility of collaboration with municipal institutions for the simple reason that in the Arab part of Jerusalem such institutions had as yet no definite existence. This early impression was confirmed on the following morning at a conference held at the headquarters of Faḍl Bey, commander of the "irregulars" of the Old City, where certain civilian notables were also present, among whom I recall Ḥilmī Pasha, chairman or leading member of the Arab Higher Committee. Both in my conversation with Dr. Ḥusaynī and in what I told the conference, I took care to insist on my firm intention of being temporary Municipal Commissioner for the whole of the city of Jerusalem and asked for the necessary facilities to be given me to set up an office and residence in the Old City, so that I could spend three or four days there every week. Dr. Mūsā Ḥusaynī took up the matter with great enthusiasm and that same afternoon arranged for two spacious rooms to be allotted to me on the top floor of the Austrian Hospice. Unfortunately there was a hitch at the last moment. As I have already said, the Austrian Hospice had been turned into a military hospital and, as such, was under the protection of the Red Cross. As soon as Dr. Marti, the representative of the Red Cross in the Old City, heard of the arrangement for my installation in the same building, he told Dr. Mūsā Ḥusaynī that he could not allow any kind of activity of a political character under the flag of the Red Cross. Needless to say, as soon as Dr. Mūsā Ḥusaynī passed on these observations to me, I said that there was no other course open but to abandon our plan and make new arrangements. Instead, therefore, of remaining to spend the night in the Old City as I had intended, I resolved to return to the Y.M.C.A. with the Belgian Consul that same afternoon. My return was certainly not without its excitements!

We went first to the British Consulate, which had just taken up its quarters in a kind of fortress, a former German boarding school, opposite the Damascus Gate, which had served during the mandate as air force headquarters.[2] From there, while the consul cheered us with a cup of tea, all the front line military posts were duly informed by telephone of our passage through the lines. In a car belonging to the consulate, with an immense white flag waving over us, we proceeded at a snail's pace as far as the Cathedral of St. George. From there we had to walk about five hundred yards to the first Jewish post at Mandelbaum Gate. Night was beginning to fall and the absolute silence and emptiness of the streets gave one an eerie feeling of disquiet and oppression; all the more so because in that apparent solitude one knew one was being intently watched by some dozens of individuals and our lives depended on the fact that all those individuals, without exception, had received the order not to fire on us and were prepared to obey that order.

*   *   *   *

2. The building subsequently reverted to its original use.

In my anxiety about the fulfillment of the obligations imposed on me by my resplendent office of "temporary" Municipal Commissioner, it struck me that, in the absence of anything more substantial, I might begin by visiting the hospitals and the municipal, cultural and religious institutions of the Jewish zone. I visited the hospitals on the afternoon of May 21, accompanied by Dr. Auster, mayor of the Jewish municipality, and Mr. Nathan, Secretary of the Vaad Leumi. The sight was a depressing one; the two that I visited, the hospital of the British Mission and the hospital at the French Monastery of St. Joseph, were absolutely full of wounded from the fighting around Jerusalem and a few civilian casualties of the bombardment by the Arab Legion artillery. Nevertheless, the standard of organization, cleanliness, order and equipment was surprising when it is remembered that they were in the front line of fire. At the hospital of St. Joseph, a shell had torn a huge hole in one of the walls and reduced to rubble the equipment of the children's clinic.

As we went out of the hospital of St. Joseph, we met Dr. Davis, Assistant Director of Hadassah Hospital, who was coming in search of me to ask me to facilitate the evacuation of the twenty-seven sick persons still remaining at Mount Scopus, with the doctors and nurses who were looking after them. The difficulty was that 'Abdallāh Tall, the officer then commanding the forces of the Arab Legion which had arrived two days previously in Jerusalem and were virtually surrounding the hospital, refused to authorize the evacuation of the patients and medical staff until the Jewish troops of the Haganah which were occupying the hospital and the Hebrew University surrendered. We went along to Dr. Auster's house and there I decided to send a message to King 'Abdallāh, suggesting the evacuation of the sick and wounded through the intermediary of the Red Cross and the suspension of hostilities, at least until the evacuation had been completed. The text of the message was approved not only by Dr. Auster and Dr. Davis, who helped to draft it, but also by Dr. Kohn of the Jewish Agency, whom they consulted by telephone. For my part, I thought it necessary to tell the Delegation of the Red Cross what I had done and I spoke to Dr. Marti on the telephone immediately. The problem of transmitting the message from the Jewish zone of Jerusalem to Amman was not without its difficulties. I called the British Consul, Mr. Beaumont; and he himself offered to telegraph the message to his legation at Amman with the request that it should be transmitted immediately to the King.

The consul also undertook to inform 'Abdallāh Tall of the step I had taken, so as to ensure that no attack should be made on the hospital until the King's reply had been received.

This reply arrived at noon on the following day (May 22) through Sir Alec Kirkbride, the British Minister in Amman, and its content could not have been more satisfactory. King 'Abdallāh agreed to the immediate evacuation of the patients and hospital staff, adding (and this was the most important thing) that if the Jewish troops guarding the hospital and University on Mount Scopus withdrew under the supervision of the Red Cross, the King would guarantee the safety of the buildings and their contents. Finally, the King declared that while his proposal was being examined, the buildings would not be attacked unless there was Jewish provocation. This reply, in substance, fully satisfied the two points on which Dr. Davis (and with him the Jewish Agency) had insisted as the essential condition on which a compromise formula could be accepted, namely, to prevent an attack, with the consequent destruction of the buildings and their contents, and to prevent the Jewish troops guarding the hospital and University from having to surrender to the Arab Legion.

The King's response was immediately communicated to Dr. Davis and the Arab High Command and in the early afternoon a cease-fire was agreed upon, which was scrupulously respected, at any rate during the twenty-four hours the negotiations lasted.

It would be tedious to describe in detail these negotiations, which were conducted by telephone from my room in the Y.M.C.A. with the Jewish Agency on the one hand and the headquarters of the Arab Legion in Jerusalem on the other, between the early hours of the afternoon of the 22nd and the morning of the 23rd. My notes for the draft of the telegram which I sent on the following day to the Secretary General record in this space of time, twenty-four telephone conversations, most of them with the contesting parties, some with the members of the Commission, particularly the American Consul, who had expressed the desire to be kept informed in detail of the course of the negotiations.[3] Justice compels me to say that the attitude of the Jewish authorities did not rise to the level of King 'Abdallāh's conciliatory ges-

3. This same night the American Consul, Mr. Wasson, died as the result of an attack on him the previous day when he was returning from a meeting of the Truce Commission. His assistants, Mr. Burdett and Mr. Stabler, gave me the sad news during the couse of one of our telephone conversations as dawn was breaking. *Vide* Chapter VII.

ture. They began by asking for explanations on points of detail relating to the form of the evacuation, to which the King sensibly replied suggesting that the practical details could be decided by the Red Cross in agreement with the respective military commands. Then the Agency said they had to consult the government at Tel Aviv, which delayed their reply for several hours. The answer came at 3:30 in the morning; it did not authorize any agreement over the evacuation of the troops but gave Dr. Davis *carte blanche* as far as the evacuation of the patients and medical staff was concerned. On the following morning the Jewish Agency issued a long statement explaining the reasons why they had not accepted King 'Abdallāh's proposals. These all revolved around the principle of the hospital's inviolability as a humanitarian institution under the protection of the Jewish equivalent of the Red Cross. What the Jewish Agency forgot was that by their insistence on maintaining a military force in the hospital, it had been impossible to place it under the protection of the Red Cross. This manner of proceeding did not appear to me very correct and I said as much to my friends in the Jewish Agency. At their request I had taken steps to procure an honorable compromise, which would prevent the destruction of the buildings and the surrender of the Jewish troops to the Arab Legion, and when the Arabs had accepted a compromise which would satisfy both these requirements, the Jewish Agency explained its refusal not as the result of examining the merits or demerits of the proposal itself, but by invoking considerations of a general character on the principle of the inviolability of the hospital as a humanitarian institution. At ten o'clock on the morning of the 23rd, I informed 'Abdallāh Tall of the Agency's negative response, adding that, for my part, I considered the negotiations closed, though I fervently hoped that the cease-fire could be prolonged indefinitely.

*   *   *   *

A few days later, on May 26, I paid my visits to the municipal institutions of the Jewish zone. The program had been devised with customary care and meticulousness by my friends of the Jewish Agency. I went to the Agency on foot; King George's Avenue was completely deserted, silence reigned supreme and on that peaceful May morning, full of the incomparable luminosity of Jerusalem, it was almost impossible to think of the existence of danger. I quickly crossed the small square opposite Terra Santa, which was the most exposed to the fire of possible snipers and arrived without incident at the Agency where Eytan and Bergman were awaiting me. There I came in for a severe reprimand for having come by way of King George's Avenue, which was then still a "no man's land" and considered dangerous, instead of taking the route through the part of Rehavia which was under the control of the Jewish police.

Accompanied by the Mayor, Dr. Auster, I attended an official session of the Municipal Council, at which remarks appropriate to the occasion were exchanged. I then visited Vaad Leumi and the Chamber of Commerce of Jerusalem and my official visits concluded with luncheon at the Hotel Eden at the invitation of the Municipal Council, followed, at my request, by a visit to those parts of the city which had been most severely damaged by the Arab Legion's bombardment. All this, apart from its symbolic value as the visible affirmation of the presence of the United Nations in Jerusalem, enabled me to form a direct idea of living conditions in the Jewish part of the city during the "siege."

The truth is that the siege, properly so-called, had by then been overcome. The worst period was the month of April when each convoy that succeeded in getting through to Jerusalem with food and war matériel from Tel Aviv had to clear a passage by force through territory which was militarily dominated by the Arabs; and it is with good reason that the Jews have inscribed in letters of gold in the annals of the struggle for Israel those legendary and heroic convoys. It is not easy to forget the wave of emotion and enthusiasm that swept the Jewish city of Jerusalem when the head of a convoy appeared in the first bends of the Tel Aviv highway. And indeed, much was at stake. Not only the military defense of Jewish Jerusalem, but the possibility of even feeding its population depended on the valor and military skill of the Haganah in its efforts to force a way for the convoys. This precarious and perilous situation began to improve from the time when, half-way through April, the Jews consolidated their position at Kastel. And from that moment the improvement was constant and favored by the departure of the British troops who, as I have said elsewhere, tried to prevent important military positions from passing from Arab to Jewish hands.

There can be no doubt that the bombardment suffered by the Jewish zone of Jerusalem from the time when, on May 18, the Arab Legion made its appearance, considerably aggravated the sufferings and privations endured by its inhabitants during that period. But, in general, the bombardment was never very severe;

the number of casualties was not high and the material damage was not very great, due in part to the circumstance that the entire city of Jerusalem is constructed of stone. This does not, however, detract from the merit of the civilian population and of the municipal authorities in maintaining a splendid morale and insuring the continuance of the city's essential public services—a merit all the more worthy of admiration since they were enduring the Arab bombardment in the most demoralizing circumstances, knowing that the Jewish forces had not, nor could have, in Jerusalem any artillery with which to reply to the fire of the Arab guns.

However, the greatest danger to the Jewish city and the origin of most of the hardships of the daily life of its population was the lack of water. Jerusalem's water supply comes from the coastal region and the water is brought to the city by means of pumping stations, the chief of which is at Latrun. When the fighting began in the neighborhood of Latrun, before the end of the mandate, the pumps were allowed to deteriorate and the water supply began to be irregular. But when the Arab Legion occupied Latrun and the pumps stopped working, Jerusalem remained practically without a drop of water. As an emergency measure, the Municipal Council had organized a remarkable system of house-to-house delivery by tank trucks of limited supplies of water, using certain reservoirs in the environs of the city. But the days of the system were numbered, not because the reservoirs were exhausted, for their capacity was such that, as Dr. Auster himself told me, the service could have been maintained for more than two months, but because it was impossible to obtain the necessary fuel for the trucks. In the circumstances I considered it to be one of the first, if not *the* first, of my "municipal" obligations to do all that lay in my power to restore Jerusalem's water supply.

Everything depended on King 'Abdallāh, whose troops were occupying the pumping station at Latrun, and during my first visit to him after my appointment as temporary Municipal Commissioner, when I was accompanying the Chairman of the Truce Commission, I had made him acquainted with my anxieties and tried to gain his consent. But it was all in vain. The King, hardly leaving me time to finish, told me peremptorily that so long as the Jews continued to fight the Arabs, not a single drop of water should reach Jerusalem.

My second attempt took place some days later. On May 22,

the Security Council had adopted one of its first resolutions prescribing a cease-fire in Palestine and it occurred to me that this
was a suitable opportunity to remind King 'Abdallāh of the question of Jerusalem's water supply. This time I put my request in
writing, but it met with no more satisfactory response than the
first. Within the space of a few days I was informed that the question would be examined jointly with the Security Council's resolution; and there the matter rested. The first truce, which was
agreed upon a few days later, enabled the Jewish Municipality of
Jerusalem to perfect its system of house-to-house distribution and
later on, the Israeli authorities endowed the Jewish city with a
new water supply which made it independent of the famous Latrun pumping station.

*   *   *   *

Meanwhile, I had heard nothing further about the arrangements for procuring an office and residence in the Old City to
enable me to establish the same sort of collaboration with the
Arab municipal authorities as I had with the Jewish authorities.
To clarify the situation I decided to go and spend a few days in
the Arab zone. Since my last visit, communication with the Arab
zone had become considerably more difficult. It was no longer
possible to cross the lines and the only means of communication
was to go by car to Government House and then on foot by path-
ways crossing great dried-up rocky ravines, when an hour and a
half's walking brought one to the eastern part of the Old City,
which was entered by St. Stephen's Gate.

This was what I did on the afternoon of May 27. I went as
far as Government House in a Red Cross car which M. de Regnier
kindly placed at my disposal; the Red Cross had already set up
a refuge for non-combatants in Government House[4] and their
chauffeurs were familiar with the route they had to take in order
to cross the Jewish zone with its innumerable control points. Accompanied by two Arab guides and with a donkey to carry my
luggage, I set off on my journey and towards nightfall arrived at
the headquarters of the Arab commandant, 'Abdallāh Tall. The
journey was uneventful; the footpath crosses great ravines with
rocky hillocks and declivities and with stretches of cultivated land
on the lower slopes, worked almost exclusively by women. The
last part of the journey, where we came out onto the road to

4. *Vide* Chapter X.

Jericho, skirted the gloomy Kedron valley or Valley of Jehosha-
phat and a little farther on we passed by the Garden of Gethsemane. This was the first time I had been able to see it close by,
and like all the holy places connected with the life of Christ in
Jerusalem, I found it very disillusioning. True, there remained
a few ancient olives, the stones, the dust, the air and the light,
but their enchantment and power to evoke the past were pro-
faned—by the commonplace Russian Orthodox monastery with
its typical belfry set on the high ground, and even more by the
blatantly modern church which the Franciscans had recently built
right beside the road. If anyone had wanted to symbolize the
exact opposite of what Gethsemane ought undoubtedly to evoke
in a sincerely Christian spirit, he could not have hit on anything
more perfect. Ostentation, frivolity, wealth—these are what its
marbles, jaspers and rich mosaics bring to the mind. How much
more "Christian" would it have been to leave the land alone with
its stones and scrub and build in a place apart a small, austere
and simple chapel where the believer could pray and meditate in
the pious atmosphere of the Gospel instead of visiting the present
church and admiring its riches with the gaping curiosity of a
tourist admiring a new movie house or theater.

The headquarters of the commander of the Arab Legion wore
its usual air of a "caravanserai," full of people continually coming and going. The commandant, 'Abdallāh Tall, received me
with his characteristic smile, but I read in his face weariness and
anxiety. Shortly after my arrival Dr. Tannūs, one of the leaders
of the Arab Higher Committee, came in and sat down by my side
and explained to me, in the midst of that scene of confusion, that
both the Arab Higher Committee and the Arab National Committee had decided not to cooperate with the Municipal Commissioner for Jerusalem appointed by the United Nations. Circumstances had changed; when the representative of the Arab
Higher Committee had given his assent at Lake Success, he had
expected a serious truce to be concerted immediately; now it was
war and there could be no other authority than the military. I
pointed out that the decision in question was too grave to be
conveyed by mere word of mouth and I asked for the Committee
to put it in writing. He took his departure saying that he would
report our conversation to the Committee; but the night passed
and I did not see him again.

'Abdallāh Tall took me to dine with him and some other officers at a kind of mess on the upper floor of the building where

he had his headquarters and which occupied the site of the ancient fortress of Antonia, Pontius Pilate's residence. Soon afterwards Dr. Mūsā Ḥusaynī arrived. After dinner, they had various consultations among themselves and, as a result, handed me a letter signed by 'Abdallāh Tall saying briefly that as an individual they welcomed my presence, but as "temporary" Municipal Commissioner they would have no dealings with me. I confined myself to reminding them that what they were saying implied the annulment of a resolution adopted by the Assembly of the United Nations with the consent of the representative of the Arab Higher Committee accredited to the United Nations, and that I could not consider a letter addressed to me by the commander of the Arab Legion forces in Jerusalem an appropriate medium for treating, much less settling, the affair. In view of my attitude, 'Abdallāh Tall took back his letter and told me he would consult his government.

I spent the night at the American School of Archaeology and the following morning 'Abdallāh Tall asked me to arrange to go to Amman as soon as possible and take up the matter there with King 'Abdallāh and the government. Two days later, after having witnessed, as related in another chapter, the surrender and evacuation of the Jewish quarter of the Old City, I returned by the same route to what was in fact my normal residence. When I arrived at the close of day at Government House, I found that telephone communication with Jerusalem had been cut off and that it was therefore impossible to telephone for a car to be sent for me. I have to confess that this apparent contretemps was really a blessing in disguise, for thanks to the cordial welcome and hospitality of the two nurses who were in charge of Government House, I was able to spend the night there and enjoy a silence, calm and tranquillity such as I had not experienced for months. Since I arrived in Jerusalem in February, apart from the brief interlude of my visit to Lake Success towards the end of April, I had not passed a single night without hearing firing and explosions of some sort in the vicinity. The previous night had passed without the mortar and cannon fire nearby ceasing for a single moment, in a room where I had to remember to stoop down when passing in front of the windows for fear of being hit by a stray bullet. It will readily be understood why that night of silence and calm in Government House has remained so deeply engraved on my memory.

The first thing I did when I was back again in our offices was to telegraph to Mr. Evans, who was waiting patiently at Shepheards Hotel, Cairo, until peace reigned anew in Jerusalem before taking up the burden of office, to let him know how the situation stood. I then began preparations for my journey to Amman and, as soon as I could, set out again for the Old City, the compulsory point of departure for Amman. This time I went to Government House in a car we had been able to procure for ourselves and we tried out for the first time a method we had evolved for reducing the serious risk which always attended the first moments of our exit from the Y.M.C.A. This new method consisted in leaving the car the previous night in front of a large gate in the wooden fence around the recreation ground, where it was hidden by the fence itself; then opening the gate quickly, driving out at top speed, taking advantage of the great width of the gate. My colleague, Mr. Macabe, assured me with the utmost conviction that the snipers who infested the neighboring houses and who had now succeeded in turning the principal exit and, above all, the corner of Mammillah Road a few yards away into a death trap, would not have time to aim if we went out by this back door at top speed. I do not know whether it was due to his great faith in his discovery, but the fact is that we escaped without hearing a single shot and were able to pick up without any difficulty the Jewish officer who was waiting for us opposite Terra Santa to accompany us through the control points to the entrance of Government House. Without more delay than was necessary to load my luggage on the donkey that my two guides had brought for this purpose, I set off with them by the now familiar footpath towards the Old City. It was June 2, well on into the morning and, needless to say, the heat was oppressive. In the Old City I stopped for a few moments to greet 'Abdallāh Tall and then left immediately in his own car for Amman.

On arrival at the Philadelphia Hotel I found a message awaiting me to the effect that the King would receive me at half past six. I was in good time for the audience and after the usual courtesies, and when I had said a few words about the admirable behavior of the Arab Legion during the surrender of the Jewish quarter of the Old City, I broached the theme of the Municipal Commissioner for Jerusalem. The King was quite prepared for the conversation and lost no time in launching forth into a long tirade in which he spoke of Jerusalem as if it belonged to him and its future destiny lay in his own hands. Naturally, he told me in the most categorical manner that in view of the fresh circumstances there was no question of accepting or recognizing any kind of international authority in Jerusalem. For the moment there could be none but military authority and, for the future, everything would depend on the solution of the Palestine question in its entirety. He then cut short the conversation on this theme, saying that the legal and procedural details could be discussed with the Prime Minister, who was present at the audience, and with whom I then and there arranged an interview for the following day.

My interview with the Prime Minister left the situation perfectly clear. His point of view was that once the Assembly had entrusted Count Bernadotte as Mediator with the mission of finding a solution to the Palestine problem as a whole, it was unreasonable to prejudice this solution by establishing an international authority in Jerusalem. Moreover, the question was irrelevant, because in the prevailing circumstances no other authority than the military would be able to function in Jerusalem. The truth is that I could not find much to quarrel with in these arguments with which I inwardly agreed.

As I was getting ready to return to Jerusalem, rumors began to circulate that Count Bernadotte was going to pass through Amman that evening. He came and went so quickly, however, that I was not able to see him, but one of his colleagues who remained behind in Amman advised me not to return to Jerusalem, but to see Count Bernadotte in Cairo, where I could also give Mr. Evans a verbal account of the situation as regards the Municipal Commissioner for Jerusalem.

On my arrival in Cairo on June 4, I first paid a visit to Mr. Evans and acquainted him with the substance of my two conversations with King 'Abdallāh and the Prime Minister. My remarks did not appear to make much impression on him. He continued to stay in Cairo, attached to Bernadotte's staff, accompanying him on his travels and more preoccupied with the possibilities of his rôle in Jerusalem as a Quaker than as Municipal Commissioner. But what finally convinced him that there was no part for him to play in Jerusalem was a short visit he paid to the city accompanying Count Bernadotte. I cannot remember whether, as a result of this visit, he decided to cable offering his resignation, but I do recall that, a few days later, instructions were received by telephone from the Secretary General that Mr. Evans should return immediately to Lake Success.

CHAPTER VI

The Surrender of the
Jewish Quarter of Jerusalem

THE PART OF JERUSALEM which is called the "Old City" is not, as is usually the case with other historic cities, a more or less ancient part of the city with somewhat indeterminate boundaries. In Jerusalem, the Old City is formed by an urban unit which is perfectly distinctive and apart—so much so that it forms a precinct entirely enclosed by the imposing walls built by Saladin and it communicates with the rest of the city by means of gates which, save for one, the Jaffa Gate, are really gates, that is to say, they can be opened and closed at will.

The Old City of Jerusalem, where the most important "holy places" of Christians, Jews and Muslims are to be found, was inhabited before the war by some twenty to twenty-five thousand Arabs (Christians and Muslims) and about 2,500 Jews, who lived in a compact group in the Jewish quarter under the southern wall of the city. This kind of Jewish incrustation on the Old City of Jerusalem, otherwise exclusively Arab, has been the source of constant difficulties and recriminations between the two sections of the population. We can all remember the incidents of several years ago relating to the famous Wailing Wall—incidents which in 1928-29 assumed such proportions that the Mandates Commission of the League of Nations and the Council itself had to deal with the matter. This Wailing Wall was situated in a place which was in fact exposed to all kinds of complications. The Jews regard it as the last remnant of the Temple of Solomon, and it actually forms part of the precinct enclosing the great court in the middle of which rose the Temple two thousand years ago. Unfortunately, the center of this same court is occupied today by the marvelous Mosque of Omar, known also as the Dome of the Rock, which is the most important Muslim sanctuary after Mecca and Medina.

64

Such intermitting has undoubtedly led to constant danger of untoward incidents; but it is necessary, nevertheless, not to exaggerate their importance. As with all questions relating to the "holy places" in Palestine, whether Christian, Arab or Jewish, the difficulties lose much of their gravity and, I might almost say, their respectability when they are looked into closely. In reality, the importance of these questions is inflated by fanaticism (which is only respectable if it is sincere) and by political interest; when it is not, as is the case, above all, with the Christian "holy places," mixed up with sordid struggles and rivalries among the various Churches and confessions.

In any case, the type and mentality of the Jews of Tel Aviv and of many of those who live in the modern suburbs of Jerusalem, not to speak of the youth working in the agricultural settlements, do not seem to me propitious for keeping alive long a sincerely religious interest in the Wailing Wall; though there is no doubt that the religious interest will continue to be wielded as a weapon in the "political" struggle for Jerusalem. And it is precisely this that can be the source of difficulties and controversies. As the problem presented itself in 1948, it was not so much a question of assuring to the Jews free and easy access to the Wailing Wall as of restoring in the whole city of Jerusalem, both new and old, normal living conditions which would insure the peaceful co-existence of its Muslim, Christian and Jewish populations. Once this normality was restored, the question of the protection of, and free access to the "holy places" would have been reduced to its proper proportions, namely, a simple and elementary question of urban policy.

During the British mandate, while Arabs and Jews were employing their combative instincts in attacking, alternatively or jointly, the British, the situation of the Jewish quarter in the Old City of Jerusalem was relatively normal, save for certain incidents already mentioned in relation to the Wailing Wall. But when in the latter days of the mandate the struggle changed in character and Arabs and Jews, instead of fighting the British, devoted themselves to fighting each other, its situation daily became more precarious and perilous. During the last months of the mandate, when I was on my first mission to Jerusalem, the Jewish quarter of the Old City, under the protection of a detachment of the Haganah, was being literally besieged by the Arabs. Supplies of food were assured by a weekly convoy protected by British troops. The Arabs demanded the evacuation of the Haganah as a condition of raising the blockade. The Jewish authorities firmly refused, saying that if the Haganah forces were evacuated, the Jewish population would be massacred by the Arabs. Thus passed the last months of the mandate; attempts at settlement by the British authorities, alternating with sporadic fighting between besiegers and besieged. When the British troops left Jerusalem on May 14, the Arab attacks redoubled in fury and, until its surrender on May 28, the Jewish quarter of the Old City was one of the most active centers of fighting in Jerusalem.

From that moment the politico-military objectives of the combatants showed up clear and undisguised. The Arabs were determined not to allow the opportunity of ridding the Old City of its Jewish incrustation to pass. It was soon apparent that their objective was not only the evacuation of the Haganah, but the complete and total expulsion of the Jewish population. The Jews, for their part, under pretext of the danger of a general massacre, persisted in maintaining within the Old City a military force which would be of the utmost military significance in the case, for example, of a general attack by the Jews on the city from the outside. It can be said, therefore, that during the last months of the mandate, and particularly during the two weeks that elapsed between the departure of the British and the Jewish surrender, the question of the Jewish quarter of the Old City was entirely dominated by strategic and military considerations.

*   *   *   *

The first suggestion of surrender was made on May 17 and 18 and it is of special interest because it was closely related to the arrival of the Arab Legion in Jerusalem.

On May 17, the Belgian Consul in Jerusalem and I had gone to Amman on our second mission to King 'Abdallāh as representatives of the Truce Commission. Returning to Jerusalem in the afternoon, we stopped at Jericho, at the headquarters of the Arab Legion, where we had a long conversation with the commanding officer at that time, 'Abdallāh Tall. This was my first encounter with this officer; during the following weeks I was in constant and close contact with him and was thus able to appreciate his qualities of character and intelligence. In the course of our conversation 'Abdallāh Tall explained to us that the Jewish quarter of the Old City was on the point of surrender; the difficulty was that the Haganah forces defending it were apparently prepared to surrender to regular Arab troops by means of a formal capitulation, but not to the irregular bands of volunteers who controlled the Old City. 'Abdallāh Tall was expecting at any moment the order to march on Jerusalem with his troops, occupy the Old City, and negotiate with the Haganah the surrender of the Jewish quarter.

We continued our journey and reached Jerusalem at twilight. As it was too late to cross the lines, and in view of the situation in the Jewish quarter, we decided to spend the night in the Old City and asked to be escorted to the headquarters of the Arab irregulars. Faḍl Bey, their commanding officer, was a young man who did not appear to be more than twenty-five to thirty years old, very erect, with a calm and pleasant expression and sober gestures and manners; he spoke English fluently but was a man of few words. He was surrounded by a large number of assistants, adjutants and guards, equipped and armed in a somewhat picturesque manner, among whom was a Catholic priest, Father Ayad. He was a short, slight, thin-faced man with a small black beard, whose figure and cassock made a singular contrast to the motley group forming what might be called the general staff of the Arab High Command. Father Ayad's presence was explained by his influence not only in the Latin Patriarchate (as the supreme Roman Catholic authority is called in Jerusalem) but on the direction of military operations by the Arab armed forces in Jerusalem.

Our visit was the occasion for a meeting of these and certain other personalities, to whom the Belgian Consul related what 'Abdallāh Tall had told us about the eventual surrender of the Jewish quarter and offered his good offices if these could contribute towards solving the problems in a manner favorable to both sides. The Arab leaders then told us that the Jews had, the day before, shown signs of being willing to surrender and had even accepted in principle the terms fixed by the Arab High Command and communicated to them by the Father Custodian of Terra Santa; but on the morning of the following day, when they should have sent their representatives to sign the capitulation, they made it known that they were not prepared to surrender to irregulars but would do so to regular troops like the Arab Legion. This had irritated the Arabs very much. The Belgian Consul reiterated his offer and it was decided to telephone the Jewish Agency in the modern part of Jerusalem and let them know the following terms of surrender: men between the age of 15 and 55 were to become prisoners of war; women under 15 and over 55, together with the seriously wounded, were to be handed over to the Red Cross; women between 15 and 55 were to be exchanged for Arab women in Jewish hands; synagogues were to be placed under the protection of the Muslim National Council or of the Latin Patriarchate; war matériel was to be handed over to the Arabs. The Belgian Consul telephoned the Jewish Agency from Arab headquarters and informed Dr. Kohn of the terms of surrender. Dr. Kohn took note of them and announced that he would be ready with his reply at half past eight; it was then approximately seven o'clock. The reply was negative; he had communicated by radio with the commandant of the Haganah in the Jewish quarter and the situation was far from being so serious as to justify acceptance of the Arab terms.[1] When we communicated this reply to Faḍl Bey and his aides they were visibly depressed; obviously, for them to continue the attack presented almost as many difficulties as for the Jews to continue their defense. Moreover, they were no doubt aware of the imminent arrival of the Legion and they knew that this was their last opportunity of receiving the surrender of the Jewish quarter. The failure of this attempt left the door wide open for the entry of the Arab Legion into Jerusalem, which, if I remember rightly, took place twenty-four or forty-eight hours later.

*   *   *   *

On Thursday, May 27, I returned to the Old City to deal with various matters connected with my functions as temporary Municipal Commissioner for Jerusalem and, in view of the attitude of the Arab authorities, I had decided to return to the Jewish part of the city on the afternoon of the following day, Friday the 28th.

Apart from an official visit to the Latin Patriarchate, I spent the morning looking around the Church of the Holy Sepulchre Anyone who visits the Church of the Holy Sepulchre (or any of the other Christian "holy places" in Palestine) in the hope of finding in them any lingering echo of the Gospel spirit is due for a great disillusionment. No sensitive person could remain indifferent to the noble and impressive structure of the Church of the Holy Sepulchre. It is enough to justify all the respect and

---

1. In fact, two days later, on the morning of the 19th, the Haganah succeeded in establishing contact with the forces defending the Jewish quarter and maintaining it for several days.

admiration which the work of the Crusaders in Palestine merits and inspires. But just as in its architectural structure it reflects that profound religious faith and astonishing dynamism with which the Crusaders were animated, it must be admitted that its interior arrangement and design are lamentable; and if one had to consider them as expressing the Christian spirit of our time, the conclusion for a sensitive Christian would be desolating. And yet where, and in what way, could the various Christian confessions give higher proof of their spirituality than in the worship of the places where Christianity was born and which ought to be for all Christians the object of the greatest veneration and reverence? The traditional site of Our Lord's crucifixion and His sepulchre are enclosed in the Church of the Holy Sepulchre in a kind of inextricable labyrinth of corridors and chapels. But let no one suppose that he is going to find any of these places in its orignal state, or even see in them anything that could remotely recall what those of us who have been brought up in the Christian faith have imagined by reading and studying the Gospels. Each one of these places is, so to speak, covered or enclosed by a chapel in which no trace of its original character and significance can be found. And as if that were not enough, the chapels are decorated for the most part in the most deplorable modern monastic style, with gold, percale, chrome and branches of artificial flowers. To sum up, in the "holy places" as they are today, there is nothing genuine, pure, really suggestive of the Gospel spirit; and one does not know whether to laugh or cry at the ridiculous arrangements which have had to be resorted to in order to organize their "distribution" among the various Christian Churches and confessions and appease the quarrels (sometimes violent) which their ignoble and puerile rivalries provoke. An essay comparing the Church of the Holy Sepulchre in Jerusalem and St. Peter's in Rome as symbolic interpretations of Christianity and Catholicism would offer a fruitful field of speculation on the true and authentic significance of each in modern life.

*   *   *   *

However, let us return to our account of the surrender of the Jewish quarter of Jerusalem. After lunching with Dr. Ḥusaynī in a monastery we went to 'Abdallāh Tall's headquarters to take leave of him and to arrange my return to Government House. 'Abdallāh Tall was not there, and after waiting for him for a short while one of his aides appeared with orders to ask me to go and meet him immediately because the Jewish quarter was surrendering that afternoon to the Legion, and he wanted me to be present as an impartial and objective witness to the capitulation of the Haganah troops and the evacuation of the civilian population. Accompanied by this officer, we made our way swiftly to the Armenian Patriarchate where 'Abdallāh Tall had set up his temporary headquarters for the capitulation. As we went along, I noticed that the streets were absolutely deserted, especially in the Armenian quarter, and the officer accompanying us explained that a rigorous curfew had been imposed to avoid possible incidents arising out of the transit of prisoners of war. We reached the Armenian Patriarchate and found the entrance so closely guarded that it was only after much argument and explanation that we were allowed to pass. But matters became worse when, on entering one of the inner courts, the guard who was protecting the entrance into the adjoining courtyard where 'Abdallāh Tall was already conferring with the two Haganah leaders, could think of no better method of checking our impetus than to let loose a burst of machine-gun fire over our heads. A few moments sufficed to clearup the matter and without further incident we gained the next courtyard where 'Abdallāh Tall and the two officers of the Haganah troops which had defended the Jewish quarter were giving the final touches to the act of capitulation.

Here is the detailed account of the surrender which I drew up the next day: In the courtyard were grouped 'Abdallāh Tall with a few officers of the Legion (all Arabs) and the commandant and second-in-command of the Haganah troops which had been defending the Jewish quarter—two young men, about twenty-five to thirty years old, well set up and of a pleasing appearance. The spectacle of the conversation between 'Abdallāh Tall and the two Jewish leaders was rather moving: the former with great affability and without a single word or gesture which could have humiliated or offended the defeated leaders in any way; the latter, calm, strong, showing not the slightest sign of submission or resentment. I approached them; 'Abdallāh Tall told them that he had summoned me so that I could be an impartial witness of everything that passed, and from that moment the two young Jews did not leave my side. They were discussing the act of capitulation. The commandant of the Jewish troops wanted the expression "able-bodied"—to describe the men who had to be con-

sidered as prisoners of war—replaced by the word "combatants."
'Abdallāh Tall agreed to this. They then discussed how the Haganah troops waiting on the other side of the wall, before the
Zion Gate, were to be informed of the hour when the evacuation
of the civilian population was to begin. 'Abdallāh Tall decided
that the Jewish second-in-command, accompanied by one of the
Arab officers, should go and tell the commandant of the Jewish
troops outside the walls and make the necessary arrangements
with him for escorting the civilian population as it went out
through the Zion Gate. The two officers disappeared through the
immense gate and about ten minutes later the gate swung open
again to admit the two emissaries returning after the completion
of their mission. They were ten minutes of nerve-racking anxiety,
the first anxious moments we had known; for who knows what
catastrophe might have occurred if the Jewish troops outside
the walls had allowed themselves to be carried away by the temptation of liberating the Jewish officer and taking the Arab officer
prisoner. However, everyone rose to the occasion and the episode
helped, on the contrary, to create an atmosphere of mutual confidence. Meanwhile, the mayor of the Jewish quarter, who was
also one of the most important Rabbis of Jerusalem, had arrived at the courtyard where we were all assembled. The poor
man, wearing a dirty overcoat and hat, was in a lamentable state,
clearly suffering from moral and physical prostration. He tried,
nevertheless, to introduce certain changes into the act of capitulation, but the Jewish commandant himself begged him not to
insist, and in my presence as a witness the document was signed
by 'Abdallāh Tall, the Jewish commandant and the mayor of the
Jewish quarter. Although 'Abdallāh Tall pressed me to add my
signature at the foot of the document, I refused. It was one thing
for me to be present in order to prevent incidents and perhaps
useless suffering; it was quite another to authorize and legalize
with my signature, on behalf of the Secretary General of the
United Nations, the act of capitulation which was the result of a
military action undertaken in open defiance of the Security
Council's reiterated decisions.

As soon as the capitulation was signed, all of us in the courtyard, some thirty persons, set off for the interior of the Jewish
quarter. On the way, I tried to give the mayor some much needed
encouragement; the two Jewish officers and 'Abdallāh Tall came
with us. As soon as we reached the first streets we began to meet
people: swarms of children, women of all ages and old men. The

suburb was already occupied by the Arab Legion and I was reassured to see that, from the first, the civilian population showed
not the slightest sign of terror. Dejection and anxiety were general, especially among the old; the young, both men and women,
were calm and appeared to get on well with the Arab soldiers;
some of the Jewish girls even joked and laughed with the men
of the Legion. The children wavered between curiosity and fright
in the midst of all that confusion. In general, there was an atmosphere of serenity and confidence and I could not help but
think that, for the immense majority of those unfortunate people,
the bitterness and moral suffering which the surrender and consequent abandonment of their homes had inevitably caused them
were at least partly compensated by an indefinable sensation of
peace and well-being at seeing the nightmare of the last two
weeks ended.

Our arrival caused a sensation. Women, children and old men
crowded anxiously around us; and it was really a pleasure to see
how 'Abdallāh Tall, with his affability, his smile and his complete equanimity, instantly confirmed the atmosphere of security
and confidence. For everybody, and especially for the old people
and the children, he had a word of comfort and encouragement;
and a few minutes after our arrival it was apparent to me that
the Arab Legion, far from constituting a menace to the Jewish
population, was a guarantee not only that the people would be
safe, but that everything would be done in such a way as to
cause them the minimum of suffering.

For a while there was some confusion. One or two attempts at
looting had been repressed by the men of the Legion with what
seemed to me excessive severity. The first case I saw occurred
while we were still in the open space under the walls, discussing
the terms of capitulation. I suddenly saw a group of soldiers beat-
ing up a man so violently that he fell to the ground. Thinking
that the victim was a Jew, my first reaction was one of indignation and protest, mingled with horror at the thought that this
was how the Legion was going to treat the Jews. But the next
moment brought me enlightenment; the man was an Arab irregular whom the soldiers of the Legion had surprised in the act
of looting. To convince me, they brought him to where we were
standing and as he was only a youth and all this had been more
or less at my insistence, they let him go free. Later I had occasion
to witness other cases of attempted looting and, as I have said,
the Legion always reacted with the greatest vigor and severity.

As the confusion increased, at five o'clock in the evening the prisoners of war (that is, men between 15 and 55 years of age who were combatants) and the civilian population were given an hour to assemble in a kind of square or open space nearby. Immediately the heart-breaking spectacle of all evacuations of civilian populations began to take shape—the all too familiar groups of women, children and old men were slowly forming, laboriously dragging bundles and suitcases with all that they had been able to salvage from the disaster. As they filed into the square they went and sat on the ground, waiting for the order to move on; and in this way the square soon became a vast camp, melancholy and silent.

Meanwhile, the three hundred prisoners of war had been formed into a column and marched off to the citadel, where they spent the night, and the following day to a concentration camp not far from Amman. In this connection, something happened which might have had disagreeable consequences for me. It occurred to me to go to the gate to see the column of prisoners march out and instead of telling 'Abdallāh Tall and getting an officer to accompany me, I set off alone through the streets, fighting my way through the throng of people who were hurrying to the square. Just as I had got through the narrowest part, I saw the commandant of the Jewish forces surrounded by a group of Arab irregulars, who were apparently trying to relieve him of a small suitcase. As soon as he saw me, he called to me for help. I approached and explained to the Arabs as best as I could that the only thing they could do was to search the suitcase to make sure that it contained no arms; but they were on no account to take it away. They then opened it in my presence and found nothing suspicious, whereupon the Jewish commandant marched off to join his companions. But the amusing thing was that hardly had the Jew disappeared than the Arabs were suddenly struck by the peculiar fact of my presence and intervention and began among the lot of them to subject me to a kind of interrogation and display a desire to search me, all rather violently and with the natural excitement created, more than anything, by the impossibility of making ourselves understood, either they by me or, what was worse, I by them. In the end, I can't quite remember how, I managed to get away and returned to 'Abdallāh Tall and his officers, who were already supervising the removal of the civilian population, now concentrated in the square, to the Zion Gate, through which the evacuation was to take place.

It is hard to imagine a sadder spectacle than that of a population forced to abandon the houses, city or fields where they have lived or worked for generations. Unfortunately, it is a scene which in the last twenty-five or thirty years has become almost a commonplace occurrence. Nevertheless, it is only just to recognize that the circumstances attending the particular case of the Jewish population of the Old City were much less cruel and grievous than in so many other cases of recent years. The bitterness of abandoning their ancient homes was inevitable, especially for the old. But even for them, to say nothing of the young, this painful sensation was appreciably lessened, as I said before, by the immense relief of knowing that the frightful nightmare which life had become for them during the last two or three weeks had come to an end. Moreover, there was no question, as there had been, for example, in the Spanish civil war, of being forced to go long distances by roads which were exposed to constant aerial bombardment, in search of a future full of uncertainty and insecurity. In this case, there was only a distance of some five hundred yards to traverse, in complete safety, with the knowledge that they would be welcomed by their own people and looked after and installed in surroundings which were superior not only to the terrible conditions in which they had spent the weeks of blockade and fighting, but in many cases to their normal living conditions. Finally, the weather was magnificent, the temperature ideal, and even if they had had to spend a night under the stars, the fresh air, the calm of the countryside and the silence would certainly have been like balm to people who had spent night after night in the indescribable stench of that heap of debris and filth which the Jewish quarter had become under the constant fire of mortars and machine guns. I myself, crossing the suburb of Katamon in the residential part of Jerusalem the day after, saw how the same families that I had seen the previous evening leaving their homes in the Old City in such a lamentable state, were installing themselves, as best they could, in the magnificent houses which had been abandoned by their Arab owners in the early days of the struggle.

As soon as the column of prisoners of war had marched off, the most pitiable part began—the evacuation of all that mass of old men, women and children, dragging their heavy bundles, suitcases and packages with all that they had been able to salvage from the disaster. The distance they had to go was, first, some three or four hundred yards through the filthy alleys of the suburb; then another two hundred yards along an esplanade under the wall. But the difficulty was that the way was strewn with obstacles: stairs, narrow passages and doorways through which it was hard to drag their burdens; blocks of fallen masonry and even fire, for one of the houses right at the entrance to the esplanade had caught fire and the soldiers of the Legion had to remove fragments of burning wood which at times blocked the path.

In spite of the slowness with which the melancholy procession advanced, the space before the Zion Gate kept filling up with people because the exodus had been arranged in such a way that they could only pass two by two. The result was that in a short time the camp in the square, where the people had been ordered to assemble, was transferred to the Zion Gate, before which the families again sat down on the ground, awaiting their turn to go out. With the exception of some young women who presented a relatively clean and tidy appearance, the scene was a depressing one. No doubt the great physical misery of which all showed signs was largely due to the terrible conditions endured by these unfortunate people during the last two or three weeks, when what remained of the Jewish quarter was so reduced that there was no possibility of keeping the civilian population separate from the zone of combat. Among the most pitiful cases, that of the old rabbis, with their greasy skull-caps and robes, remains engraved on my memory; for them, the abandonment of their homes and synagogues was obviously the end of everything. Their dejection and despair was moving; I saw some who, on passing their homes, desperately kissed the usual sign on the lintel of the door. The women and even, surprisingly, the children remained calm, and in general it can be said that all showed great self-control.

During all this painful and delicate process, the Arab Legion and its commanding officers in Jerusalem behaved in an admirable manner. The soldiers spontaneously helped the old people and children with their burdens; they carried in their arms children who had become separated from their mothers; they shared the water from their own flasks; in short, they did everything they could to lessen the inevitable sufferings of the evacuation. I remember my reaction on seeing four soldiers carrying a sewing machine; at first I thought it was a case of looting, but afterwards I realized that they were doing it for the owner, a buxom housewife who was following them full of gratitude—though I doubt if the sewing machine arrived safely at the end of its eventful journey.

Seeing that night was drawing on before there was any likelihood of all that crowd being evacuated, I myself urged 'Abdallāh Tall to hurry them on, fearing that in the dark some incident or provocation might occur. But I met with a blank refusal to exercise any pressure; he insisted on letting the people advance with the calm and moderation which their condition and, above all, their burdens required, assuring me that there was nothing to fear and that all would end well.

The case of the military hospital in the Jewish quarter deserves special mention, primarily because the installation, organization and management of that kind of oasis of cleanliness and beauty in the midst of the indescribable accumulation of filth and rubbish which, as we have seen, the entire Jewish quarter had become, was proof of extraordinary merit. The hospital was installed in a large one-storied house (if my memory serves me right) and on crossing its threshold one began to doubt whether not only the order with which everything was set out, but even the whiteness of the doctors' and nurses' overalls and of the great pieces of linen with which they had covered the walls, was a reality or an illusion.

On our arrival we were met by the assistant director, a relatively young man who had the greatest difficulty in controlling his nerves and restraining his irritation; many complaints, not a few recriminations and various demands, not all justifiable. Shortly afterwards the director, Dr. Laufer, appeared, still wearing the rubber gloves in which he had just been operating on a wounded man. Dr. Laufer was an older, more self-possessed man, an Austrian Jew and a doctor of the University of Vienna. The tone of the conversation changed immediately; the tension disappeared and we were able to discuss the best means of evacuating the hospital and, above all, the thorny question of how to classify the wounded since, in accordance with the terms of capitulation, the slightly wounded were to be considered as prisoners of war, while the gravely wounded were to be handed over to the Red Cross. As the afternoon was now far advanced, we had to give up the idea of carrying out the inspection and removal that day and 'Abdallāh Tall proposed that the wounded and all the hospital staff should spend the night in the Jewish quarter under the protection of the Arab Legion. On the following morning an inspection of the wounded by three doctors, one Arab, one Jewish and a third from the Red Cross, could be carried out so as to decide which were the slightly wounded to be sent to Amman as prisoners of war, and which the serious casualties to be handed over to the Red Cross.

This proposal caused great alarm among the doctors and hospital staff. The assistant director came and told me in a state of great excitement that he accepted no responsibility if the proposal were put into practice, as he was sure that the Legion would leave not a wounded man alive during the night. Such was the atmosphere created by Jewish propaganda against the Arab Legion! I spoke to 'Abdallāh Tall and even for a moment considered the possibility of staying myself and spending the night in the hospital. But 'Abdallāh Tall was so emphatic in his assurances and accepted so absolutely and unreservedly full responsibility for the protection of the hospital, that it seemed to me unhelpful to do anything that might be interpreted as a sign of distrust. I explained the situation to the doctors and told them that I would be responsible for the safety of the hospital during the night. They calmed down a little and went off to take the necessary measures for this, their last night in the Jewish quarter.

I spent the night at Dr. Ḥusaynī's house and would have slept very comfortably after the nervous tension of the day had it not been, on the one hand, for my anxiety over the hospital (a rash word, a gesture wrongly interpreted, even an act of provocation, could have precipitated a catastrophe for which I might reasonably have been held at least partly responsible, through my excess of confidence) and, on the other, the constant shelling by a Legion battery of the Jewish and modern part of Jerusalem from a nearby hill.

The following morning I returned to the Jewish quarter to witness the inspection of the wounded by the doctors and their evacuation, and was surprised to find that all the wounded had been transferred during the night to the Armenian Patriarchate because some fires in the Jewish quarter had spread so as to threaten the hospital and render its evacuation necessary. And here is the interesting part; it was those same soldiers of the Legion who had remained to guard and protect the hospital and who, according to the assistant director, were not going to leave a single wounded man alive on the following morning, who removed them to the Armenian Patriarchate and saved them from the fire. I confess that this was a great source of satisfaction to me, especially when Dr. Laufer, the director of the hospital, beckoned me to one side and said more or less as follows: "You will remember my fear and mistrust when it was decided last night to leave the hospital under the protection of the Arab Legion. Well, now I want to tell you that the Legion has behaved as well as the best disciplined force of any European army, and I may say that I have served as a doctor first in the Austrian army and afterwards in the British. Thanks to the soldiers of the Arab Legion and their magnificent behavior, we have been able to save our wounded from the fire that was threatening the hospital."

With the arrival of Dr. Marti of the Red Cross, who had turned up during the night, I thought my own presence was unnecessary and even indiscreet, and I decided to consider my part in this episode of the struggle in the Old City of Jerusalem at an end.

* * * *

Thus it was that on May 28, 1948, the entire population of the Jewish quarter departed sadly from the Old City of Jerusalem. For the first time in the three thousand years of its history, the Old City of Jerusalem was going to be without a single living Jew within its walls. The disappearance of the Jewish quarter in the Old City was an inevitable consequence of the struggle between Arab and Jew arising out of the establishment of the State of Israel in Palestine. As Jerusalem was when the British mandate came to an end, the days of the Jewish quarter in the Old City were numbered, unless (an altogether impossible hypothesis) the Jews had been capable of seizing the whole of the Old City in the first few days after the departure of the British. The only thing that was in doubt was whether the disappearance of the Jewish inhabitants would come about by an orderly evacuation or by their extermination and the destruction of their homes.

We have already seen that, regarding the inhabitants, the evacuation compares favorably with similar operations carried out during the last twenty-five years in various countries of Europe.

In contrast, the disappearance of the Jewish quarter has meant, in practice, the total and complete destruction of Jewish homes. But in the interests of truth and justice it should be said that, contrary to what has been asserted, that destruction was not deliberately engineered either by the Arab Legion or by the civilian population of Jerusalem. It was simply the result of the struggle that raged for three weeks in the streets and the physical impossibility of dealing effectively with the fires which were caused by that struggle. The Jewish quarter was not large; it was formed of houses piled on top of one another, separated by a positive labyrinth of narrow streets, and it was hard to imagine that the battle for it could have had any result other than its complete destruction.

The case of the great Hurva synagogue deserves special mention. It was deliberately mined and destroyed by the Arab Legion on the afternoon of May 27, and no one can deny that this was a considerable loss to the artistic and archaeological treasure of Palestine. But the question of whether the responsibility for its destruction should rest on the shoulders of the Arab Legion, whose hand actually struck the blow, or on the Haganah, who had turned it into their last redoubt, is difficult to answer.

To appreciate the operation in its entirety, we must take into account two considerations which ought to appear on the credit side of the balance sheet. The first is that, with the disappearance of the Jewish quarter of the Old City, one of the most insalubrious urban agglomerations, perhaps, in the world has been wiped out; so that however bad the present or future conditions in which its population may be obliged to live, they could never be worse or even equal in squalor to those which surrounded it in its sordid dwellings in the Old City of Jerusalem. And the second is that, however cruel and painful this veritable surgical operation on the living body of a human group (and we know that it was less so than other similar operations), thanks to it, a constant source of quarrels and disputes capable of lapsing at any moment into armed conflict has been eliminated. One of the most difficult and delicate aspects of the problem posed by the political and administrative organization of the city of Jerusalem has thus been solved. With the conquest by the Jews of the Arab districts of the modern city and the evacuation and destruction of the Jewish quarter of the Old City, the almost complete homogeneity of the population in the two areas of Jerusalem, the Arab and the Jewish, has been assured—no slight advantage to the normal functioning of its municipal life.

CHAPTER VII

The Cease-Fire:
The Consular Truce Commission

FROM THE SPECIAL ASSEMBLY of April-May, 1948, until the conclusion of the armistices a year later, the action of the United Nations in Palestine was concentrated on achieving a truce and ensuring the observance of it. In accordance with the Charter, this action devolved upon the Security Council; it was, therefore, this Council that adopted all the resolutions which served as a basis for the activities of the various bodies sent to Palestine to try to prevent war, or at least to obtain a suspension of hostilities. The United Nations action had three phases: in the first, the stage was occupied by the Consular Truce Commission; the second was dominated by the brilliant personality of Count Bernadotte and his tenacious efforts to secure acceptance of, and respect for, the first and second truces; the third was characterized by the conclusion of the Rhodes armistices under the auspices of Ralph Bunche.

The Consular Truce Commission was set up by the Security Council on April 23, 1948, in order to supervise the implementation of the Council's resolution of April 17 summoning the interested governments and authorities to accept a truce in Palestine. It was composed of the Belgian, American and French Consuls in Jerusalem and its active life lasted about five weeks, until the time when the task of concerting a truce and enforcing its observance was handed over to Count Bernadotte, the recently appointed Mediator of the United Nations in Palestine, by a resolution which the Security Council adopted on May 29. In contrast, its official existence seems likely to stretch to eternity, for the negligence shown by the Security Council and the Secretary General of the United Nations to this "Cinderella" of international commissions, and the oblivion they have condemned it to, have reached the point where they have never even thought of going through the formality of dissolving it and thanking it for its labors.

When I reached Jerusalem on my return from the Special Assembly, I found the Commission already constituted under the chairmanship of the Belgian Consul and with the French Consulate as its regular meeting place. The Commission usually met every morning and afternoon; in the days that followed the departure of the British, it can be said to have been in permanent session. We always had the impression that the conditions in which the Commission worked and the constant risks everyone ran in keeping it functioning were but imperfectly realized at Lake Success. In order to attend the meetings, the Chairman and, at times, the American Consul used to come to the Y.M.C.A. and from there we all went to the French Consulate. We never made up our minds whether it was better to go on foot or by car. The first fifty yards as far as the corner of the King David Hotel were comparatively safe, except for the risk of snipers who infested the neighboring houses. But between the corner of the King David Hotel and the consulate there were about three hundred yards entirely in the open and in a direct line of fire from the walls of the Old City; and although Colonel Roscher Lund assured us that the distance was too great for accurate aim to be taken, we were not at all reassured when we thought of the consulate employees and guards who had been wounded at its very entrance. When we went on foot, our exit in single file from the King David Hotel to the consulate must have struck anyone who could contemplate it with serenity as comic. We ran the gauntlet one by one, at intervals of a few minutes. We each had our own tactics: Colonel Roscher Lund used to go very quickly, zig-zagging along the center of the road; the Belgian Consul and I preferred to cling to the wall and cross the street in one bound. Once inside the consulate we still had to take care crossing the garden and the great vestibule, where some of the guards were wounded.

The first and second day we met in the consul's study which was on the ground floor in the front of the building, facing the Old City. The windows were practically covered with sandbags, and protected by them and by the consulate's thick stone walls, we ran no risk at all. But we were obliged to transfer our meetings to an inner room, with windows overlooking a courtyard, because the noise of bullets and shrapnel striking the wall and sandbags made conversation impossible at times. I have already said something elsewhere about the living conditions in the French Consulate during that period; to perpetuate the memory, the consul has formed a collection of fragments of projectiles of all descriptions (mostly mortar bombs) picked up within the precincts of the consulate and has carefully preserved the bullet marks on the inside walls. It may be asked whether, in these circumstances, the French Consulate was the right place to choose for the Commission's meetings. But any other place would have had similar disadvantages and at the French Consulate we had the compensation of always being able to count on a cordial welcome and hospitality from M. and Mme. Neuville.

*   *   *   *

The Truce Commission met the sad fate which is almost always reserved for pioneers, namely, to open up the road with their failures for the success of those who follow. The determination and disinterestedness which the three members of the Commission displayed in the discharge of their functions are beyond all praise. They did all that the circumstances and the scanty means at their disposal allowed; and they did it without heeding personal discomforts and dangers. In this connection, the conduct of the Belgian Consul, M. de Nieuvenhuys, who never hesitated in braving whatever difficulties and dangers were necessary to accomplish the tasks the Commission set him to perform, is worthy of special mention. Nevertheless, in spite of everything, the Commission never succeeded in achieving the objective for which it had been created—the conclusion of a truce. During the five weeks of its active life, the struggle went on incessantly, with varying intensity, in Jerusalem and in the rest of Palestine. This does not mean that the experience of those five weeks was wasted; on the contrary, thanks to that experience, a whole series of methods and systems was put to the proof and clearly demonstrated to be useless. Men who can see in a flash what to do in order to reach the goal they have set themselves are very exceptional; the majority have found the trail blazed by pioneers who, with their failures, have shown what was useless to attempt. Such has been the contribution of the Truce Commission to the work of pacifying Palestine: to demonstrate that, in order to concert a truce, it was necessary to use greater energy and be able to command on the spot far more potent means than those which had been placed at its disposal—the negative and preliminary phase which is almost indispensable to all great human enterprises.

Apart from the neglect that failed to provide for the Commission even the most elementary means of transport, what most stultified its action to the point of rendering it inoperative was the multiplicity of agents, each working as a separate unit, which were initiating truce negotiations with the two contestants and the inevitable confusion which this deplorable system was bound to create.

I have already said something about the difficulties which had arisen between the Commission on the one hand and the British High Commissioner and the Red Cross, on the other. Towards the end of April (that is, at the beginning of the Commission's existence), the High Commissioner had succeeded in persuading the Jewish Agency and the Arab Higher Committee to accept a precarious cease-fire in Jerusalem, which was respected in a fashion until May 14, when the British evacuated the city. For their part, the delegation of the International Committee of the Red Cross in Palestine, under M. de Regnier, was conducting negotiations with Arab and Jewish authorities and personalities with a view to converting the entire city of Jerusalem into a security zone under the flag and protection of the Red Cross. These negotiations, which were initiated verbally at the end of April, resulted in a written plan which M. de Regnier communicated to the two parties at the beginning of May and of which he sent me a copy for the information of the Commission, with the suggestion that the latter should notify both Arabs and Jews of its approval.

All these proceedings were viewed by the members of the Commission with marked suspicion and, at times, irritation. Their attitude was not unreasonable, if one reflects for a moment on the manner of negotiating a truce during those last days of April and the beginning of May. The leaders of both the Jewish Agency and the Arab Higher Committee had, in the course of each day, to negotiate first, with the High Commissioner about the cease-fire in Jerusalem, its violations and the manner of extending or consolidating it; secondly, with the Truce Commission, or with its individual members, or with its secretariat, about the methods of putting into practice the truce called for by the Security Council in its resolution of April 17; thirdly, with M. de Regnier, about his plan for making Jerusalem a security zone under the protection of the Red Cross. Can anyone be surprised if, in such conditions, the truce negotiations led to no positive result during that period?

On top of all this, there was the defective coordination between the members of the Commission, often due to the physical difficulties of communication and liaison, and the lack of understanding among the governments of the immense limitations
imposed by circumstances on the action of the Commission and
of each one of its members. This applies almost exclusively to
the United States government, for I have no recollection that
any other government exerted itself to send to the Commission,
or to any of its members, any kind of suggestions or exhortations
regarding its activities. Almost always, the communications the
Commission received from the American government, through its
representative, were the source of difficulties not only in our negotiations with Arabs and Jews, but inside the Commission itself. On one occasion, the State Department's proposal was immediately followed by instructions to the consul to regard its
text as *ne varietur* and submit it to the two parties in the name of
the American government if his two colleagues on the Commission did not agree to submit it in the latter's name. This manner
of proceeding was bound to create a certain "malaise" inside the
Commission, all the more so since the proposals were far from
reasonable and betrayed a complete ignorance of local conditions
on the part of their authors.

*   *   *   *

On the morning of May 12, the Commission examined a truce
plan for the whole of Palestine, which the American Consul had
just received from the State Department with instructions to communicate it immediately to the Jewish Agency, the Arab Higher
Committee and the Arab League. Somewhat reluctantly, the Commission agreed to forward the plan itself and that same day the
document was in the hands of the Jewish Agency and the Arab
Higher Committee. Forwarding it to the Arab League presented
greater difficulties, for the League's official domicile was in Cairo
and, as I have said, the Commission had no means of transport.[1]
However, we discovered that 'Azzām Pasha, the Secretary General of the League, was on a visit to Amman and the Commission decided that its Chairman, accompanied by the Secretary,

1. Transport was a great problem at that period. The Secretary General refused
to sanction the purchase of a car for the Commission, but he did authorize us to
hire one through the consulates. To hire a car in Jerusalem at that time! The result was that we had to use cars lent either by the Red Cross (which owned a
fleet of four or five cars) or by the consuls themselves, which gave rise to remarks
to which it was not always easy to find an adequate answer.

should go to Amman the next day, try to see 'Azzām Pasha and at the same time establish contact with King 'Abdallāh and the government of Transjordan (as it was then called), whose co-operation in arranging a truce in Jerusalem might very soon be decisive.

As a result of this decision, on the following day, May 13, the Belgian Consul and I left for Amman in his car at seven o'clock on a luminous and transparent morning, such as can only be found in Jerusalem. This first expedition to Amman had for me all the savor of a real adventure, full of mystery; and I confess that I approached it with curiosity, not unmixed with appre-hension. After all, it was the first time that I was going to have personal and direct contact with the Arab world and, what was almost as exciting, I was going to travel around Palestine by my-self, without any kind of military escort or protection.

As soon as we had passed the outskirts of Jerusalem and the village of Bethany, we entered the impressive and austere coun-try of Judaea with its bare, dun-colored hills separated by harsh, rocky ravines. All was silence and solitude. From time to time we saw a Bedouin encampment, with its dark, ragged tents, sur-rounded by goats and camels; and it seemed a miracle that men and beasts could find a living in the midst of such desolation. Half way through our journey we came to the inn of the "Good Samaritan," now an Arab Legion post, so called because it is built on the site where, according to tradition, the events recorded in the parable of the Good Samaritan took place. A few miles further, not far from the Jordan, a notice board informs the reader that he has arrived at sea level and, after about a quarter of an hour, the road debouches into the great plain which forms the valley of the Jordan, against the imposing background of the mountains of Moab in Transjordan. About a mile more and we reached Jericho, a green and smiling oasis in that forbidding set-ting; another mile or so, across a somewhat lunar landscape be-tween strange cones of sand and we were at the Jordan—and the frontier between Palestine and Transjordan. The British had abandoned the police post, which was already occupied by forces of the Arab Legion. While the consul's chauffeur attended to our passports (I was worried because I had no papers except the United Nations "laisser passer" and I was by no means sure they would accept it), I was able to look at the Jordan for the first time, little thinking that all those places were going to become familiar to me during the next four years. Truth to tell, if it were not for its historical interest, no one would pay much attention to the little river which flows between rushes and sand, with nothing to make it worth a minute's contemplation. The road crosses it over a commonplace steel bridge built by the English and dedicated to General Allenby, the conqueror of Palestine in the 1914-1918 war. Looking right from the bridge, one guesses at rather than descries the merging of the Jordan into the Dead Sea. The road runs then in a straight line across the other half of the valley and, after passing through Shuneh, a wretched Bedouin village with nothing worthy of note save the proximity of the winter palace of the Kings of Jordan, begins the ascent of the great mass of the mountains of Moab. The road winds upwards nearly all the time on the edge of a precipice, following the slopes of deep, abrupt and rocky ravines with green and leafy depths. Quite high up, we passed by Salt, a town of very remote Biblical memories, which clings picturesquely to a high cliff with fig and pomegranate gardens below. A few minutes later we reached the plateau and Amman.

Amman is of very ancient origin and the marvelous ruins of its Roman amphitheatre attest to its importance in other periods of history. In the early days of that summer of 1948 it was no more than a dirty and poverty-stricken Bedouin town, with the kind of seething life that is characteristic of the East; its narrow streets were as malodorous as they were picturesque and its tiny shops full of the most diverse and peculiar merchandise.

Amman is situated at the foot of a ravine and was then already beginning to be surrounded, as it were, by a residential zone of magnificent buildings ascending the slopes of the ravine, among them, of course, the Royal Palace and most of the legations and consulates. During the four years that followed, it was astonishing to see the almost daily transformation and urban progress of this part of what could already truthfully be called a real city— all due, chiefly, to the initiative and enterprising spirit of the refugees from Palestine.

As is *de rigueur* in Amman, we went straight to the Philadelphia Hotel, which is situated directly opposite the magnificent ruins of the Roman amphitheatre, but apart from that was then more like a country inn than a hotel.[2] The Philadelphia Hotel was the center of all the political gossip of Transjordan; diplomats, journalists, Arab or European notables who were passing

2. Since then the Philadelphia Hotel has been considerably modernized.

through Amman—all forgathered at the Philadelphia; and in its lounge, which then resembled the parlor of a provincial inn, conferences and interviews were held, whose repercussions might easily reach London or New York. There we had an interview, shortly after our arrival, with the Mayor of Jaffa,[3] who took advantage of our presence in Amman to describe to us in detail his city's situation as the result of its occupation by the Jews a few days previously. All this took up the best part of the morning. The Belgian Consul then decided to go and visit the Lebanese Minister, who was a personal friend of his and who, in the twinkling of an eye, arranged for us by telephone an audience with King 'Abdallāh for half past two that afternoon. We then paid a visit to Sir Alec Kirkbride, the British Minister, of whom, recalling what Cervantes says about the innkeeper, it might be remarked that being very big, he was very mild, but concealed behind a phlegmatic manner a strong character and a great personality.

We had been warned that the King expected his visitors to be punctual, so we presented ourselves at the Royal Palace at 2:30 sharp. We were accompanied by the Lebanese Minister who acted as our interpreter, for the King always spoke Arabic and everything had to be translated into that tongue. An aide-de-camp, an officer of the Arab Legion, was waiting for us at the outer gate and escorted us to a room where we were met by the Minister for Foreign Affairs at that time, Fawzī Pasha al-Mulki. Shortly afterwards the King came in alone, without having himself announced and without ceremony. He was dressed in Arab garb and, in spite of his small stature, he had an unmistakable air of majesty. What most impressed me about him was his particularly lively and penetrating glance.

After a few brief words from the Belgian Consul explaining our mission of peace, the King took the floor and launched into a long diatribe against the Jews, followed by a no less elaborate disquisition emphasizing the peaceful intentions which had inspired the sending of the Arab Legion to Palestine; for it was by then an open secret that the Legion had occupied a considerable part of the Arab zone in Palestine. With great emphasis, the King stressed the point that the Arab Legion had been sent to Palestine to restore the order which had been disturbed by the Zionist "gangs" and to protect the Arab population against their

3. Later appointed Jordanian Minister in Washington.

terrorist activities. When he had finished he rose, without giving us time to say anything, and took leave of us with every sign of cordiality. It was obvious that the time was not yet ripe.

At ten o'clock that evening we had our interview with 'Azzām Pasha at the Egyptian Consulate. The Secretary General of the Arab League was without doubt one of the most outstanding figures in the Arab political world. The "crusade" for the liberation of Palestine had strengthened the precarious unity of the Arab countries by presenting them with the opportunity of co-operating in a common task. The League was the natural instrument for achieving this task and the general recognition that 'Azzām Pasha was its moving spirit gave him, at that moment, an almost decisive influence in such matters as the struggle in Palestine, which was of common interest to the Arab countries as a whole. 'Azzām Pasha was about fifty years of age; tall, lean and sallow, with deliberate, assured gestures, he had a certain gravity of manner and a lively and intelligent glance, resolute but not hard. As soon as he came into the room where we were waiting, I realized that he was extraordinarily tired and had consented very unwillingly to the interview. He listened indifferently and in silence while the Belgian Consul explained to him the plan for a cease-fire which we had instructions to hand to him and later asked us who was the body responsible for the proposals in the plan. Our reply was vague, as it could not help but be, since we ourselves were not very sure of its true origin. Then 'Azzām Pasha told us courteously, but quite categorically, that he was not prepared to receive the document or to acquaint himself with its contents; the Arab League would not intervene in something that concerned the Arab Higher Committee; the latter body had its representative at Lake Success and he saw no reason why such a communication as this should not be addressed to that representative. And here the interview ended: 'Azzām Pasha obviously annoyed that we had forced him to adopt this attitude and we ourselves confused and irritated. Was 'Azzām Pasha afraid that the communication to the Arab League concealed a maneuver to provoke dissension and suspicion between the League and the Arab Higher Committee? It might well be so, given the atmosphere of mistrust in which official Arab circles moved with regard to anything originating, either directly or indirectly, with the State Department. But I sincerely believe that in this case the suspicion was not justified. During the following months when we were in Cairo, we sometimes laughed over that first interview at Amman, which certainly gave no hint of the mutual confidence which was later to be established between us.

Our audience with King 'Abdallāh was followed some days later by another interview, in much more difficult circumstances. Jerusalem was already a battleground and we had to ask the Red Cross for the loan of a car to take us through the lines to the Herod Gate where a car had been sent from Amman to pick us up[4]. The King received us this time in European dress. He was wearing sports clothes with the *kaffiyah* of the Arab Legion, and I must confess that with the change of apparel he had lost a great deal of the stateliness and majesty which had so impressed me at our first meeting. He was on the point of reviewing units of the Arab Legion which were setting out for Palestine, and he began, with ill-concealed impatience, by asking us to be brief. The Chairman of the Commission made a short statement expressing not so much the Commission's anxieties about the approaching arrival of the Legion in Jerusalem, because we all thought it to be the only way of ending the semi-chaotic situation in the Old City, but our fears lest the Legion's presence give rise to an intensification of the struggle in the city. The King, who obviously had not listened very attentively to what the Chairman had been saying, confined himself to telling us that so long as a single Jew remained in Palestine, the Arab Legion would not abandon the struggle nor would a single drop of water reach Jerusalem.

The failure of these two interviews and the ever increasing isolation of the Commission limited its activities during the last two weeks of its active life to sending daily telegrams to the Security Council, giving such information as it was able to procure, necessarily incomplete and fragmentary, on the course of the struggle in Jerusalem.

*   *   *   *

May 22nd was undoubtedly the most tragic and dramatic date in the brief annals of the Consular Truce Commission. We had held the usual meeting in the morning and at lunch time we all went, with the customary precautions, to the Y.M.C.A. We were staying to lunch there and Thomas Wasson, the United States Consul General and member of the Commission, was going on to his consulate. I still remember that before separating we stayed

---

4. On the return journey the car was fired upon, in spite of the Red Cross markings, and the chauffeur, who was employed by the Delegation, received a wound in the face from which it took him months to recover.

a few minutes—only a few, because the place was not safe—talking at the entrance of the Y.M.C.A. Two hundred yards further on, as he had just turned the corner of the road to the consulate, and under the very eyes of his guards, Thomas Wasson fell wounded in the chest by a sniper's bullet. The steel vest he always wore and which we used to joke about when he took it off on arriving at our meetings and hung it over the back of his chair, availed him nought; whether it was mere chance or the sniper's good aim, the bullet penetrated clean through the right armpit. He was taken by ambulance immediately to Hadassah Hospital and operated on in the course of the afternoon; but in spite of all their efforts the doctors were unable to save him and he died in the hospital at six o'clock in the morning of the following day, May 23.

A funeral service was held according to the Protestant rites on the afternoon of the same day in the courtyard of the convent of the Sisters of the Rosary, adjoining the consulate. This service also commemorated one of the consulate guards who had been killed a few days before when he imprudently went out alone and at night to walk around the consulate. Apart from the consulate staff, headed by the consuls, Mr. Burdett and Mr. Stabler, the service was attended by representatives of the Red Cross, a few Americans who were still resident in Jerusalem, some journalists, and the Belgian Consul and myself, representing the Truce Commission and the Secretary General of the United Nations. The place and the road leading to it were dangerous owing to snipers in the neighboring houses, but I find that the entry in my diary referring to this sad ceremony records the fact that during the service not a single shot was heard in the vicinity. The atmosphere was, however, tense and on the faces of all present could be read not only natural emotion but a certain note of anxiety. The common danger to which we were all exposed gave to our feelings and reactions at that moment a peculiar intimacy and fellowship. We all felt the death of Thomas Wasson touched us closely; the same fate might have befallen any one of us and might still befall us at any time.

The Chairman of the Commission hastened to inform the Security Council of the attack of which his American colleague had been the victim. I never found out whether the Security Council adopted a special resolution or expressed their feelings in any other way about the tragic death of the American member of the Truce Commission. In any case, the Commission never received any communication from the Security Council about the melancholy incident and this silence made a deplorable and painful impression on us all. Thomas Wasson died when he was returning from a meeting of the Truce Commission, that is, in the fulfillment of his mission not as the United States Consul, but as a member of the Truce Commission appointed by the United Nations. He had, therefore, the tragic privilege of being the first victim sacrificed to the cause of peace in Palestine.

CHAPTER VIII

Count Bernadotte, Mediator
of the United Nations for Palestine

The Truces

THE POST of United Nations Mediator in Palestine was created by a resolution which the Assembly adopted late in the afternoon of May 14, 1948, that is to say, a few hours before the official expiry of the British mandate and when the High Commissioner, the British administration and the British armed forces had already evacuated Jerusalem. Without loss of time, Count Bernadotte was invested with the high functions and grave responsibilities which the Assembly had conferred on the holder of the new post, and from that moment until his tragic death by assassination four months later in Jerusalem, his dynamic personality filled the international stage of Palestine.

In substance, the mandate entrusted to the Mediator by the Assembly was a twofold one. In the first place, the Mediator was to "use his good offices with the local and community authorities in Palestine to promote a peaceful adjustment of the future situation of Palestine." Desirous, no doubt, of carrying out his mandate to the full, Count Bernadotte immediately set in motion negotiations with the Arab governments and the Israeli government about the questions of substance which divided them and, as a result of these negotiations, drew up a series of proposals which he submitted to the two parties and which figure in the first part of his report to the Assembly. These proposals were rejected by both Arabs and Jews; and the Assembly which met at Paris in the autumn of 1948 abstained from any expression that might be interpreted as assent.[1]

The failure of this attempt at mediation cannot have come as a surprise to Count Bernadotte. As he stated in his report, the indispensable condition for mediation to be attempted with any

1. *Vide* Chapter XI.

chance of success was a suspension of hostilities, and the truces were too precarious and the time that elapsed before his death too short for this condition to be regarded as fulfilled. The very terms in which this part of his report is couched clearly show the scepticism of the Mediator himself as to the probability that his proposals would be accepted by the combatants or confirmed by the Assembly. It is obvious that the proposals were drawn up rather hastily, principally in order not to leave that part of his mandate unfulfilled; but what was undoubtedly the essential and almost exclusive object of his attention during those four months, what consumed almost all his astonishing energy and dynamism, was the titanic task of achieving the acceptance of a truce and the observance of its terms and conditions by both parties.

The Assembly's resoluton defining the Mediator's mandate relegates to a secondary place, and hardly mentions in passing, his participation in concerting a truce; it confines itself to stating that the Mediator ought to "co-operate with the Truce Commission for Palestine appointed by the Security Council" in its resolution of April 23, 1948. It was the Security Council itself which, by its resolutions of May 29, ordaining a four weeks' truce, reversed the terms, making the Mediator responsible, in agreement with the Truce Commission, for supervising the conclusion of the truce and enforcing respect for it. It was not long before events proved that the allusion to the Truce Commission was not much more than a polite formula. In reality, this resolution made the Mediator the organ of the United Nations responsible for concerting a truce and supervising its observance; consequently, it put an end to the active life of the Truce Commission. In any case, the latter had anticipated the inevitable and, before the Security Council had adopted its resolution of May 29, had decided to suspend its activities in order not to interfere with any steps the Mediator might think it advisable to take on his arrival in Palestine.

This change in the United Nations attitude to Palestine affected me personally. On June 4, I arrived in Cairo.[2] The same day, Bunche introduced me to Count Bernadotte and we all three had a preliminary conversation. I got the impression of a man wholly preoccupied with the idea of speed and activity, anxious to appear as someone who came to the point at once and knew his own mind. But was all this genuine? There was rather too much activity, too much coming and going, counting the

2. *Vide* Chapter V.

minutes, taking rapid decisions and carrying them out without time for proper reflection—and all in a somewhat confused and chaotic manner. I find the following note in my diary for that period: "The Count gives me the impression of a man who is lost in a labyrinth, who yet continues walking with great speed and decision as if he knew exactly where he is going." And today it seems to me that that remark contains more than a grain of truth. But whatever the external characteristics of his personality and methods, no one could refuse to pay a tribute of admiration and respect to the wholehearted devotion with which he flung himself into his task, or to his impartiality and his fervent desire to accomplish a work of peace and justice in Palestine.

Shortly after my arrival in Cairo, the Mediator decided to appoint me his representative with the Egyptain government and the Arab League, and with these functions I remained eight months in Cairo, until, in January 1949, I was appointed Principal Secretary of the recently created Palestine Conciliation Commission.

* * * *

The first truce was concluded on the basis of the resolution adopted by the Security Council on May 29, 1948. This resolution summoned all the interested governments and authorities to order a cease-fire for four weeks, and to undertake not to introduce into their territories during that period either fighting personnel or war matériel. The resolution instructed the Mediator to supervise, in agreement with the Truce Commission, the implementation of these measures and, for this purpose, laid down that an adequate number of military observers should be placed at his disposal. The resolution ended with a penal clause: if either of the parties rejected the resolution or if, having accepted it, they repudiated or violated it, the situation in Palestine was to be the subject of a fresh examination in order to decide whether to apply Section VII of the United Nations Charter.[3] The Council authorized the Mediator to fix the date when the four weeks' truce was to begin and, in general, to deal with any problem that might arise in connection with the implementation of the resolution.

The lesson of the Truce Commission had not been forgotten and its recommendations in favor of energetic action had not

3. This chapter under the title "Action with respect to threats to the peace, breaches of the peace and acts of aggression" contains the measures relating to the application of political, economic and military sanctions.

fallen on deaf ears. Everything went to show that the Security Council was determined to procure a cease-fire in Palestine and this determination was manifested in a concrete and positive manner by the number of means and facilities with which the Mediator was provided as the person responsible for assuring on the spot the conclusion and observance of the truce. He was furnished with a staff that was imposing both in number and quality, with Ralph Bunche at its head. A team of observers to supervise the truce, consisting of American, Belgian, French and Swedish officers, was rapidly organized and set up its headquarters at Haifa. From the outset, the Mediator had at his disposal practically unlimited means of transport, beginning with a special airplane, with Red Cross and United Nations markings, in which he made his spectacular arrival in Cairo and which was constantly at his disposal for travelling to and from the Middle East. This airplane proliferated during the following months, and the Mediator's mission at Rhodes ended up with fourteen or fifteen airplanes of different types and categories. It is possible that all these were necessary for an operation of such complex nature as the supervision of the truce, but the prodigious use of them on operations of doubtful necessity provoked justifiable criticism and even bitter reflections on the part of those who could not help comparing this prodigality with the parsimony displayed a few weeks previously towards the Truce Commission. This abundance of material means, taken in conjunction with the publicity with which the Mediator's mission was always surrounded and Count Bernadotte's marked predilection for the spectacular and the ostentatious, undoubtedly helped to create a propitious atmosphere in which the personal action of the Mediator, in spite of its logical deficiencies, could produce the desired result. Thus it was that on June 9, the two parties declared themselves ready to accept the concrete conditions proposed by the Mediator for a four weeks' truce to start on the 11th of the same month.

Four weeks later, this first truce came to an end, and after two attempts by the Mediator to have it prolonged, first for thirty days and then for ten days, both frustrated by the refusal of the Arab states, hostilities broke out again, with the result that the Jews conquered three important positions—Nazareth, Lydda and Ramleh—without counting several small Arab villages isolated in Jewish-controlled territory.

Faced with such a grave situation, the Security Council, with Count Bernadotte present, adopted its famous resolution of July

15, *imposing* a truce of unlimited duration under the direct threat of sanctions against the Arab states. The effect was immediate, almost overwhelming. The resolution contained an order, not an invitation or an appeal; and the order was obeyed within forty-eight hours. The only thing the Mediator had to do was to fix the time when hostilities were to cease. That time was July 16 for Jerusalem and July 18 for the rest of Palestine.

*　　*　　*　　*

It is not my proposal, nor indeed would it be to the purpose, to write a detailed chronicle of the truces. The interested reader will find such a chronicle, in very complete and authentic form, in the report which the Mediator submitted to the Assembly of the United Nations which met at Paris in the autumn of 1948. In any case, since I remained in Cairo as the Mediator's representative with the Egyptian government and the Arab League during the whole period while the two truces were in force, my personal information about what happened at that time is necessarily incomplete and even, perhaps, biased. For all that, a view of the truces from Cairo, however incomplete and biased, forms a part of the picture as a whole which is too important to be ignored.

My functions as an intermediary between the Mediator and his mission in Rhodes, on the one hand, and the Egyptian government and the Arab League, on the other, brought me into contact with a great many Egyptian politicians, outstanding among whom was Nuqrashī Pasha, who was Prime Minister during the whole of my mission in Cairo. I confess that I never succeeded in familiarizing myself sufficiently with Egyptian domestic politics to form a precise idea of the part played in them by Nukhrashī Pasha. In a society composed of a peasant majority and a minority of great landowners, living at the two extremes of misery and opulence, and without the regulating action of a real public opinion, domestic politics in Egypt consisted of a kind of game of "give and take" between a few families represented by pseudopolitical parties, the King, the army and the fanatical and intransigent Muslim hierarchy. But whatever his political significance, Nuqrashī Pasha possessed in the highest degree the art of maintaining the most acrimonious discussions and controversies in an atmosphere of cordiality and mutual understanding. He had the great merit in that country of concentrating attention on the substance of the matter, ignoring with the gesture of a *grand seigneur* questions of prestige and *amour propre*. He was clear and direct in the presentation of his arguments, and succeeded in reconciling the most unshakable firmness in the defense of his point of view with a constant affability and perfect courtesy.

At our first interview in the early days of June, Nuqrashī Pasha told me that he was directing the Palestine negotiations himself and gave me clearly to understand that he wanted me to approach him personally over any question, great or small, relating to my functions as the Mediator's representative. The result of this was the establishment of very cordial personal relations, for there were times when I had to see him not only daily but several times a day, and on occasions our official conversations ended in informal chats which, little by little, changed our formal relations into a real personal friendship. On the other hand, I found myself in trouble with the Minister for Foreign Affairs, Khashabah Pasha, through whom I should, in principle, have established and maintained my relations with the government. This situation caused some offense which I regretted, for I held the minister in great esteem; but everything continued in an atmosphere of cordiality and I can truthfully say that my relations with the Ministry of Foreign Affairs, like those I enjoyed later with the Ministry of Defense, were always marked by mutual confidence. It will readily be understood from what has gone before that the assassination of Nuqrashī Pasha on December 28, 1948, was a source of profound personal grief to me. He died a victim of his laudable endeavor to free his country's public life from the secret influence of fanatical terrorists. His funeral was the occasion of a striking demonstration of popular sorrow, in the oriental manner: noisy, disordered, with clear signs of collective hysteria, bordering on violence and even aggression.

The other great personality with whom my functions brought me into frequent and cordial contact during this period was 'Azzām Pasha, Secretary General of the Arab League. I have already described the circumstances of our first meeting at Amman[4] and how, contrary to what that encounter augured, our personal relations could not have been more friendly in the months that followed. But 'Azzām Pasha constantly employed his extraordinary intelligence and tremendous powers of persuasion in defense of the most extreme and intransigent stand against every idea of peaceful coexistence with the Jews or the State of Israel. It is difficult to say how far 'Azzām Pasha helped to create

4. *Vide* Chapter VI.

the state of popular opinion which crystallized into the formula "liberation of Palestine and extermination of the Jewish invaders"; but there is no doubt that, with his characteristic lucidity, he immediately saw the value which a "crusade" to liberate Palestine could have in consolidating the still wavering Arab League. And with this fundamental consideration as the pole star of its policy, the League and its Secretary General became the most authoritative exponents of the policy of unbending opposition to any compromise formula and, hence, to the truces.

There could have been no objection to this attitude, from the point of view of what is called "realist" policy, had the Arab states been in a position to put it into practice and bring it to a successful conclusion. But here we are touching on something that has been the constant characteristic of Arab policy during the Palestine crisis and one of the causes of its failure: defective coordination between the political or military plans and adequate means to carry them out. This is what important and responsible leaders of the Egyptian army reproached 'Azzām Pasha and the Arab League with, in terms of great vehemence and bitterness. The Egyptian army, they said, lacked everything that was necessary for a campaign such as the one in Palestine;[5] they accused the "politicians" of having forced the army to advance rapidly and at all costs, resulting in a strategic disposition of the front which had made Egyptian staff headquarters a laughing stock in the eyes of the world; they maintained, finally, that this campaign represented a sacrifice which was out of all proportion to Egypt's interest in the liberation of Palestine.

*   *   *   *

The truces were received with ill grace by the Arabs and particularly by the Egyptian government. This is not surprising if we remember that, when the Mediator began his lightning negotiation to procure acceptance of the first truce, supply difficulties and the lack of water had created in the Jewish part of Jerusalem a situation of extreme gravity. Moreover, at that same period, official communiqués were announcing that the Egyptian army, destined to perpetuate the glories of the great Muḥammad 'Alī and his son Ibrahīm Pasha, was advancing rapidly on Tel Aviv, which was about to fall into its hands. What, after all, was the destruction of a handful of Jews, clinging to their precarious foothold in Palestine, compared with the fabulous campaigns of

5. It was said in Cairo that the army did not even have the necessary water trucks for crossing the Sinai desert.

Ibrahīm Pasha, threatening Constantinople itself? In this atmosphere which the Egyptian government had imprudently created with its bombastic propaganda, it was not at all strange that the truce should be regarded as a device to frustrate a great Egyptian victory by saving the Jews of Palestine from the extermination which so closely threatened them.

The reality, however, was far from corresponding with this picture, which the Egyptian government had prepared for internal consumption. There is no doubt that, without the first truce, the situation of Jerusalem would have become desperate; and in this sense, the reluctance of the Arabs to accept it is understandable. But the truth is that the first truce, far from having frustrated an imaginary Egyptian victory and a still more imaginary conquest of Tel Aviv, came in the nick of time to save the government and the army from the ridicule which would have been their portion, once it was discovered in what a dangerous situation the army lay as a result of this same rapid and reckless advance of which official circles had boasted so vaingloriously.

The sober truth is, however, that, taken as a whole, the first truce favored the Jews; not only in the particular case of Jerusalem, but also because, as the Mediator himself recognized in his report to the Assembly, any truce, by its very nature, hinders the attacking forces in pursuing their objectives and makes it possible for the defenders to consolidate and improve their positions. Dominated by this idea, the Arab states put up a determined and tenacious resistance to the Mediator's proposals for the prolongation of the first truce—a resistance which only yielded to the direct threat of sanctions contained in the Security Council's resolution of July 15. In principle, the Arab attitude appears understandable and even justified; and I confess that, at the time, I judged the conduct of the Mediator and of the Security Council harshly, seeing that they were *imposing* the prolongation of the truce on the Arab states in full knowledge of the fact that, in itself and apart from the degree of impartiality with which it was administered, it was bound to favor the Jews. What I was not then in a position to appreciate and what gave the Arab attitude a certain humorous and paradoxical savor, was the extent of Arab military impotence, not so much on account of the poverty of their means as of their lack of coordination and their internal rivalries and disputes; and in the particular case of Egypt, the dangerous situation of the Egyptian army as the result of its rapid and imprudent advance, leaving intact in its rear numerous and important Jewish settlements which already, with their armed forces, their organization and their war matériel, constituted formidable military positions. This slight air of paradox in the obstinate Arab resistance to the prolongation of the truce is emphasized by the fact that, during the eight or ten days between the two truces and while Arab politicians were pouring out a flood of eloquence against prolongation, Arab generals were unable to defend three positions of such capital importance as Nazareth, Lydda and Ramleh, which thenceforth became part of the State of Israel.

The second truce came into force on July 18, and lasted on paper and so far as Egypt was concerned, until the armistice was signed on February 24, 1949. On the spot, and in actual fact, the truce was broken by the Jewish offensive in the Negev on October 15. The system of inspection and supervision functioned with greater efficiency, though not with greater impartiality, than during the first truce. I was always doubtful about the wisdom of having established the headquarters of the system at Haifa in Jewish territory; though it was true that the Jews regarded this as a sign of partiality towards the Arabs, since it rendered possible a particularly strict control over the Port of Haifa. Until the assassination of Count Bernadotte, the truce control services were headed by General Lundstrom, of the Swedish air force, a man who no doubt possessed the highest qualities as a military leader and an aviator, but who was certainly not gifted with the necessary tact and prudence for the successful discharge of functions as delicate as those involved in effectively supervising the observance of the truce. When Ralph Bunche succeeded Count Bernadotte as "temporary" Mediator, General Lundstrom was replaced by General William Riley, of the American Marines. The apparatus which had been created for these functions was excessively complicated. Its "committees," examining and deciding by majority vote, accusations of violations by either party, with the inevitable accompaniment of legal opinions, were insensibly losing the necessary elasticity for the practical and concrete mission on which they ought to have been engaged, and becoming pseudo-courts of justice, taking rigid decisions which, for the most part, only aggravated the situation instead of facilitating a practical and reasonable solution. In contrast, the supervision of the truce on the spot by teams of official observers gave positive results and constituted as a whole one more demonstration of the possibility of creating really international teams, with a truly international spirit and ready not only to work, but to run personal risks for an international cause.[6]

The observance by the Egyptian authorities of the truce terms relating to the import of war matériel or the increase and training of military effectives was never subject to regular and effective control. I remember that on one occasion the thought must have struck someone that, if only in order to preserve the formalities, a team of observers ought to be stationed in Alexandria. Forthwith, without even warning the Mediator's representative with the Egyptian government, the Haifa "headquarters" dispatched to Alexandria a young marine officer, who presented himself one fine day at the customhouse and insisted on inspecting the cargo of a ship that had just arrived. This produced, of course, the inevitable incident: the port authorities refused, the matter was referred to the central authorities, and it took me several days to calm the excitement caused by a manner of proceeding which the Egyptian government not unreasonably considered offensive. But this manner of proceeding was characteristic of the state of mind then prevailing among those who were responsible for supervising the truce. Their functions demanded that they should frequently interfere in matters which were normally reserved to the internal sovereignty of states and their tendency was to interfere without tact or reflection, and without taking account of the hypersensitiveness which still afflicted both the Arab states and the State of Israel with regard to anything affecting their sovereignty as independent states, precisely because that independence was so recent and at times so precarious.

The stationing of observers in military airports was another source of prolonged discussion with the Egyptian authorities, who refused to allow observers in their airports so long as the airfields which Israel was using to supply her settlements in the Negev by air were not subject to supervision. To the best of my recollection, Haifa headquarters never succeeded in placing observers in Egyptian military airports.

The Egyptian front in the northern Negev was naturally subjected to continuous and rigorous supervision by teams of observers stationed at Gaza. Until the Jewish offensive of October 15, the greatest difficulties arose in connection with the passage through the Egyptian lines of supply convoys destined for the

6. The Mediator's report to the third session of the United Nations Assembly held in Paris contains all kinds of details on the organization and functioning of all these services.

Jewish settlements which, lying to the south of these lines, were cut off from Israeli territory. The difficulties started in June, at the beginning of the first truce, and continued without interruption until the Jewish offensive of October 15. The terms of the truce provided for the supplying of these settlements and the obstacles which the Egyptian authorities placed in the way of the convoys were an open breach of the truce. On the other hand, the Egyptian government complained that the settlements were continuing to receive supplies by air which were transforming them into regular military positions, and that though this was equally a breach of the truce, because it was not controlled by the observers, the Mediator was taking no effective steps to prevent it. The incidents and interminable discussions to which this situation gave rise have remained, above all else, engraved on my memory because of the anxieties we went through to see that either the local commandants were advised in time to let the convoy pass or, in the contrary case, that headquarters were notified so that the convoy could be held up—and all this with an urgency that brooked no delay, at any hour of the day or night, with all the difficulties of communication between Cairo and Haifa, in Israeli territory.

What most disturbed me in all these negotiations relating to the application of the truce terms was the Egyptian authorities' growing lack of confidence in the impartiality with which supervision was exercised, especially since the death of Count Bernadotte. And whatever the intimate convictions and personal preferences of those who were chiefly responsible for exercising this supervision (a field which I took good care not to enter), it is fair to say that appearances often lent color to the misgivings and suspicions of the Egyptian authorities. Incidents like those I have described were certainly not the most likely to persuade the Egyptians that those responsible for supervising the truce were animated by sentiments, if not of sympathy, at least of respect and consideration for them. Among a series of incidents that were continually inflaming this mistrust, a typical case is that of the capture and destruction by Jewish forces of three Arab villages south of Haifa. The facts were reported to the Mediator by the Arab League, but the accusation remained unanswered for six weeks under the pretext of investigations on the spot. This prolonged silence provoked a violent protest from 'Azzām Pasha, the Secretary General of the League, in the course of one of his customary attacks on the truces and the system of supervision.

Within forty-eight hours the League received a reply saying that the charges made had been confirmed by investigation and that a report had been adopted condemning the Jews. It was an easy task to persuade malicious minds in Cairo that, without 'Azzām Pasha's energetic intervention, the question would have been interred forever in the voluminous archives of the truce control "headquarters."

During all those months the general atmosphere in Cairo was tense and at times threatening to all foreign elements. Air raids, whether real or imaginary, by the Israeli air force provoked violent popular demonstrations, which more than once cost the life, in the very center of the city, of innocent tourists or European residents in Cairo. The three or four days that followed the explosion of the bomb which destroyed one of the great shops in the center of Cairo were days of real anxiety. For several hours the Jewish quarter was exposed to the fury of the mob, and the number of victims and the extent of material damage were never known. In the rest of Cairo there were only a few isolated cases of attacks on Europeans who had been mistaken for Jews, but it was dangerous to go about the streets and we spent several days shut up in Shepheards Hotel under police protection. As could have been foreseen, the anti-Jewish fury of the mob provoked by the war in Palestine spread rapidly to other aspects of Egyptian political and social life and offered a fruitful field to the activities of ultra-nationalist clandestine and fanatical organizations. In November agitation started among the students who, at the beginning of December, barricaded themselves in the university, forcing the police to undertake real military operations which resulted in the death of the Cairo Chief of Police. All this culminated in the assassination of Nukhrashī Pasha, towards the end of December, by a member of the powerful political-religious organization known as the Muslim Brotherhood, which was characterized by its nationalist and religious fanaticism. It was from the terrorist activities of this organization that Nukhraskī Pasha had tried to free Egyptian public life.

*   *   *   *

During the night of September 17, the first news reached Cairo of the assassination that same afternoon in Jerusalem of Count Bernadotte and Colonel Serot. The crime was a particularly odious and repulsive one and the circumstances in which it was committed shrouded it in an atmosphere of equivocation and suspicion which has taken a long time to disperse. As to the re-action of the Israeli government, the report drawn up by the then United States Ambassador in Tel Aviv, Mr. James Mac-Donald, of his interview with Mr. Sharrett during the night fol-lowing the day of the assassination, bears clear and irrefutable witness to this.[7] The ambassador wholeheartedly threw all the weight of his enormous personal and political authority into per-suading the Israeli government to adopt the most energetic mea-sures to meet the grave international repercussions which the crime was bound to provoke. The government, in the ambassa-dor's graphic phrase, must prove itself a real government and not a political *junta*. Nevertheless, neither the actual assassins, nor those who were behind them, have ever been discovered and the crime has remained unpunished to this day. But what most helped to create the atmosphere of equivocation and suspicion which surrounded the tragic event was the difficulty of under-standing how the Israeli authorities, knowing the hostility of the extreme nationalists to Count Bernadotte and aware of the fact that he had been threatened with death, could have allowed him to traverse a part of Jerusalem which was in fact under the con-trol of these same extremist groups, without a police escort or any protection whatever. The ambassador must no doubt have thought that any reference to this aspect of the question would have put the minister in a somewhat embarrassing position and, remembering that tact is one of the qualities most esteemed in a diplomat, carefully refrained from mentioning it in his conver-sation with Mr. Sharrett.

The Security Council at once appointed Ralph Bunche tem-porary Mediator and, as I have said, when General Lundstrom resigned his post as chief of staff to the truce control service a few days later, the temporary Mediator replaced him by the as-sistant chief of staff, the American General Riley.

The tragic death of Count Bernadotte had a curious effect on my daily life in Cairo. The authorities decided to provide me with a police escort which accompanied me during the day and spent the night outside the door of my room at Shepheards Ho-tel. Following the rule laid down by Count Bernadotte himself not to ask for special protection or to reject any measures adopted by those who were responsible for his personal safety, I bowed to the decision, but I confess that I never got used to this form

7. MacDonald, James G. *My Mission in Israel 1948-1951*. (New York: Simon and Schuster, 1951) p. 81.

of servitude. And my scrupulous respect for religious sentiments ended by making me adjust my comings and goings to the hours of the Muslim believer's morning and evening prayers; for nothing outraged my conscience so much as to find, on leaving my room, that my guard had taken off his shoes in the middle of the corridor and was engaged in the genuflections appropriate to his devotions—devotions that he was obliged to abandon precipitately in order to follow me.

*   *   *   *

On October 15, 1948, the Israeli army launched what can properly be called today its offensive in the Negev, thus putting an end to the truce between the Egyptian and the Israeli forces. If my memory is not at fault, the initial attacks were the result of one of the continuous incidents provoked by the passage through the Egyptian lines of a supply convoy destined for the Jewish settlements in the Negev; but the scope of the operations very soon made it plain that this was a regular offensive, carefully planned and prepared down to the last detail. At eleven o'clock that same night, I was urgently summoned to the Ministry of Foreign Affairs, where I was handed a note denouncing the bombardment by Jewish forces of various Egyptian positions, some of them in Egyptian territory. The text of the note was immediately telegraphed to the Mediator in Paris. On the following day, October 16, headquarters at Haifa ordered a cease-fire, to take effect at two o'clock in the afternoon of the same day. Two days later the Mediator telegraphed to me from Paris a proposal to suspend hostilities for four days, which was accepted at once by the Egyptian government. During the night of the 19th to 20th I received, also from the Mediator in Paris, the text of the resolution adopted by the Security Council on the 19th, ordering an unconditional cease-fire, the withdrawal of the troops to the positions they had occupied on the 15th, before starting the attack, the acceptance by the Egyptian government of the "decision" relating to the supply convoys for the Jewish settlements in the Negev and, finally, the opening of negotiations on other questions pending between the two parties.

This rapid succession of decisions, each virtually contradicting or at least ignoring the previous one, was not the most appropriate method of bringing home to the Israeli government the conviction that the Security Council and its executive organs were sincerely resolved to put an end to the Jewish offensive. As seen from Cairo, everything indicated that the United Nations were reacting with singular mildness and resignation to the offensive, which the Mediator himself described to the Security Council as a "unique incident," implying a struggle of "much greater scale than any that had occurred during either of the two truces." The well-intentioned did their best to find an explanation for this attitude; the malicious openly attributed it to complicity on the part of the United Nations in order to give the offensive time to achieve the desired results before intervening in a really effective way. Those weeks left a bitter taste in my mouth, because more than once I found myself unable to give a satisfactory answer to the criticisms and questions which politicians, soldiers and journalists addressed to me. The harshest criticism referred to the contrast between the terms employed by the Security Council when forcing the Arabs to accept the second truce, naming them explicitly as the guilty party and threatening them unequivocally with sanctions, with those now employed in the resolution of October 19 to deal with the gravest violation of that same truce. Those terms were drafted so skillfully that a perusal of them would not even make it clear whether the violation had been committed by the State of Israel or by the Arab states. Nor was it easy to explain satisfactorily why this last resolution omitted any reference to the manner of determining the precise moment when the cease-fire was to become effective, without which, as is well known, any cease-fire order is practically inapplicable; and the correspondence that was necessary before the hour was finally fixed for two o'clock in the afternoon of October 22, by dwelling upon the suspicion aroused by this omission in Egyptian official circles, did not help to allay the growing distrust with which the United Nations intervention on this occasion was viewed in Cairo.

This distrust was the more understandable since each of these resolutions became a dead letter before the ink in which it was written had time to dry. During the two weeks when resolutions were following hard on each other's heels, the Jewish offensive had achieved its principal objective: Beersheba, the capital of Negev, had been captured by Jewish forces on the second day of the offensive and, in the latter days of October, one of the best divisions of the Egyptian army had already been cut off at Faluja—an incident that, as we shall see, became a determining factor in the course of events during the following weeks. Not a day passed without the liaison officer at the Ministry of Defense coming to announce fresh attacks by the Jews on the Egyptian positions. The accusations were frequently accompanied by urgent messages from the minister asking me to inform the Mediator that, if the attacks did not cease within a few hours, the Egyptian government would regard its promise not to attack as cancelled and the Egyptian forces would recover their freedom of action. However, I soon realized that all this was pure arrogance; any pretext served to revoke the summons and forget the threat. The truth is that the front had collapsed and the Egyptian army was not in a position to take the offensive. But the days passed, the Jewish attacks continued, and distrust of the United Nations among those politicians or soldiers who were following the course of events closely was becoming more profound and deeply rooted.

While the Mediator and his representatives in Palestine were trying with more or less urgency to carry out the resolution of October 19, prescribing the withdrawal of the armed forces to the positions they had occupied on the 15th, before the offensive, the Security Council, ignoring these efforts, brusquely abandoned this formula, and in its resolution of November 4. replaced it by another, according to which the armed forces were to withdraw not to the lines they had occupied before October 15, but to new provisional lines which the Mediator was to trace. At the same time, it was ordered that the parties were to come to an agreement, either directly or through representatives of the United Nations, about the demarcation of permanent lines and the establishment of neutral and demilitarized zones considered appropriate for the maintenance of the truce. It was a hard blow to the Egyptian government; for the first time it found itself confronted during this crisis with a decision that not only evaded the question of responsibility for the violation of the truce, but opened the door to a solution of the conflict that was based on acceptance of the *fait accompli*. However, the Egyptian government, plucking up heart, and urged on by a military situation that was deteriorating hour by hour, accepted the Security Council's resolution; and on November 14, a few hours after having received the Mediator's note with the demarcation of new provisional lines and the plan for the consequent withdrawal of the troops, appointed the high-ranking officer of the Egyptian army who was to contact General Riley with a view to discussing this operation. In the eyes of the Egyptian government, the resolution of November 4, with all its drawbacks, made it still possible to liquidate the situation created by the Jewish offensive without inflicting a defeat on the Egyptian army. In fact, the new provisional lines fixed by the Mediator would have implied the abandonment of Beersheba by the Jewish army and the liberation of the Egyptian division cut off at Faluja, the two most painful and humiliating reverses suffered by the Egyptian army.

But it was precisely this which provoked the opposition of the Israeli government which refused, not unreasonably, to renounce at the last hour and for what in their view was no more than a legal scruple, the two principal results of a military operation which had cost so much effort, so many sacrifices, and no small risk. This opposition on the part of the Israeli government was singularly facilitated by the resolution adopted by the Security Council on November 16, that is, three days before the date when, according to the Mediator's plan, the armed forces should have withdrawn to the new provisional lines, ordering the conclusion of armistices in all sectors of Palestine. This resolution was followed two days later by an urgent message from the Mediator asking the interested governments to let him have as soon as possible their opinions on the procedure to be adopted for negotiating the armistices. Thus the way remained open, not only to negotiation for implementing the resolution of November 4, with the consequent withdrawal of the troops to new provisional lines, but to parallel negotiations for the conclusion of the armistices prescribed by the resolution of November 16. The Egyptian government refused to accept the latter resolution until the former had been implemented, which provided the Israeli government with an excellent excuse for refusing to sanction the withdrawal of troops demanded in the resolution of November 4, until the Egyptian government had agreed to negotiate an armistice in conformity with the resolution of November 16. This curious duel went on for about three weeks until, after the lightning visit of the Mediator to Tel Aviv and Cairo in the early days of December, the Egyptian government announced that it was prepared to take part in armistice negotiations, once the resolution of November 4 had been implemented, that is, when the troops had withdrawn to the provisional lines fixed by the Mediator. This ushered in a new phase of the transaction, which now concentrated on the search for a formula which, on the one hand, would offer a reasonable guarantee to the Israeli government that once the troops had withdrawn to their new lines, the Egyptian government would fulfill its promise to negotiate an armistice and, on the other, would satisfy the Egyptian government that the division which was cut off at Faluja would be evacuated before the armistice negotiations began.

As the talks continued it became more and more evident that the key to the conflict lay in the evacuation of the Egyptian division at Faluja. The Egyptians resigned themselves to the fact that the evacuation of Beersheba would figure among the questions to be discussed during the actual course of the armistice negotiations (and Beersheba was finally incorporated, with the rest of the Negev, into the State of Israel); but they insisted to the very last that the division which was cut off at Faluja should be liberated before the armistice negotiations began. And though there were good reasons to hope that the Israeli government would facilitate the evacuation of the Faluja division if Egypt agreed to negotiate an armistice, a more intransigent attitude prevailed at the last moment and the result was that the armistice negotiations opened with the best division of the Egyptian army locked up in Faluja. Personally, I believed, and I still believe, that the Israeli government threw away on that occasion a unique opportunity for winning over Egyptian military opinion; for, as I have said, there were important elements in the Egyptian army which were, at heart, favorable to a policy of collaboration with Israel and resolutely opposed to the "crusade" for the liberation of Palestine preached by the Arab League. It does not seem to me to be straining the possibilities to think that a gesture by Israel, agreeing to the evacuation of the forces at Faluja, in conformity with the resolution of November 4 and as a pledge of good will, would have enabled her to obtain from her victory fruits of more permanent value to her future relations with Egypt than the unstatesmanlike satisfaction of humiliating an enemy who was conquered more by internal weaknesses than by anything else.

But having said this, it is fair to recognize that the profound humiliation which Egypt was forced to endure was the result of her attempt to consolidate her supremacy among the Arab countries by posing as the chief instrument in the liberation of Palestine and the extermination of the Jews there. Egyptian statesmen should have made themselves better acquainted with the international setting of the Palestine question and with conditions in their own country, before launching themselves on an adventure which was beyond their strength and in which they had nothing to gain and much to lose.

Israel put into practice for the first time the policy of the *fait accompli,* and did it with an impetus, a confidence and a mastery which command admiration. From a moral point of view, this policy no doubt deserves to be condemned. But before judging its use by the Israeli government in this particular case, we must stop and consider the circumstances. It was not Israel, but the Arab states which decided to resort to force and, as we know, this is a decision which is charged with dangerous consequences if, as occurred in this case, the one who adopts it is defeated. Experience shows that, when the door has been opened to force in a dispute, it is impossible to eliminate it entirely in the final decision. What was censurable in Israel's policy during this period was her duplicity in accepting the truces, on the one hand, and in continuing, on the other, her preparations for the struggle and the struggle itself when a favorable opportunity occurred. But was it in reality such a grave offense when we remember that the Arabs, under the leadership of Egyptian politicians, were continually fanning the sacred flames of the "crusade" for the liberation of Palestine?

The successive resolutions adopted by the various organs of the United Nations between October 19 and November 16 made possible a notable operation, in virtue of which not only was the Jewish offensive of October 15, the most serious violation of the truces in all their history, consigned to oblivion, but its perpetrator, the Israeli government, was able to open negotiations for an armistice with its victim, the Egyptian government, without having to abandon a square yard of the territory it had conquered through its offensive. I cannot say whether this was the result of a deliberate policy; and no doubt the need to take facts into account, that is, Israel's victory, will be urged in its defense. But what can be said is that the operation did not help to raise the moral authority of the United Nations in Egypt, still less to foster among the Arabs respect for the impartiality and objectivity of its decisions.

CHAPTER IX

Ralph Bunche, Temporary Mediator:
The Armistices

THE EFFECT of the Security Council's resolution of November 16, 1948, was to displace the center of gravity of the Palestine question from the truces to the armistices. The truce, the observance of it and its violations, immediately lost actuality and was relegated to the limbo of things past; what was important, what was urgent, what ought to be the object of all the United Nations efforts was the new idea of the armistices. From that moment no one seriously thought either of exacting responsibility for the continued violations of the truce which had been going on since October 15 or, still less, of restoring the *status quo*. These same violations showed, according to the apostles of the new creed, the state of dilapidation into which the truce had fallen and the urgency of substituting for it armistice agreements.

There is no need to say that this shift of attention from the truce and its violations to the armistices made it easier for the government of Israel to continue the military operations deemed necessary for consolidating its conquest of the Negev. The Egyptian army remained concentrated in a narrow zone along the coast between Gaza and the frontier of Egypt, from which, for political or military reasons, Israel never tried to dislodge it. On the other hand, the Israeli forces, in the impetus of their advance, actually crossed the frontier between Egypt and Palestine, penetrating several miles into Egyptian territory; and, as we shall see, the withdrawal of these troops to the other side of the frontier ended by being the one and only condition laid down by Egypt in exchange for her participation in the armistice negotiations. It must fairly be recognized that, in this extreme case, United Nations intervention, coupled with diplomatic pressure exercised by certain Great Powers, satisfied the Egyptian government's demand; Israel withdrew her troops from Egyptian soil and Egypt was able to take part in the armistice negotiations with her territory freed from enemy occupation. But the position of the Faluja garrison in the early days of 1949 had become indefensible as a result of Israel's persistent military activity, and the Egyptian government found itself obliged to go one step further along the road of its humiliation and abandon the liberation of Faluja as a precondition for entering upon armistice negotiations. If the Mediator was able to procure an immediate suspension of hostilities, the Egyptian government would send a delegation to Rhodes with powers to negotiate and concert an armistice.

This was, in substance, what Colonel Nūḥ and Colonel Sharīn Bey[1] came to tell me, on express instructions from the Minister of Defense, in the late afternoon on January 4, 1949. The ceasefire was to become effective on the following day, the 5th, at two o'clock in the afternoon; the aim of the negotiations was to be the implementation of the Security Council's resolutions of November 4 and 16; they were prepared to negotiate with an Israeli delegation, under the aegis of the United Nations, but the negotiations were to be exclusively military in character. In the presence of the two emissaries, I drafted a telegram conveying their message to the Mediator; they thought it advisable to obtain the approval of the Minister of Defense, which they did by telephone from my office at Shepheards Hotel. The telegram to the Mediator at Lake Success was dispatched that same evening, after a telephone conversation announcing its dispatch and giving a brief summary of its contents.

A few days later I learned from a reliable source the inner history of this episode, which was going to have such a decisive influence on the future evolution of the Palestine question.

Ibrahīm 'Abd al-Hādī Pasha, who had succeeded Nuqrashī Pasha as Prime Minister, was much more inclined than the latter to liquidate the Palestine adventure rapidly. This predisposition on the part of the new Prime Minister facilitated the task of the Minister of Defense, since he was much more receptive to arguments in favor of immediate negotiations with Israel and of ignoring legal scruples about the danger that these negotiations

---

1. During the whole of my mission in Cairo, Colonel Nūḥ was the liaison officer at the Ministry of Defense and in the most critical circumstances, showed an intelligence, an objectivity and an integrity of mind worthy of the highest praise. Colonel Sharīn Bey had accompanied me on a visit to the front; he later became a member of the Royal Family through his marriage to a sister of King Farouk (Fārūq).

might be interpreted as an implicit recognition of the State of Israel. The minister apparently successfully argued that Egyptian delegates were already negotiating with official representatives of the State of Israel around the table of the Security Council and other United Nations organizations, without this implying recognition, either direct or indirect, of that State. The result was a decision in favor of accepting armistice negotiations and the visit of the two colonels on January 4.

It proved to be physically impossible to arrange a cease-fire on the 5th, as the Egyptian government had proposed. After several attempts and many exchanges, it was finally arranged that the cease-fire should come into effect at noon on January 7. At last it seemed that everything was settled: the Mediator was already on the way to Rhodes, and in Cairo and Tel Aviv the delegations were getting ready to go and meet him as soon as they heard that he was prepared to begin the negotiations. But fate still had one last trial in store for us; on the 8th, Colonel Nūḥ arrived at my office and announced in melancholy tones that Jewish forces had crossed the frontier between Egypt and Palestine the previous night and were occupying a position in Egyptian territory dominating the main road between El-Arish, an Egyptian air base near the frontier, and Rafah, a small sea-side town on the same frontier. The colonel informed me, on behalf of the Minister of Defense, that the Egyptian delegation would not leave Cairo until the Israeli troops had withdrawn to the positions they were occupying at noon on the 7th, the hour when the cease-fire was supposed to have taken effect. As I have said, this time international political pressure prevailed over the policy of the *fait accompli*. On January 10, the Israeli troops withdrew to their original positions and on the 12th, an imposing delegation, consisting of three army colonels, with a legal adviser and certain other officials, landed at Rhodes airport. The delegation properly so called was accompanied by two high officials of the Ministry of Foreign Affairs, who did not form part of it and whose presence at Rhodes, according to the official version, was strictly personal and private. Their absence from the official meetings did not, however, preclude them from playing the decisive rôle in the negotiations to which both their rank and their authority entitled them.

*   *   *   *

I arrived at Rhodes with the Egyptian delegation after landing by mistake on an abandoned airfield in the interior of the island. Ralph Bunche was already in Rhodes with all his staff. The Israeli delegation, led by Walter Eytan and with Eliah Sassoon as its most important civilian member, had arrived the same day or the previous day. On the afternoon of January 12, there were official meetings between the Mediator and each delegation, in preparation for the official opening session which took place on the following day and at which the two delegations, under the chairmanship of the Mediator, sat down for the first time at the same table.

In our first talks, Eytan and Sassoon, old friends of mine since my first mission to Jerusalem a year before, expressed great eagerness to meet in private and in a strictly personal capacity the two high officials of the Ministry of Foreign Affairs who had accompanied the Egyptian delegation. This was easy from a physical point of view, since the two delegations and the Mediator's mission were installed at the Hotel of the Roses, on the sea front at Rhodes, where Count Bernadotte had set up his headquarters on first taking over his functions. I spoke to my friends in the Egyptian delegation and they agreed, though not very enthusiastically, to establish private and personal contacts with the members of the Israeli delegation. As I later ascertained, the contacts duly took place, and they no doubt contributed to the success of the negotiations.

I can say nothing about these negotiations from my personal knowledge, for on my arrival at Rhodes I found a telegram from the Secretary General of the United Nations appointing me Secretary of the Palestine Conciliation Commission, set up by the Assembly a few weeks previously. Two days after arriving at Rhodes I left for Geneva, where the Commission was holding its constituent session a few days later. But it is public knowledge that Bunche conducted the negotiations with great intelligence and exceptional energy. His unlimited capacity for work, enabling him to ignore the difference between night and day that the normal man has to take note of, must have tried the stamina of his own staff and that of the two delegations to the utmost. And I have a shrewd suspicion that on more than one occasion, agreement was reached as a result not so much of concessions freely and voluntarily obtained as of the physical and mental exhaustion of the delegates—very tempting tactics for those who, like Bunche, are lucky enough to be able to preserve intact their mental lucidity and will power throughout the twenty-four hours of the day, but which introduce into agreements so obtained, psychological elements which, in the long run, can be the source of considerable difficulties in application.

Without trying to decry the great merit of Dr. Bunche's achievement in concluding these armistice agreements,[2] the truth is that once the *fait accompli* of the conquest of the Negev by Israel in open breach of the truce was accepted, the negotiation of the armistice between Israel and Egypt presented no fundamental difficulties. Reduced to its essential elements, the object of the negotiations was to procure the acceptance by Egypt of the conquest of the Negev by Israel in exchange for the evacuation of the Faluja garrison and the undisputed possession by the Egyptian army of the coastal zone between Gaza and the frontier, where it was then concentrated. It was inconceivable that Israel would raise objections of principle to a formula which, in practice, legalized her conquest of the Negev. As far as Egypt was concerned, no doubt the formula was a great humiliation and if her army had been in a position to fight, neither persuasion nor exhaustion could have wrung consent from her. But her best division was cut off at Faluja and the rest of her army was concentrated in the Gaza zone, in a strong defensive position, but without the slightest possibility of taking the offensive—its only line of communication with Egypt across the Sinai desert being constantly threatened by the Israeli forces. Moreover, the formula, though humiliating, would divert the eyes of the world from the spectacle of the military débâcle and this was now the only thing that really interested the government: the Faluja division would be liberated and its surrender avoided and the army would remain on Palestinian soil and not have to return empty-handed to Egypt, a difficult thing to explain away after all the paper victories the army had won in official accounts of the campaign. The basic elements of the armistice agreement had been, therefore, clearly defined before the negotiations opened, by the victory of the Jewish troops in the Negev campaign. This does not mean that the negotiations were easy; on the contrary, the adjustment of the details relating to the evacuation of the Faluja garrison, the drafting of texts, the demarcation of armistice lines and the elaboration of the system of supervision by Mixed Commissions —all these must have presented grave difficulties in the day to

2. The armistices gained for him the Nobel Peace Prize in 1950.

day discussions; and no doubt the Mediator and his aides found infinite opportunities for making extensive use of their intelligence, ability and inexhaustible capacity for work. Six weeks after the start of the negotiations, the armistice between Egypt and Israel was signed at Rhodes on February 24, 1949.

The conclusion of the armistice with Egypt greatly facilitated the negotiation of the other three armistices with, respectively, Lebanon, Transjordan and Syria: in the first place, because the Egyptian armistice served as a model for the general clauses, thus avoiding much of the work of drafting; in the second, because these three countries were not as heavily committed to the war as Egypt was. Lebanon and Syria had made a modest contribution to the "crusade," sending limited forces; and the Transjordan Arab Legion had studiously avoided any serious encounter with the Jewish army and was practically intact. On the other hand, the demarcation of the armistice lines presented greater difficulties in the cases of Syria and Transjordan than in the case of Egypt, since, unlike the latter country which had no territorial ambitions properly so called in the Negev, Syria and Transjordan had very substantial territorial ambitions in the upper valley of the Jordan and in central Palestine, respectively. True, the armistice agreements contained clauses emphasizing its provisional and strictly military character and reserving for future peace negotiations the solution of political and territorial questions pending between the parties; but the unlimited duration of the armistices much reduced the effective value of these reservations and the interested governments rightly foresaw that, with the lapse of time, the demarcation lines traced by the armistices would be converted into real political frontiers. The guaranteeing of these lines by the three great Western powers in 1950 has done no more than confirm this foresight.

In the case of Transjordan, the Mediator was fortunate enough not to be obliged to solve the difficulty, for the demarcation of the boundaries in the central zone of Palestine known as the "triangle,"[3] which was undoubtedly the most sensitive spot, was the subject of an agreement between representatives of the Israeli government and King 'Abdallāh, entered upon as the result of secret conversations held in the King's winter palace at Shuneh. All that had to be done at Rhodes was to incorporate the demarcation of the boundaries agreed upon at Shuneh in the ar-

3. This name applies to a region between Jenin, Nablus and Tulkarm, which was one of the strategic bases of the Arab armed forces during the war.

mistice agreement. The armistices with Lebanon and Transjordan were signed, respectively, on March 23 and April 3, 1949.

The armistice with Syria was undoubtedly the one that presented the most difficulties, for the tracing of the demarcation line along the upper valley of the Jordan directly affected the political frontier of Syria, which explains and even justifies the tenacity with which the Syrian government defended its point of view. The controversy had its origins in the demarcation of the frontier between the two mandates, the British mandate over Palestine and the French mandate over Syria, at the end of the First World War. Since then, first France as the Mandatory Power and later Syria, after gaining her independence, had claimed the Jordan as the frontier with Palestine in place of the frontier that had been fixed some miles to the east of its left bank, leaving the river with both its banks in Palestinian territory. It was not surprising that the ancient controversy should be revived on the occasion of the demarcation of the armistice lines between Syria and Israel. The negotiations lasted four months and took place in an atmosphere of considerable tension. In the end, agreement appeared possible, thanks to the expedient of creating extensive demilitarized zones between the lines, placed under the immediate authority of the Chairman of the Mixed Commission charged with supervising the conclusion of the armistice. This expedient enabled the difficulty to be overcome and the armistice was signed on July 20, 1949. But its uncertain and temporary character was obvious and was somewhat brusquely thrown into relief by the incidents at Lake Hulé in the spring of 1951. To these intrinsic difficulties of the negotiation must be added the obstacles arising out of the unfavorable physical conditions in which they took place. In contrast with the splendid surroundings at the Hotel of the Roses on the seafront at Rhodes, the meetings between the delegations of Israel and Syria were held in a tent in the no man's land between the military lines, and to get to it from Damascus or Tel Aviv meant a journey of several hours by car. The winter was a severe one; and I am sure that the temperature in the tent did not contribute much to creating an atmosphere of cordiality and mutual understanding. Bunche had returned to Lake Success from Rhodes as soon as the negotiation of the armistice with Transjordan was concluded and, though he kept in daily touch with the course of the negotiations for the armistice with Syria, the effective chairmanship devolved upon his principal assistant, Henri Vigier, aided by General Riley, chief of staff of the truce control services.

*   *   *   *

It is not entirely correct to say that the armistices put a stop to the struggle in Palestine. In actual fact, when the armistice negotiations began in January, 1949, the real struggle had already ceased on all fronts. In the Negev, the only front where effective military operations had taken place during the last few months, the fighting had ceased, for the reason that most fighting does cease; because one side, in this case Israel, had gained its objective, the conquest of the Negev, and had defeated the enemy army. The armistice came, then, at the right moment according to the rules of the military art: when one of the parties had gained the immediate objective of its operations and the other either could not, or did not want to, continue the struggle. At the end of 1948, Israel had not only contained the attack launched by the Arab states to destroy her, but had incorporated into her territory important regions which, at the beginning of the war, were under the domination of the Arabs, as for example, the region of Lydda and Ramleh in central Palestine, western Galilee with Nazareth, to the north, and the Negev with Beersheba, to the south. For their part, the Arab states had failed in their attempt to destroy the State of Israel and had found that, for military reasons in some cases and political reasons in others, it was a practical impossibility for them to continue the war. The struggle was, therefore, at an end and, according to the rules of the game, the moment for the armistices had arrived.

In the armistice texts themselves and in the report which the Mediator submitted to the Security Council when the four agreements were signed, stress was laid on the fact that they should be regarded as a first step along the road to the establishment of peace in Palestine. Leaving aside legal technicalities, this seems to be, in effect, the character of an armistice which, as a general rule, implies a favorable disposition on the part of the combatants to enter into peace negotiations. But the armistices between Israel and her four neighbors proved a clear exception to this rule. With the possible exception of Transjordan, it is obvious that, in spite of all the declarations, more or less in the nature of formulas, contained in the texts of the armistices themselves, the Arab states have never considered the armistices as the first step along the road to the establishment of peace with the

State of Israel. If we take peace in its *negative* meaning, that is, the absence of war, there is not much sense in talking of a first step along the road that leads to it, for the armistice agreements establish it and perpetuate it in the most complete and final manner. If we take peace in its *positive* meaning, that is, the recognition of the State of Israel and the establishment and cultivation of diplomatic, economic, cultural and other relations, it can be categorically stated that neither the Egyptian government nor the Lebanese government nor the Syrian government have ever considered that, by affixing their signatures to the bottom of the armistice agreements, they were setting out on a road which would lead them to the recognition of Israel and the establishment of diplomatic, economic and cultural relations with her. The obstinacy and tenacity with which these governments have systematically refused to make the least gesture which could be interpreted as a step forward along the road to positive peace with Israel is the best proof of the correctness of this interpretation of the armistices in relation to peace.

As the Mediator himself emphasized in his report to the Security Council, the armistices are real and authentic pacts of non-aggression, of unlimited duration, between Israel and her four Arab neighbors; and in conformity with this character, the documents are signed on behalf of the respective governments, and not on behalf of the commanders-in-chief of the two armies, as is the traditional practice in the conclusion of armistices. This character of non-aggression pacts is what makes these agreements original, almost revolutionary documents, which break with the classic order of gradation in the relations between states; for according to that order, the conclusion of a pact of non-aggression would have been inconceivable between two states which had not recognized one another either *de facto* or *de jure* and which, if they did recognize one another, would be in a state of war, as a result of the refusal by one of them to begin peace negotiations.

In the field of practical politics, and although, at first sight, it may appear paradoxical, the fact that the armistices have this character of non-aggression pacts has slowed the advance towards the establishment of a positive peace between the Arab states and the State of Israel. The armistices have guaranteed "security" to the Arab states without placing them under the necessity either of recognizing the State of Israel or, consequently, of making peace with it; and in the case of Egypt, what is perhaps more serious, without the Egyptian government having committed itself in any way to abstain from hostile acts towards Israel, save strictly military ones.

This difference between the armistice agreement with Egypt and the other three agreements merits a few moments' attention. Among the general clauses at the beginning of the agreements prohibiting, in admirably precise terms, all military action by one of the parties against the other (it is these clauses that give the documents the character of non-aggression pacts), there is a paragraph in the armistices with Lebanon, Syria and Transjordan which extends this prohibition to "acts of hostility" directed from the territory under the authority of one of the parties against the other, without specifying that the acts referred to are military acts carried out by land, sea or air forces. This paragraph does not appear in the armistice with Egypt, where all the clauses prohibiting acts of hostility by one of the parties against the other refer explicitly and narrowly to military acts carried out by land, sea or air forces. This difference between the texts of the armistice agreements acquired particular importance when the Security Council examined, in 1951, Israel's complaint against the restrictions imposed by the Egyptian government on the passage through the Suez Canal of ships with cargoes for Israel. Without pretending to go very deeply into the legal aspect of the question, it seems clear that the thesis that these measures violated the armistice agreement would have been more easily defended if the agreement had contained the paragraph prohibiting in general terms "acts of hostility" directed against one of the parties from the territory of the other; while its absence makes it difficult to regard the measures as violating the *letter* of the agreement. All that could be maintained is that they might be considered to violate its *spirit*.

The practical consequences of this difference were shown during the course of the conference with the Arab states and the State of Israel which the Palestine Conciliation Commission convened at Paris in September, 1951. The Commission attempted to create an atmosphere propitious to negotiation by means of a declaration of peaceful intentions to be accepted by the two parties. The negotiations failed, partly, because of the impossibility of getting the Egyptian government to agree to a text which would have virtually implied its acceptance of the same undertaking to refrain from general "acts of hostility" which the other three Arab states had accepted in their respective armistice agreements; while the Israeli government refused to agree to a text which did not even contain the same obligation accepted by these three States with regard to abstention from hostile acts.

The report which the Mediator submitted to the Security Council, giving an account of the signing of the armistices, contains no explanation of this difference; nor do I know of any official document which affords an inkling of its origin and *raison d'être*.

CHAPTER X

Government House

"GOVERNMENT HOUSE" was the name of the official residence of the High Commissioner during the British mandate. At the beginning, and until 1927, the High Commissioner had his official residence in the colossal edifice which Kaiser Wilhelm II built on the top of Mount Scopus as the visible and permanent symbol of his interest in the Holy Land and Jerusalem. The building is characteristic of modern German architecture: massive, heavy, with a marked tendency to the grandiose. Its tower, with the campanile of the Russian Orthodox Monastery on the Mount of Olives, is the first thing the traveler sees of Jerusalem as he approaches from the direction of the Jordan. The building was, I believe, originally intended to serve as a hospice for German pilgrims and it was called "Augusta Victoria" in memory of the Empress. When the British High Commissioner installed himself in the present Government House, the Augusta Victoria passed through many vicissitudes, ending up as a hospital which, first under the management and control of the Red Cross and afterwards of UNRWA, was used mainly, if not exclusively, for Arab refugees.

During the early 1930's the British government built the present Government House in the southern environs of Jerusalem, on top of a hill, or rather a plateau, dominating a landscape that is at once one of the noblest in the world and the most evocative of the past: to the north, Jerusalem, with the Old City enclosed in its walls—a view which, in its general lines, recalls El Greco's painting of Toledo; to the east, the valley of the Jordan as far as the extreme north of the Dead Sea, with the huge mass of the mountains of Moab sharply outlined in the background; and on the south and west, the gentle hills through which winds the road to Bethlehem.

Government House, built of white stone rather in the manner of a fortress, without any great architectural pretensions, im

122

presses by its dignity and simplicity of line, so much in harmony with the surrounding landscape. On the east side, there is a garden of local wild plants, the whole enclosed in a fairly extensive park surrounded by barbed wire. I do not know how Government House would be guarded in normal times, if times were ever normal during the mandate; but during the latter months, when Jerusalem and the rest of Palestine were already in actual fact a battleground, the protection of Government House devolved upon a company of infantry, which was encamped inside the grounds and had posted guards not only at the entrance, but at intervals along the barbed wire surrounding the park.

What was to be the fate of Government House after May 15, 1948, when the High Commissioner left Jerusalem and the armed forces protecting it withdrew, was a source of constant and growing anxiety to everyone during the last months of the mandate. At that time I used to see Sir Alan Cunningham, the last British High Commissioner, once or twice a week, and during our conversations, which frequently took place as we walked through the park, he never ceased urging me to point out to the Palestine Commission at Lake Success the grave responsibility which the United Nations was going to incur if, for the lack of suitable protection, Government House and all in it was destroyed, looted and sacked by the Bedouins of the nearby villages. This, in his opinion, would inevitably occur within twenty-four hours of the departure of the British guards, unless appropriate methods were taken to prevent it. In all our conversations the High Commissioner always assumed that, at the end of the mandate, Government House would be taken over by the United Nations, which would be responsible, from that moment, for everything, good or ill, that happened there. I confess that the fear of seeing the gloomy prognostications of the High Commissioner come true was one of my greatest anxieties, in the midst of so many other grave preoccupations; an anxiety that was aggravated by the Palestine Commission's total lack of response at Lake Success to my persistent and importunate warnings.

So the days and the weeks passed, until at the beginning of April, it was evident that however much dynamism and energy the Palestine Commission displayed (and these were certainly not its characteristics!) it was now impossible to arrange for the adequate protection of Government House and its contents when, on May 15, it was abandoned by the High Commissioner and the British guards withdrew. It was then that M. de Regnier, the representative of the International Committee of the Red Cross in Palestine, took the initiative of creating two security zones where noncombatants could take refuge under the protection and guarantee of the International Red Cross during the struggle which we all now considered to be inevitable. One of the zones was to include the King David Hotel and the Y.M.C.A. building; the other, Government House, the Arab College and the School of Agriculture. Having obtained the consent, in principle, of the Arab Committee and the Jewish Agency, M. de Regnier approached the High Commissioner with a view to securing the British government's approval for Government House to be included in the proposed safety zone. The High Commissioner replied in the affirmative, but on condition that the United Nations also gave its consent. The British government's argument was that, as from May 15, Government House would pass into the hands of the United Nations and that, therefore, without the latter's consent, the British government could not accept any obligations regarding Government House extending beyond that date.

The High Commissioner and M. de Regnier then approached me as the representative in Jerusalem of the Secretary General of the United Nations; the former, to advise me of M. de Regnier's action and his reply; the latter, to ask me to obtain United Nations' consent for Government House to be included in the projected safety zone. For me this was a tremendous relief, for not only did it appear to offer the best possible guarantee that Government House would be protected from the risks and perils that seemed very real at that moment, but it relieved the United Nations of a responsibility which it was not then in a position to shoulder. Time was short: M. de Regnier wanted an immediate answer in order to prepare the execution of his plan; neither the Palestine Commission nor the Secretary General, in spite of my pressing request, seemed to understand the urgency of the case. In the end, without waiting for the Commission's reply, I decided to accept M. de Regnier's proposal on my own responsibility; but I expressly stated, in a letter I sent to M. de Regnier on April 17, 1948, that the consent of the United Nations was subject to the condition that Government House was to be handed over to the United Nations whenever the latter desired. My acceptance was later confirmed by the Palestine Commission (or the Secretary General); and thus was formalized, so to speak, the operation whereby, on the morning of May 14, when the High Commissioner and all his staff left Government House, the Brit ish flag which had waved for twenty-five years from its tower, was replaced by the flag of the Red Cross.

In the course of the morning of the same day, the company of infantry which had guarded and protected Government House while it was the official residence of the British High Commissioner withdrew, and its place was taken by two efficient and attractive Swiss nurses of the International Committee of the Red Cross, who took over the whole property as a matter of course and, without more protection than was afforded by their flag, accepted the tremendous responsibility, in the midst of a chaotic situation, of enforcing respect for it, not only from the more or less "regular" forces of the Arabs and Jews, but from the Bedouin population of the neighboring villages. All this was done in particularly difficult conditions, for the British troops (as the two nurses told me two or three days later when I stopped at Government House on my way to the Old City) had left them with the telephone disconnected and the larder empty, no doubt as the result of a too slavish adherence, at the wrong moment, to the rules applicable to the evacuation of military positions in the event of a withdrawal.

It must be acknowledged, in justice to the Arab and Jewish troops and, above all, the populations of the neighboring villages, that the prognostications of the British High Commissioner were happily not fulfilled. Neither during the night of May 14-15, which the two Red Cross nurses spent alone at Government House without a telephone—and without dinner—nor during the two following weeks until the first truce, did the most trivial incident or the slightest difficulty occur. During that period I stopped at Government House several times on my journeyings between the Arab and Jewish sectors of Jerusalem. Though the number of persons who had sought refuge in the safety zone was never large, every day saw more women and children from the neighboring villages attending the small clinic which the two nurses had instituted. I remember that on my return from the Old City the day the Jewish quarter surrendered, I spent the night at Government House and, on rising the next morning, I was surprised to see a group of Bedouin nomads encamped in the grounds, not more than two or three hundred yards from the house. When I voiced my alarm, the two nurses assured me that they were very peaceable folk to whom they were most grateful; while they were here, they had helped them in a thousand small ways as, for example, bringing water up to the house, which in those days was one of the greatest trials of domestic life in Government House.

In the early days of June, 1948, I left Jerusalem and was absent until February, 1949, when I returned as Principal Secretary of the Conciliation Commission. I never found out in detail when and how the United Nations took over Government House; but among the territorial adjustments which accompanied the two truces imposed by the Security Council and negotiated by Count Bernadotte, there was one which provided that Government House, with its park and a certain area around it, was to be neutralized under the control and guarantee of the United Nations.

This surrounding zone had been steadily encroached upon and incorporated bit by bit in the territory occupied by Israel and Jordan, as the result of a series of small advances which the Truce Supervision Organization (TSO) had tolerated. The last and most important advance took place in August, 1948, when Israel occupied the Arab College and the School of Agriculture, situated right in the neutral zone, barely three-quarters of a mile from the entrance to Government House. This brought a protest from the Mixed Commission, but, needless to say, the affair ended with the acceptance of the *fait accompli*. The situation was confused. Israel invoked an agreement with Jordan for the division of the neutral zone between them, an agreement which was apparently later repudiated by the government of Jordan. According to a letter which Dr. Eytan, the Secretary General of the Israeli Ministry of Foreign Affairs, wrote to the Conciliation Commission during its meetings at Lausanne, the proposed division of territory excluded the actual grounds of Government House, thus implying that the two governments recognized the rights of the United Nations over the property.

When the Conciliation Commission arrived in Jerusalem in February, 1949, one of its first decisions was to establish its official seat at Government House—a measure that was fully justified in principle, but which, in practice, considerably complicated the work of the Commission in the initial stage of its existence Without counting the difficulties caused by the precautions with which the Israeli authorities had surrounded the movements of the members of the Commission,[1] communications between the King David Hotel, where we were staying, and Government House were not, at that moment, either easy or rapid. The direct road could not be used, because it traversed an area which

1. *Vide* Chapter XI.

had not yet been cleared of mines; this meant that we had to go a long way round through the modern districts with their various control points,[2] the last of which gave access to the neutral zone and was closed relatively early in the evening. It was, therefore, difficult to arrange meetings of the Commission in Government House, since we never knew how long they were going to last. Finally, the interior of the house and its fittings still showed signs of its recent adventures; several months between the lines, temporary occupation by Israeli troops and sporadic, and no doubt involuntary, bombardment by Egyptian artillery, not to mention a highly precarious and irregular telephone service, total lack of running water and even, I believe, of electric light.

But the most difficult problem in connection with the installation of the Commission's official seat in Government House was that of providing a minimum of protection for the Commission, its secretariat and its archives. Partly as a matter of principle and partly out of respect for the terms of the truce agreement which created the neutral zone of Government House, the entrance to the zone was strictly barred to anyone belonging to the armed forces or police forces of either Israel or Jordan. On the other hand, it was obvious that the United Nations could not create, train, and send to Jerusalem, with the speed that the case demanded, an international force capable of adequately protecting the Commission, its secretariat and its archives in Government House.

Someone suggested that the Israeli and Jordan authorities in Jerusalem should be asked to take joint responsibility for ensuring the protection of Government House, as the official seat of the Conciliation Commission. At first, none of us took the suggestion seriously; but Colonel de la Rue, the head of the Jerusalem group of "observers," enthusiastically supported it and offered to discuss it with the Arab and Jewish commanders-in-chief of the Jerusalem area. He was so confident that, in the end, he succeeded in overcoming my natural resistance to a solution which seemed to me to be full of dangers, and that same night I submitted the proposal to the Commission at a meeting where the Colonel himself supported it with characteristic ardor and impetuosity. The Commission authorized us to find out what the reaction of the military authorities would be. The negotiations thus begun produced results as swift as they were satisfactory. On the following day Colonel de la Rue announced that the two

2. The way Count Bernadotte was taking when he was assassinated.

commanders-in-chief had immediately accepted the idea and were awaiting detailed proposals for putting it into practice. The arrangements were quickly made by the colonel and his group of observers, and within twenty-four hours the system was inaugurated with a simple ceremony at which, in the presence of the Commission, and with the two Arab and Jewish detachments, in full uniform, drawn up opposite one another in front of the principal entrance of Government House, the flag of the United Nations was hoisted over the building. From that moment, the Israeli detachment mounted guard over the western entrance to the grounds of Government House, while the Arab Legion mounted guard over the eastern entrance. Inside the grounds there was a system of mixed patrols, composed of one soldier of the Arab Legion and one Israeli, who kept a twenty-four hour watch over the park and the area around the house. How many hours we spent at my office window, watching the two soldiers chatting together in the most amicable manner, so far as their linguistic abilities permitted, in spite of the difference in their uniforms! The two detachments, composed, naturally, of the same number of men and commanded by officers of the same rank, were under the superior command of Commandant Loriaux of the Belgian army, the "observer" officer in charge of the Government House post.

It must be recorded, to the credit of all those who took part in this bold experiment, that the result could not have been more satisfactory. For several weeks, until the United Nations was able to send to Jerusalem a sufficient number of guards to provide adequate security for Government House, the system of joint protection by the Arab Legion and Israeli detachments functioned perfectly efficiently and without any untoward incidents. And what was no less remarkable, as soon as the United Nations was in a position to provide its own guards, the Arab and Jewish forces withdrew without the least difficulty, satisfied, no doubt, that they had on this occasion won the respect and gratitude of the United Nations.

It was during that period that an incident occurred which illustrates the conditions then still prevailing at Government House. One evening one of the United Nations guards discovered by the roadside some five hundred yards from the entrance to the grounds, half hidden in a heap of gravel, a steel box which turned out to be a mine connected by an electric wire with the first Jewish post on the other side of the demarcation line of the neutral zone. The discovery caused a sensation. That same night I called on Colonel Dayan (as he was then), commandant of the military district of Jerusalem, to ask for an explanation of this alarming find. His explanations were confused; he himself did not know of the existence of the mine; he would take measures to deal with the commander of the post; it was, undoubtedly, not a recent mine, but one planted there during the military operations and which the officer commanding the sector had not had removed, either through pure negligence or intentionally. The Commission thought it best to accept these explanations. The mine disappeared and after a time no more was heard of it.

It must be admitted, in justice to the administrative services of the United Nations in Jerusalem, that the situation improved considerably during the next months. By the autumn of 1949, progress in all directions was noticeable and, in 1950, the United Nations administration had solved very satisfactorily the arduous problem of adapting the British High Commissioner's official residence to its new functions as the seat of a great political and administrative center of the United Nations. The secretariat of the Conciliation Commission, General Riley and the officers of his organization, a large radio station, administrative, financial and transport services, even a small clinic—all found adequate and, in some cases, even luxurious accommodations. Within a few months, the new status of Government House as the headquarters of the United Nations in Palestine was confirmed in the eyes of all, natives and foreigners—a status that was publicly and solemnly confirmed when the Secretary General of the United Nations and Mrs. Lie, on the occasion of their visit to certain Middle Eastern countries, decided not only to visit Government House, but to spend there the night which, according to their itinerary, they were due to spend in Jerusalem.

One of the most effective contributions the United Nations can make to preserve the peace in Palestine is to keep possession of Government House and to defend, against pressure from any quarter, its character as a neutral zone under United Nations control and guarantee. Even those not versed in military strategy can grasp the significance of Government House in relation to the maintenance of order between Arabs and Jews in Jerusalem. If this peaceful coexistence is to be achieved and assured through the complete or partial internationalization of Jerusalem (a hypothesis whose probabilities diminish with every day that passes), the possession of Government House by the representative of international authority in Jerusalem is the absolutely indispensable condition for the viability of that internationalization. If the partition of Jerusalem between Israel and Jordan is to be continued, it is inconceivable that the equilibrium on which the physical peace enjoyed by Jerusalem is based can be maintained for an hour if Government House ceases to belong to the United Nations and passes under the control of either Israel (which would appear the most likely) or Jordan. As I had occasion to say to Mr. Lie, when he was looking at the admirable panorama of Jerusalem from one of the balconies of Government House, against the background of the Mount of Olives and Mount Scopus, the guarantee and symbol of peace in Jerusalem is the flag of the United Nations waving both over Hadassah Hospital and the Hebrew University on Mount Scopus, and from the tower of Government House.

CHAPTER XI

The Road to Peace

THE ESTABLISHMENT of a political régime which would ensure not only passive coexistence but collaboration and intercourse between Arabs and Jews was, in the last analysis, the final aim of every effort directed towards the pacification of Palestine. England, after twenty-five years of endeavor, had had to admit failure, bringing to an abrupt end the mandate which had been entrusted to her by the Peace Conference immediately after the end of the First World War. The United Nations, with the generosity and impetuosity of a young institution, agreed to step into the place England had vacated and, as a first measure, decided to send out to Palestine a committee of inquiry[1] which, after an intensive, though rapid, study of the matter, submitted to the Assembly, at its session in the autumn of 1947, a plan for the partition of Palestine based on the three following principles: the creation of two states, respectively Arab and Jewish; the establishment of an economic union between them; the internationalization of Jerusalem. This plan of partition was adopted by the Assembly on November 27, 1947; and in order to implement it, the Palestine Commission was appointed and functioned at Lake Success between January and April, 1948.

1. The Bernadotte Plan and the 1948 Assembly

We have seen in previous chapters how this Commission was unable to fulfill its task, partly on account of its own deficiencies and partly as a result of the violent opposition of the Arabs to the implementation of the plan of partition. We have also seen how the Assembly, at its extraordinary session of April-May, 1948, after having dissolved the Commission, entrusted Count Bernadotte, as the United Nations Mediator for Palestine, with

---

1. United Nations Special Committee on Palestine (UNSCOP).

the mission of "promoting a peaceful adjustment of the future situation of Palestine."

In his report to the Assembly which met at Paris in the autumn of 1948, Count Bernadotte gave a detailed account of his negotiations with the parties in order to fulfill this part of his mandate. These negotiations were cursory in the extreme; beginning on June 15, immediately after the acceptance of the first truce, the Mediator brought them to a close at the end of July, when his conversations with Arab statesmen had convinced him that the Arab states would reject any suggestion implying the acceptance or recognition of the Jewish state or even a meeting between their representatives and the representatives of the new State of Israel. Negotiation at such a breakneck speed, justifiable perhaps when it was a question of putting an end to hostilities by means of the truce, was not only inappropriate but actually harmful when dealing with the fundamental problem, the difficulties of which were so great that not all the resources of England, nor her centuries of experience, had sufficed to overcome them during twenty-five years of continuous effort.

But where the Mediator and his immediate advisers were guilty of an even grosser error of judgment on this occasion was in their decision to submit to the parties *and to make public,* barely two weeks after having initiated the conversations, a series of "suggestions" to serve as a basis for a possible peaceful adjustment of the future situation of Palestine. These suggestions, which are reproduced in full in the Mediator's report to the 1948 Assembly, can be summarized as follows: a) Palestine, as delimited in the original British mandate of 1922 (that is, including the kingdom of Transjordan) was to form a "union" with two members, one Arab and the other Jewish; b) each member was to have full control over its immigration policy, but at the end of two years either member of the Union would have the right to demand a review of the other's immigration policy by the Council of the Union; and if the Council of the Union found itself unable to adopt a resolution, the matter should be submitted to the United Nations Economic and Social Council; c) the frontiers between the two members of the Union were to be determined by negotiation with the aid of the Mediator and on the basis of the following suggestions which formed an appendix to the document communicated to the parties: 1) all or part of the Negev was to be included in Arab territory; 2) all or part of western Galilee was to be included in Jewish territory; 3) the Jerusalem area was to be included in Arab territory, with municipal autonomy for the Jewish community; 4) Jaffa was to have a special status; 5) there was to be a free port at Haifa and a free airport at Lydda.

These proposals, though they bore witness to a vein of fantasy and imagination in their author, were of little practical value and, in fact, were violently and categorically rejected both by the Israeli government and by the Arab states. Count Bernadotte, realizing no doubt that the difficulties in the way of accomplishing his mission as Mediator were greater than he had imagined, decided to throw in his hand and refer the matter back to the Assembly. The melancholy result was to add one more failure to the list of abortive attempts to find a political formula which would enable Arabs and Jews to live together peaceably in Palestine.

In the conclusions of his report to the Assembly, the Mediator reproduces, with important variations, the suggestions he had submitted to the parties towards the end of June. No mention is now made of the famous "union," in which "Greater Palestine," including the kingdom of Transjordan, was to have been incorporated. On the other hand, the Arab territory was demarcated in such a way as to comprise the localities of Madjal, Faluja, Ramleh and Lydda. Moreover, the Jerusalem area, instead of forming part of Arab territory, was to remain under the authority of the United Nations, with the greatest possible local autonomy for the two communities, Arab and Jewish. Finally, the United Nations was to confirm the right of the Arab refugees to return to their homes in territory under Jewish control. Their repatriation, resettlement and economic and social rehabilitation, together with the payment of compensation for the property of those who decided not to return, was to be carried out under the supervision and with the aid of the United Nations, which, for this purpose, as well as for the purpose of continuing the efforts to procure a peaceful adjustment of the future situation of Palestine, was to appoint a Conciliation Commission.

The Mediator's report was the focal point of the far-ranging discussions on the Palestine question which took place in the Assembly of the United Nations when it met at Paris during the latter months of 1948. These discussions resulted in the resolution adopted on December 14, in which only two points of importance among those that figured in the conclusions of the Mediator's report were incorporated, namely, the appointment of the Conciliation Commission, though with a mandate rather different from that proposed by the Mediator, and the affirmation of the Arab refugees' right to return to their homes, to be economically and socially rehabilitated, and to receive due compensation for the property they had abandoned in Israel.

2. *The Conciliation Commission*

In accordance with the procedure laid down by the Assembly in its resolution of December 14, 1948, the Conciliation Commission was composed of the United States, France and Turkey. Its members, as the resolution expressly declares, are the three states, represented by their governments which, in their turn, are represented by persons appointed by them to take part as their delegates and on their behalf in the Commission's deliberations. This, though it is perfectly clear, was the source of continual discussions and misunderstandings during the three years of the Commission's "active" life, for some governments, notably the Egyptian, refused to admit that the members of the Commission represented their governments. They maintained that the Commission was an organ of the United Nations and that its members ought only to obey instructions emanating either from the Assembly or from the Security Council, and not those sent them by their governments. The misunderstanding sprang from a confusion as to who should be regarded as members of the Commission. If the actual persons who attend the Commission's meetings are to be regarded as its members, there is no doubt that their conduct in the Commission could not fail to be dictated by the governments they represent. But if when speaking of the members of the Commission, we think, not of the actual persons present at the meetings, but of the governments they represent, the Egyptian thesis is indisputable; as members of a United Nations commission, those governments are obliged, if they are not to betray the confidence placed in them by the Assembly, to base their conduct not on their own convenience, but on the general interests represented in the United Nations. These confusions arise through not giving heed to the difference which separates the two categories of international commissions which the League of Nations, in its day, and now the United Nations, set up as special organs for the study or solution of given problems. Some commissions are composed of states which, through the medium of their governments, appoint freely and without the intervention of the United Nations, the actual persons who, as their representatives, have to attend meetings of the commission and take part in all its activities. Others are formed of individuals chosen and appointed directly by the United Nations. Both categories are and ought to be regarded as international bodies and hence, in both, the delegates, that is to say, the actual persons taking part in their activities, have the character of representatives of the United Nations. But while in commissions of the second category, they are, so to speak, representatives of the first degree, in commissions of the first category they are representatives of the second degree, that is, they act on behalf of and through the medium of their respective governments; hence the danger that the purity of international intentions may be sullied by the impurities of the national interests and convenience of their members. This disadvantage might appear to be offset by the advantage that greater political pressure can be brought to bear by a commission composed of states than by one composed of individuals. But this advantage is illusory since (as we shall see later in the case of the Conciliation Commission) governments are only too apt to cold-shoulder commissions on which they themselves are represented, withholding their support and denying solidarity with them, so as not to appear involved in their difficulties; and only acknowledging the tie that binds them if the harassed commission happens to achieve a real miracle in obtaining a positive result in such conditions.

                *   *   *   *

The Palestine Conciliation Commission was set up in Geneva on January 17, 1949. Two of its members, France and Turkey, were already represented at this inaugural meeting by the same persons who were going to be their delegates for the greater part of the Commission's life. The French delegate, M. Claude de Boisanger, was regarded as one of the most brilliant diplomats of the younger generation; intelligent, quick-witted, objective and impartial, a connoisseur of painting and a lover of literature, his collaboration might have been most valuable had it not been for the indifference of his government and his own intimate conviction that the American government held all the cards and that it was therefore useless to wear himself out in endeavors which would be sterile without American support and rather naïve with it.

The Turkish government had appointed as its representative Mr. H. C. Yalcin, a man of astonishing physical and intellectual vigor for his age (he was nearly eighty years old) and one of the patriarchs of Turkish literature and journalism in the last fifty years. My impression was that he always acted on his own account, taking advantage of his enormous personal authority as a great figure in literature and journalism, an authority that extended not only to his own country but to the whole of the Middle East, so that both the Arab delegations and the Israeli delegation were well aware of it. His presence on the Commission was, therefore, surrounded by that aura of admiration which talent, independence of judgment and objectivity arouse. But his efficiency was impaired by lack of liaison with his government.

During the latter months of the Commission's active life, M. de Boisanger was replaced by M. Léon Marchal and Mr. Yalcin by Dr. Rustu Aras. Marchal was a more active and dynamic personality than Boisanger, but his dynamism did not succeed in dragging the Commission out of the morass into which it had fallen as the result, partly, of the circumstances inherent in the situation and, partly, of the constant instability and vacillation of American policy. Rustu Aras was a veteran of Genevan days, and during his long spell as Minister for Foreign Affairs under Atatürk had played an important rôle in the League of Nations, especially as co-author, with Venizelos of Greece, with Titulesco of Rumania and Wintchitch of Yugoslavia, of the Balkan Pact. The years had blunted his sensibilities, so that he was unable to perceive the phychological nuances of such a complex situation as that which confronted the Commission, and he soon realized that his personal authority, which was based on his services during the period of the League of Nations, did not, as he had expected, make much impression on the Arabs or on the Jews— or on the Americans. This disillusionment induced in him a mood of peevish scepticism which considerably detracted from his worth as a member of the Commission.

The United States government, for reasons which have never been clear, was not represented by a titular delegate at the Commission's first meetings. One of these meetings at Geneva was attended, for form's sake, by the American Minister in Berne; but until the arrival of Mr. Mark Ethridge, the first American delegate, when the Commission had already set up its headquarters at Jerusalem, the United States was represented temporarily by the two officials whom the State Department had appointed as advisers to the titular delegate. Ethridge was a businessman-cum-intellectual, for his business consisted mainly in running the highly influential newspapers of Louisville, Kentucky. Like so many of his compatriots who found themselves brusquely involved in the political and psychological complexities that are characteristic of international questions in the Middle East, Mr. Ethridge soon showed a tendency to impatience and irritation when confronted with the impossibility of breaking the slow and tortuous rhythm of the negotiations. To this source of irritation was added another—no less comprehensible. Not only were direct and rapid methods impossible because of the obstacles and stumbling-blocks that were constantly arising, but the American delegate was soon to discover, not without surprise, that rapidity in negotiation is conditional upon a clear and precise notion of the aim pursued and when this notion does not exist, speed loses its purpose and becomes little more than the meaningless jerkings of marionettes. The truth is that neither the United States government nor its representative on the Commission had a clear idea of how to approach the mission entrusted to that Commission by the Assembly of the United Nations. After four months Ethridge had had enough; he resigned and was replaced by a famous Washington lawyer, Paul Porter, who told me ingenuously on his arrival in Lausanne at the end of June, 1949, that according to his information, everything was now ripe for the peace treaties between the Arab states and the State of Israel to be signed within a matter of weeks, and he had therefore agreed to sacrifice his vacation in order to represent the United States during the final period of the negotiations. Two months later, seeing that the signing of the peace treaties was a product of his informant's feverish imagination, he resigned and returned to Washington to busy himself with his lawsuits. After an interval, when American representation temporarily devolved upon a distinguished official of the State Department, Mr. Hare, a model of good sense, objectivity and deliberation, the American government, realizing the inconveniences of such frequent changes in its representation, decided to adopt a new system and appointed as its delegate a diplomat, Mr. Ely E. Palmer, who had had a long and meritorious career as a consul and diplomat in a great many posts, among them the consulates of Beirut and Jerusalem, and who had recently filled with distinction the post of American Ambassador in Kabul. The emotional temperament of the new American delegate, coupled with an inclination for social life and the cultivation of personal friendships, resulted in a marked tendency to consider questions from the human and personal angle rather than from the point of view of general political interest. This tendency, together with the inconstancy and volatility of the

American government's policy (if it can be called policy to have none), left the Commission without the moral and political support which was the indispensable condition for its very existence and functioning.

*   *   *   *

The Conciliation Commission came into being, practically speaking, without a secretariat. As I have said elsewhere, when I arrived at Rhodes in the early days of January, 1949, accompanying the Egyptian delegation which was going there to embark upon the armistice negotiations, I found a telegram from the Secretary General of the United Nations appointing me Principal Secretary of the Commission, and I barely had time to get to Geneva to take part in the first meetings of the Commission.

I was accompanied to these meetings by Mr. Russell Cook, who was on the administrative staff of the Mediator's mission in Rhodes and who was sent to Geneva specially to take charge of the administrative problems to which the meeting of the Commission and its transfer to Jerusalem gave rise. But we had to apply for help to the European Office of the United Nations even for the typing of the minutes and the few letters and telegrams we sent from Geneva. All this was fortunate for the Commission, and particularly for its Principal Secretary, since it enabled us to build up a secretariat without haste and by means of careful selection. It was thus possible to get together a staff which, during the three years of its existence, not only proved to be very efficient but—what was perhaps more important—gave evidence of a genuine team spirit founded on common devotion to a task for which we all felt ourselves jointly responsible. In my twenty-five years of service as an international official I have never had colleagues who worked better together or who were more efficient and full of zeal. When the time came for the Commission to end its active life, what saddened me most was the breaking up of the secretariat and the parting from those who, in three years of daily collaboration, had succeeded in transforming the formal companionship of office life into the more human and fruitful ties of friendship.

The establishment of the Commission took place without any kind of ceremony or formality. On January 17, 1949, at eleven o'clock in the morning, the French and Turkish delegates, with their advisers and the two American advisers, met at the Hotel de Bergues, Geneva, and in less than an hour had not only officially constituted the Commission but had decided, first, to establish a system of indefinite rotation for the Chairmanship and, secondly, to appoint Mr. Yalcin as the first Chairman. Apart from official communications to the Secretary General of the United Nations and to the Arab and Israeli governments informing them of the constitution of the Commission, two more resolutions were adopted during the three or four meetings which the Commission held at Geneva. The first resolution laid down that the Commission should always act *in corpore,* that is, all the activities and negotiations which were necessary for the accomplishment of its mission should be carried out jointly by the three members of the Commission. The second resolution, which was due to the insistence of the French delegation, stipulated that the Commission should move to Jerusalem, its official seat, and set up headquarters there before the elections which Israel was to hold in a few weeks' time took place.

During those initial contacts with the delegates I was astonished to hear them talk, as of something not only possible but imminent, of convening a peace conference in Geneva after a brief period of negotiation in or from Jerusalem. This seemed to me a delusion; but I refrained from showing my astonishment and even skepticism at such rosy visions, hoping that they were based on more complete and authentic information than I had been able to glean here and there, during my stay in Cairo and Jerusalem. As soon as the Commission came into contact with the parties, all these visions dissolved into thin air and no one ever referred to a peace conference again during the three years of the Commission's existence.

*   *   *   *

The mandate conferred on the Conciliation Commission by the Assembly is defined in the resolution of December 14, 1948, in terms which, by their inarticulateness and confusion, bear witness to all the chopping and changing which had preceded the adoption of the text by the Assembly.

The general mission of conciliation between the Arab states and the State of Israel is defined in article 6 of the resolution in the following terms: "The Assembly . . . instructs the Conciliation Commission to assist the governments and authorities concerned to achieve a final settlement of all questions outstanding between them."

Apart from this general mission of conciliation, the Assembly charged the Commission with the following concrete tasks: a) to submit to the Fourth Ordinary Session of the Assembly detailed proposals for the establishment of a permanent international régime in the Jerusalem area, with recommendations relating to the Holy Places there; b) to obtain from the political authorities concerned formal and satisfactory guarantees with regard to the preservation of, and free access to, the Holy Places situated in the rest of Palestine and to submit these guarantees to the Assembly for its approval; c) to conclude agreements between the governments and authorities concerned with a view to facilitating the economic development of the region; d) to facilitate the repatriation, resettlement and economic and social rehabilitation of the refugees and the payment of compensation.

I shall describe later how the Commission interpreted this mandate and how far it was able to accomplish each of these tasks.

The Commission moved to Jerusalem at the end of January, 1949. The King David Hotel had already been more or less requisitioned by the United Nations and was used as a residence and headquarters for its personnel in Jerusalem, which at the time of our arrival consisted exclusively of the military observers who were responsible for supervising the truce demarcation lines in the Jerusalem area. Here the Commission took up its quarters, with the members of the secretariat as and when the latter were recruited. But as the hotel was in the part of the city under Jewish control, the Commission decided at its first meeting to establish its official seat at Government House, which was situated in a neutral zone under the protection and flag of the United Nations.

Life in the King David Hotel afforded a curious contrast between the luxurious furnishings of the rooms which had been provided for us and the austerity of everything else—no hot water, no telephone, no elevators, no bells, inadequate service and food which could not be described as either abundant or varied. Nevertheless, it must be admitted that Mr. Hamburger, the manager of the hotel, had done the best he could for us, considering the chaotic conditions in Jerusalem at that time.

Having solved the problems of settling ourselves, in some sort of fashion, we had to cope with other difficulties relating to personal security and transport for the members of the Commission. Incredible as it may seem, the United Nations administration had taken no measures to ensure that the Commission had adequate means of transportation on its arrival in Jerusalem, and several weeks passed before, in response to our urgent requests, we were finally authorized to acquire three light cars and a station-wagon. This delay considerably hampered the work of the Commission during this initial period, lowered its prestige (so dependent, in the East, on outward marks and signs) and caused the administration no small expense which might have been avoided with a little more foresight and quickness of decision.

The arrival of the Commission in Jerusalem and its installation in the King David Hotel (which was situated, as I have said, in the Jewish part of the city) met with open disapproval from the local authorities. The visit which I paid on my arrival to Dr. Joseph, Governor of the Jewish city, in company with Colonel de la Rue, head of the team of observers in Jerusalem, was an eye-opener to me. He told me angrily, almost violently, that he had no means of guaranteeing the safety of members of the Commission, nor was he prepared to accept any responsibility in this respect, and that therefore the best thing the Commission could do was to take up its quarters in the Arab part of the city. The Commission's reaction to this outburst was energetic, and a few days later we received from the government of Israel a written statement expressing in eloquent terms the government's satisfaction at the presence of the Commission on Israeli territory and undertaking to adopt all the necessary measures to guarantee not only the safety, but the complete independence and freedom of movement of its members. I never found out whether this incident had any connection with the replacement, shortly afterwards, of Dr. Joseph as Governor of Jerusalem by Dr. Biran, whose relations with the Commission and its secretariat during the next three years were very cordial.

There were two circumstances which, to a certain extent, explained, if they did not justify, the Jewish authorities' attack of nerves when the Commission took up its quarters in the King David Hotel. In the first place, Jerusalem was still a front line military area, where hostilities were in suspense thanks to a truce which was universally regarded as more precarious with every day that passed; isolated bursts of firing occurred with relative frequency and the armed forces on either side of the truce line were in a constant state of alert. Moreover, it was not a flight of fancy to assume that military circles were still cherishing deep-laid plans and that the presence of an important international commission in Jerusalem was, if not an obstacle, at least a serious hindrance to the execution of these plans. In the second place, the assassination of Count Bernadotte, four months previously, in the streets of Jerusalem was still fresh in the minds of everyone and it was known that the terrorist elements which had instigated the outrage were still at work, the government of Israel not having succeeded as yet (as it did some months later) in incorporating them into the regular armed forces of the state. The result was that whether the authorities thought that prevention is better than cure, or whether they were anxious to erase the bad impression which the fact that they had left Count Bernadotte completely defenseless and unprotected had made throughout the world, they bestowed upon the Conciliation Commission and each of its members a system of protection so meticulously elaborate in all its details that we used at times to joke about it. Apart from the permanent police guard in the hotel, the Commission and each of its members were accompanied wherever they went by two jeeps filled with policemen armed to the teeth, one jeep at the head and the other at the tail of the convoy—for they were indeed convoys, especially when the whole Commission set out as a body, with all its members, legal advisers and secretarial staff. During those first weeks there was something rather ridiculous, even perhaps humiliating, in the contrast between all that ostentatious display of force for our protection, and the shabby, battered-looking taxis (the only ones then available in Jerusalem) which the United Nations had provided for the Commission.

Once these preliminary problems had been solved and as soon as the American delegate, Mr. Ethridge, had arrived in Jerusalem, the Commission set about establishing contact with the governments of the Arab countries and the State of Israel. This was simple as far as Israel and Jordan were concerned, for their capitals, Tel Aviv and Amman, were readily accessible from Jerusalem by car. In fact, the Commission's first contacts consisted of a long conversation with Mr. Sharrett on February 7, at his own home in Jerusalem, and a luncheon followed by a conference with the Prime Minister of Jordan, Tawfīq Pasha Abū al-Hūdā, at the Winter Palace Hotel at Jericho, on the eleventh of the same month. Neither of these interviews produced concrete results, nor indeed had they been planned with that end in view; but they made it possible for the members of the Commission to gain a first impression, at once realistic and comprehensive, of the respective Arab and Jewish points of view. True, the Prime Minister of Jordan hinted at the possibility of bilateral negotiations between his country and the State of Israel, but the Commission did not think it prudent to take the hint, at least until it had sounded out the other Arab governments. Today, after years of fruitless attempts at conciliation, it is easy to say that the Commission ought to have taken the chance offered by the Jordanian Prime Minister and concentrated its efforts on obtaining a separate peace treaty between Israel and Jordan. But at that moment the Commission had no real cause to think that it would fail in its attempt at general conciliation. Moreover, its mandate referred to all the states concerned in the Palestine question and the Commission would not have been able to justify to the Assembly a decision to limit its efforts to two of these states before having attempted general conciliation between them all. Lastly—and this, in my opinion, is the decisive argument in favor of the attitude adopted by the Commission—the least gesture on its part which could have been interpreted as favoring the conclusion of a separate peace between Israel and Jordan would have immediately ruined whatever possibilities existed of negotiating with the rest of the Arab states; and this without there existing the remotest probability of a positive result in the limited field of relations between Jordan and Israel. This business of direct negotiations between Israel and Jordan has been a kind of bait which the government of Israel has dangled before the eyes of the Commission, seeking to paralyze its activities by suggesting that any inopportune interference on its part might cause the negotiations to fail. And on more than one occasion I had the impression that influential elements in the Secretariat of the United Nations had allowed themselves to be won over by this kind of campaign which tended to represent the Conciliation Commission as little less than the obstacle to peace in Palestine. Nothing, however, was farther from the truth! In reality, there was only one firm supporter of direct negotiations and a separate peace with Israel in the kingdom of Jordan, and that was King 'Abdallāh. But King 'Abdallāh himself knew that he was powerless to overcome the unanimous opposition which his policy aroused among the small group of outstanding personalities which represented the active political elements of the state—an opposition which was intensified when the incorporation of the Arab part of Palestine into the kingdom of Jordan and the constitutional reforms which King 'Abdallāh introduced in 1950 opened the door to the expression of a public opinion, rudimentary perhaps, but unanimous and forthright in its antagonism to any dealings with Israel or any sort of direct and separate negotiations. That this was so is shown by the fate of the famous secret agreement negotiated in the Palace of Shuneh and initialled by a "personal" representative of King 'Abdallāh and a "personal" representative of President Weizmann. King 'Abdallāh's "personal" representative, who was made Prime Minister a few months later in order to give the Shuneh agreement official and public status, failed in his task and the document, of which no one is willing to acknowledge the paternity, is passing gradually from secret into legend, until, possibly, a change in the political set-up in the Middle East gives it practical significance again. How far King 'Abdallāh's policy of *rapprochement* with Israel and his decision to annex to Jordan the Arab part of Palestine had undermined his political and moral position was shown by his tragic death by assassination in Jerusalem on July 20, 1951. Whether the assassination was the work of a conspiracy and if so, how widespread it was, is something that has never been cleared up. In the days immediately following the outrage, public opinion in Jerusalem credited the Muftī and his adherents in Palestine with a more or less direct share in its preparation. However this may be, several leading Palestinian Arabs were brought to trial and sentenced to heavy penalties; some of them, as in the case even of a person so well-known and respected in Jerusalem as Dr. Mūsā Husaynī, being sentenced to death. But it is significant that underlying the profound indignation which the assassination naturally provoked among the Arab population of Palestine, there was a certain satisfaction at the disappearance of the principal, if not the only, supporter of a policy of collaboration and *rapprochement* with Israel which everyone condemned.

To sum up, the prudent and cautious attitude of the Commission in ignoring the hint thrown out by the Prime Minister of Jordan (in very veiled terms, it is true) during the interview at Jericho, to the effect that the Commission should officially endorse bilateral negotiations between Jordan and Israel for a separate peace, was fully justified. Subsequent events have shown that any other policy would have been a gamble, as unprofitable as it was risky.

These two interviews with Mr. Sharrett in Jerusalem and the Jordanian Prime Minister at Jericho were in the nature of preliminary and, to a certain extent, semi-official discussions. Official contact between the Commission and the various governments concerned was established by a series of visits paid by the Commission *in corpore,* accompanied by its advisers and part of its secretariat, to the capitals of the five Arab states[2] and the State of Israel, between February 12 and 25. The capitals were visited in the following order: Cairo, Jedda and Riyadh, Baghdad, Amman, Damascus, Beirut and Tel Aviv. All these visits were cut on the same pattern: official interviews with Prime Ministers and Ministers for Foreign Affairs, official banquets and receptions, private conversations between the members of the Commission and their respective diplomatic agents in each capital. The cycle of visits was of real interest and importance to the future work of the Commission, for both sides, the Arab states and the State of Israel, thus had an opportunity of explaining to the Commission, through the mouth of their own governments and in clear and unmistakable terms, the positions which were, in substance, going to be maintained without appreciable alteration throughout the three years during which the Commission attempted to reconcile their points of view or mediate in their disputes. With remarkable unanimity the five Arab governments informed the Commission that, until steps were taken to ensure the return of the Arab refugees to their homes, as directed by the Assembly in its resolutions of December 14, 1948, they were not prepared to discuss any other question relating to the situation in Palestine. For its part, the government of Israel declared that it was not prepared to give facilities for the return of the refugees to the homes they had abandoned in Israel, except within the framework of general peace negotiations between Israel and the Arab states, insisting that these negotiations should be opened immediately. After these preliminary encounters, the Commission could be under no illusions as to what lay in store for it; conciliation between the Arab and Jewish attitudes was impossible unless either Arabs or Jews or both made substantial concessions beyond the limits of what could be expected as the result of mere persuasion, exercised in a friendly manner by the members of the Commission, with the vacillating and formal support of their governments. It is difficult to say whether political pressure, mobilizing all the resources of those governments, would have sufficed to clear a path to conciliation, and even if it would have been desirable and justifiable. But the truth is that the governments members of the Commission never had the slightest intention of putting such pressure on the parties as would, per-

2. A visit to the Yemen was not considered necessary.

haps, have enabled the Commission to achieve positive results. The three governments, and particularly the United States government, had many other interests of their own in the Middle East and were never prepared to waste their influence (for influence, like money, can be wasted) in supporting a cause which could only indirectly affect their immediate, concrete and tangible interests.

Our round of visits to the capitals of the Arab states and the the State of Israel was made by air, thanks to the generosity of the Turkish government in placing an airplane at the disposal of the Commission. This gesture by the government at Ankara put an end to one of the most irritating disputes between the Commission and the United Nations administration. Knowing that the journey could only be made by air, and in spite of the fact that the Commission was engaged in carrying out the Assembly's direct instructions, the administration declined to provide an airplane for the Commission and, what was worse, supported the temporary Mediator in his refusal to comply with the Commission's suggestion to use one of the aircraft which the Secretary General of the United Nations had placed at his disposal and which were stationed at the airport at Rhodes during the armistice negotiations. All this had profoundly irritated the members of the Commission; but just when I had begun to despair of averting a violent clash between the Commission and the Secretary General, the Turkish government saved the situation with its offer. The Commission was thus able to make its journey in a comfortable and safe airplane with an excellent crew, while the publicity which the Turkish government gained by its gesture served both to increase its prestige in the Middle East and to lower that of the United Nations.

During the flight from Cairo to Jedda, after crossing the impressive and austere massif of Sinai and the Gulf of Akaba, flying low all the time to enable us to enjoy the view, it occurred to Yalcin, the Turkish member of the Commission and a perfect type of old Muslim, at once believer and skeptic, that we might land at Medina and visit the Tomb of the Prophet. After circling over the city for a while, the pilot, no doubt excited by the prospect of a visit to the second most important Muslim sanctuary in the world, thought he saw something which might be, if not an airport, at least a moderately good landing place. But, when we were already circling over the spot and losing height, he realized that it was only a small patch of sandy ground without

enough room to land, and he succeeded in putting the nose of
the plane up just in time to enable him to clear the roofs of some
houses there. Some members of the delegations or secretariat who
had served with the air forces during the war assured me that
we had run a great risk and only escaped a real catastrophe
through the pilot's presence of mind and the exceptional quickness of his reactions. For my part, everything appeared quite
simple and natural and without the explanations of the experts
I should never have noticed that anything was wrong. Where ignorance is bliss. . . . !

We arrived at Jedda at one o'clock in the afternoon and, after
getting settled in our quarters, spent the rest of the day and a
good part of the night, first at an interview with the Saudi
Arabian Minister for Foreign Affairs, the Amīr Fayṣal, eldest son
of King Ibn Saʿūd, and afterwards at a great banquet and reception to which the minister invited the Commission at his official
residence. At the banquet and reception, the drab clothes of the
Western diplomats, with their starched shirtfronts and black ties,
contrasted unfavorably with the flowing, majestic Oriental robes
not only of the Amīr, his brothers and their retinue, but also
of the Bedouin chiefs, real feudal lords of the desert, who formed
with the King and his family the politically active and conscious
part of the state. When the reception was over and, nearly drop-
ping with fatigue, we were preparing to make the most of our
primitive sleeping quarters, we were astonished to learn that
Yalcin, in spite of his seventy-five years, had just set off by car
for Mecca, some forty-five miles way, and that he would be returning the following day in time to catch the plane at seven o'clock
in the morning. And what crowned our astonishment was to see
him actually arriving at the airport punctually at seven o'clock,
alert, dressed and groomed with his usual care and attention,
with the air of one who had spent the night in peaceful and refreshing slumber, instead of being bumped about for several
hours in a car over a rough road, and the serenity which a visit
to the sanctuary at Mecca could not fail to induce in a sensitive
and cultivated mind such as his.

*   *   *   *

On its return to Jerusalem the Commission weighed the results of these first contacts with the parties and quickly came
to the conclusion that its immediate objective must be to get
rid of the obstacle which prevented its mission of conciliation from

even starting—the obstacle, on the one hand, of the Arab attitude, opposed to any kind of negotiations, whatever their object, until the return of the Arab refugees to their homes had been assured; and, on the other, Israel's refusal to discuss the return of the Arab refugees except within the framework of general peace negotiations. It is fair to recognize that the Arab attitude was based on less solid and justifiable grounds than that of Israel; and the Commission considered that its immediate efforts ought to be directed to persuading Arab states not to insist upon a prior solution of the refugee question before agreeing to discuss other outstanding issues between them and the State of Israel.

This was the origin and purpose of the conference to which the Commission convened the Arab states at Beirut between March 21 and April 5, 1949. The oft-repeated accusation that in convening this conference the Commission had helped to create the Arab "bloc" is as gratuitous as it is unjustified. The Arab "bloc" vis-à-vis the Palestine question was formed when the United Nations Assembly approved the partition plan of November 27, 1947. When the Commission began its mission of conciliation, the "bloc" was not only in existence, but was being firmly maintained by the vigorous hand of the Arab League and its Secretary General, 'Azzām Pasha. The only crack that appeared in it was the dissidence, not so much of Jordan, as of King 'Abdallāh; and how difficult and dangerous it would have been for the Commission to concentrate its efforts on this has already been explained. The existence and solidarity of the "bloc" had been so clearly revealed to the Commission during its visits to the Arab governments, that to talk of the danger of strengthening it, still less of forming it, was sheer nonsense. It might be said that by its initiative the Commission, if it did not form or strengthen the "bloc," extended to it a kind of recognition or official sanction. But this criticism, too, does not fit in with the facts. The Commission strove then, as it continued to strive during the three years of its active life, to maintain clearly and unequivocally the individual and separate character of its relations and dealings with each of the Arab states. Hence, the invitations to the Beirut conference were sent to each government separately, proposing the continuation at Beirut of the conversations begun during the Commission's visit to the respective capitals; and most, if not all, of the meetings held at Beirut, except the purely formal inaugural meeting, were held between the Commission and each individual delegation, which, besides being a source of discontent to the delegations, helped to prolong the conference beyond the allotted time.

To sum up, the Beirut conference was the only thing the Commission could do to avert the danger of finding itself paralyzed before having advanced a single step along the road the Assembly had marked out for it. And the conference was fully justified by the results. In the midst of a mass of declarations overflowing with acrimony and, at times, violence, and worthy to go on record as models of irrelevance and futility, the Commission succeeded, thanks to the patience of its members, in securing acceptance by all the delegations (except that of Iraq) of a final "statement," whose recondite significance—perceptible only to the initiated— lay in the agreement of the Arab states to negotiate with the Commission on *other* outstanding issues without insisting on a prior solution of the famous refugee question. The Commission had, therefore, succeeded in removing the first obstacle to their mission of conciliation. And having made a start, they decided, as a first step, to continue their negotiations with the parties in a neutral place (Lausanne was chosen by common consent), for which purpose they invited the Arab states and the State of Israel to send delegations with the necessary powers.

*　　*　　*　　*

The conference opened at the Beau Rivage Hotel, Ouchy, on April 27, and lasted until September 15. Four Arab states—Egypt, Jordan, Lebanon and Syria—and the State of Israel sent delegations composed of eminent and respected men, with whom the Commission, its members and assistants and the staff of the secretariat, established and maintained relations of great cordiality and mutual confidence.

The Arab states had accepted the Commission's invitation on the express condition that they should not have to attend meetings with the delegation of Israel. The Arab delegations went to Lausanne to negotiate with the Commission with the firm intention of ignoring the presence of the Israeli delegation in the city. Their attitude was so resolute in this respect and they had been so determined to make the point clear and final, that the Commission thought it best, when entertaining the delegations, to space their invitations in such a way that the Arab delegates and the Jewish delegates never met at the same function.

This state of affairs permitted few illusions as to the eventual results of the Lausanne conversations, and such illusions as existed received their death blow, while still in embryo, when a misunderstanding arose over the interpretation of the document since known to us as the "protocol" of Lausanne. The drafting of this document, both in content and in form, was the subject of so many and such extensive changes and retouches that, as usually happens in these cases, its final text became a monstrosity, undecipherable even by its authors. Translated into plain language, the document states that, in order that the Commission may rapidly fulfill its mission with respect to the refugees and in relation to territorial and other questions, the parties have accepted the Commission's proposal to take as a basis for negotiation the map of Palestine traced according to the partition plan of November 27, 1947, it being, however, clearly understood that these negotiations should deal with such territorial adjustments as might be necessary to achieve the above-mentioned objectives. As if the text did not lend itself sufficiently to ambiguities, the Israeli delegation added to the confusion by introducing a reservation, according to which its signature of the "protocol" did not prejudice its right freely to express its opinions on the matters under discussion on which it entirely reserved its government's position.

On May 15, 1949, this curious document was signed by the members of the Commission and by the four Arab delegations present in Lausanne[3] and the delegation of Israel, respectively, at two consecutive sessions and in separate documents. From that moment the Arab governments have not ceased to use the Lausanne "protocol" as one more occasion for invective and attacks on Israel for her bad faith in international affairs. They claim, in effect, that in signing the Lausanne "protocol" the Israeli government had accepted as the frontiers of Israel those shown on the map of the plan of partition. This claim is manifestly indefensible, whatever the interpretations to which the obscurity of the text of the "protocol" lends itself; particularly if we bear in mind the reservation formulated by the Israeli delegation on signing, a reservation which was accepted by the Commission and communicated in due course to the Arab delegations. The map of the partition plan was accepted as a *basis* for negotiation between the delegations and the Commission, in the sense of a starting-point, and I do not recall that anyone, when the docu-

3. Iraq had informed the Commission that, as her frontiers were not contiguous with those of Israel, her interest in the negotiations was limited and did not justify the sending of a delegation. Saudi Arabia was represented by the Egyptian government.

ment was drawn up and signed, gave it the interpretation which the Arab governments later gave it. I think, therefore, that the accusation repeatedly launched by the Arab governments against the Israeli government that the latter had not honored its signature is unjust and has no foundation in the spirit of the document.

The truth is that neither Arabs nor Jews took into account at all the spirit in which the Commission had suggested their acceptance of the "protocol" when, after three months of intensive effort, they submitted their proposals on the territorial question: the Arab governments proposed the plan of partition of November 27, 1947; the Israeli government the lines of demarcation fixed in the armistice agreements with Egypt, Lebanon, Jordan and Syria. The Arabs demanded, in substance, that the Commission should ignore the war that they themselves had launched against this same plan of partition and over their defeat, and impose on Israel the return, pure and simple, to the *status quo*. A curious demand which, if it was accepted, would fill future aggressors with hope! On the other hand, Israel's suggestion would mean the recognition of territorial conquests which had been the product of offensives and attacks launched in open violation of the truce. The Commission's disillusionment at these proposals, after three months of patient effort, was the chief cause of its decision, on September 15, to suspend the Lausanne conversations and resume them in New York a month later.

It was, however, the question of the Arab refugees which took up most time and effort during the Lausanne negotiations. Neither the energy displayed on one or two occasions by the American delegate, nor persuasion by way of personal and friendly contacts, to which the members of the Commission were always much addicted (too much so, perhaps, for in many cases their private conversations with members of delegations only served to increase the confusion) succeeded in substantially modifying the attitudes adopted by the Arab and Israeli delegations, as summarized earlier in this chapter. Nevertheless, in the interests of accuracy, it is necessary to mention certain results which, though modest and partial, are not without a certain interest.

On being pressed by the Commission, the Israeli government announced that it was prepared to accept the repatriation of 100,000 refugees. The Commission considered this figure not only unacceptable, but so far removed from what it thought reasonable that it did not even communicate it officially to the Arab delegations. Months later, the Israeli government, tired, according to its own expression, of "holding out its hand," withdrew the proposal.

The Arab delegations, for their part, proposed that, as a first step in the repatriation of the refugees, a start should be made by returning to their homes the natives of territories which were under Jewish control, but which did not form part of the State of Israel according to the plan of partition of November 27, 1947. The Israeli government's refusal cut short all discussion of this proposal.

The Israeli government accepted a suggestion by the Commission to facilitate the reunion of Arab families which had been separated, some in Israel and others in Arab territory, and announced that it was prepared to authorize the return of the families of Arabs who had not left Israeli territory. The execution of the agreement was entrusted to the Truce Supervision Mixed Commissions, which had the material means, on the spot, for implementing the plan they themselves had drawn up, in agreement with the Arab and Jewish authorities, for transporting across the lines the individuals included in the scheme of repatriation. In this way, several thousand refugees were able to return to Israel and rejoin their families.

In response to a proposal by the Commission, the government of Israel accepted, in principle, a limited and conditional "unfreezing" of the blocked accounts which the Arab refugees had left in Israel. To carry out this operation, a mixed committee was formed, composed of an expert appointed jointly by the Arab governments, another appointed by the Israeli government and a neutral chairman appointed by the Commission. With their usual inconsistency, the Arabs, after having accepted the mixed committee on condition that it was to be strictly technical and not political, appointed as the Arab member, Mr. Labbanī, the second Egyptian delegate, a distinguished career diplomatist who later became counselor to the Egyptian Embassy in Washington. The government of Israel, for its part, seized the opportunity to try to establish political contacts with the Arab delegations and appointed Mr. Sassoon, their chief expert, not on finance and banking, but on Arab questions. The committee met several times in private at Lausanne, the one and only occasion, up till then, that Arab and Jewish delegates (even though disguised as financial experts for the occasion) had sat at the same table, except at meetings of a general character, to discuss questions outstanding between them. At the end of one of the first meetings the two "experts" continued to converse amicably for more than two hours in Arabic (a language that Mr. Sassoon speaks at least as well as he speaks Hebrew), in terms of mutual respect and with a complete lack of constraint. But in spite of these favorable auguries, no concrete result had been achieved by March, 1952, when the Commission ended the first stage of its active life. The technical difficulties arising out of the conditions and limitations attached by the Israeli government to its acceptance in principle, were insurmountable without an initial basis of general good will—and this good will and spirit of cooperation was conspicuous by its absence both in the Israeli government and the Arab states. The former can hardly be blamed for this, since, when all is said and done, it was the one called upon to make concessions; but the indifference of the Arab governments, except when they were exploiting the theme in their constant diatribes and invectives against the State of Israel before the Assembly of the United Nations, was incomprehensible and inexcusable. This attitude, more than anything else, convinced me that the interest which the Arab governments appeared to take in the refugees was mainly political and polemical in character and that they regarded them chiefly as a platform from which to launch accusation after accusation against the government of Israel for its refusal to carry out the Assembly's resolutions. It must be admitted that the Israeli government's obstinate rejection of any concession in favor of the refugees, whatever the justification, played straight into the hands of the Arabs.[4]

It must in fairness be acknowledged that the Commission's efforts in regard to the reunion of families and the unfreezing of Arab bank accounts in Israel, like others which were not even the subject of preliminary negotiations (the return to Israel of the owners of abandoned orange groves, with their laborers; the repatriation of religious personnel, etc.) had their origin in the report of a Technical Committee. The Commission had appointed the Committee and sent it to Jerusalem to prepare, on the spot and in collaboration with Arab and Jewish authorities, a series of concrete proposals relating not only to the return of

4. When I was no longer Principal Secretary of the Commission and had left the service of the United Nations, the question of the blocked accounts in Israel became the subject of new proposals by the Israeli government.

the refugees to their homes, but to the protection of their rights and interests while awaiting repatriation.

Judged by the usual standards of American life, both public and private, which ignore nuances and imponderables and only appreciate rapid and direct action and immediate, concrete results, the Commission's activities during this period must have made a thoroughly deplorable impression. That impression was reflected in the state of mind with which Mr. Porter, the new representative on the Commission of the United States government, arrived in July to take up his functions. He came to Lausanne (as I have said elsewhere) with the idea that everything had been virtually settled and that all that remained to do was to put the final touches to the agreements and convene a peace conference. Being a man of great intelligence, with a realistic outlook, Mr. Porter soon discovered his error and adjusted his attitude rapidly to the real situation. But whether it was the result of his desire to achieve something positive in the short space of time he proposed to remain on the Commission (the length of his vacation!), or whether (as seems more probable) it was due to the growing maturity of American policy in the Middle East during those months, the fact is that in the last weeks of the Lausanne negotiations the Commission's attitude became firmer and its attention was concentrated on more concrete aspects of the refugee question. Everything leads to the belief that, in that summer of 1949, the idea took shape of articulating the activities of the Conciliation Commission, especially with regard to the refugees, with the American policy of economic and political intervention in the Middle East. The first indications the Commission had of this came from Mr. Porter on his arrival from Washington towards the end of July. Porter dropped some hints to his colleagues about the existence of a "plan" of economic and technical aid to the Arab states (called the McGhee plan after its principal author, the Assistant Secretary of State dealing with Middle Eastern affairs).

Such was the sense of the proposal Mr. Porter submitted to the Commission on his return from a lightning visit to Washington in the middle of August. According to this proposal the Conciliation Commission was to appoint and send immediately to the Middle East an economic survey group, with an American chairman and three vice-chairmen, one French, one English and one Turkish. The group was to be composed of a team of experts (Mr. Porter suggested between thirty and forty), specializing in

different subjects, who would draw up a comprehensive plan for
the economic development of the Middle East. The group was
to function under the Commission's authority and was to submit its report to that body about the end of October when it was
expected to finish its survey.

The link between this general plan of economic development
in the Middle East and the concrete and limited mission of the
Conciliation Commission, and the reason for having the survey
group appointed by and responsible to the Commission, was the
hypothesis that the economic development of the Arab states,
which the McGhee plan was intended to foster, would make possible the absorption into their economy of the Arab refugees
who did not wish, or who were unable, to return to their homes
and properties in Israel. This idea is expressed, in the circum-
spect terms rendered necessary by the circumstances of the moment, in the second paragraph of the mission's terms of reference.
As proposed by the American government and approved by the
Commission, it ran as follows: "To facilitate the repatriation, resettlement and economic and social rehabilitation of the refugees and the payment of compensation . . . in order to reinte-
grate the refugees into the economic life *of the area* on a self-
sustaining basis, within a minimum period of time." But this
hypothesis, which was in any case rather rash, lacked all foundation so long as the Arab states persisted in their refusal to consider final settlement in their territories as a means of contributing to the solution of the refugee problem and continued to
maintain that the solution ought to consist, solely and exclusively,
in the return of the refugees to the houses and lands they had
abandoned in Israel. In order to obtain a definite reply to a point
of such importance, the Commission sent a memorandum to the
Arab delegations and the delegation of Israel, asking them if they
were prepared to recognize that the solution of the refugee problem should be sought, jointly, through the return to their homes
in Israel and through final settlement in the Arab states. The
replies were not enthusiastic and were so hedged about with conditions and safeguards that the reserve and unwillingness to cooperate that had dictated them were clearly apparent. In the end,
however, while Egypt and Lebanon pleaded over-population as
an excuse for their refusal to accept refugees in their respective
territories, Jordan and Syria announced that they were prepared,
in principle, to accept refugees who were unable to return to
their homes.

The Commission adopted the American proposal without discussion and thus, towards the end of August, the United Nations Economic Survey Mission for the Middle East was set up as a subsidiary organ of the Conciliation Commission. The appointment of Mr. Gordon R. Clapp, Chairman of the Board of Tennessee Valley Authority, as chairman of the mission followed swiftly, as also the appointment of the three vice-chairmen[5] and the group of experts who were to carry out the survey. On September 12, the mission established its offices at Beirut and two months later submitted its preliminary report, exclusively devoted to the refugee question. This was followed six weeks later by its final report on the general economic situation in the Middle East.

These reports were discussed in another chapter; here I only want to say that the Economic Survey Mission, or Clapp Mission, as it was known in its shorter and more familiar form, in my opinion, carried out its task in a more complete and satisfactory manner than any other body during the Palestine crisis. I should add that its dependence on the Conciliation Commission was purely formal. Mr. Clapp, aided by the three vice-chairmen, assumed full responsibility for the mission's work; the Conciliation Commission took care to keep entirely apart from the activities of the mission and the relations which the latter established not only with the Secretary General of the United Nations, but with the governments concerned, were maintained by its own means and without any interference by the Commission.

*   *   *   *

Having brought the Lausanne conversations to an end in the middle of September, the Commission resumed its activities in New York on October 19. During this new period, nothing worthy of note marked the course of its negotiations with the parties, which kept up, both as regards the territorial question and the problem of the refugees, the same extreme and stubborn attitudes which provoked the closure of the Lausanne meetings.

Attention in the Assembly was concentrated almost exclusively on Jerusalem. In fulfillment of the specific mandate which it had received from the Assembly in 1948,[6] the Commission had prepared a draft international statute which was communicated to

5. M. Eirik Labonne (France), Sir Desmond Morton (Great Britain) and M. Cemil Gökçen (Turkey).

6. Resolution of December 14, 1948, art. 8.

the Assembly at its session in 1949. I shall say something later about the merits and demerits of this draft in the chapter dealing specifically with Jerusalem,[7] but I must mention here the curious reception accorded to it both by the United Nations Secretariat and by the delegations. The Palestine "experts" in the Secretariat, influenced as usual by the multiform, subtle and intelligent campaign inspired by the Jews against the very idea of internationalizing Jerusalem, prophesized that the Assembly would reject the Commission's draft on the grounds that it went too far along the road to internationalization. As it happened, the effect was exactly the opposite; the immense majority of the delegations thought that the draft stopped so far short of internationalization that it could not even serve as a basis for discussion. And, in fact, the long, confused and tedious discussion about the matter in the Political Committee of the Assembly, in the Special Committee appointed to examine it and in the plenary sessions, was conducted with hardly any reference to the Commission's draft. The truth is that, right from the outset, it was ignored, not, as the Secretariat's "experts" had foretold, because of its excess of internationalism, but, quite to the contrary, because it did not go far enough in the direction of internationalization.

The 1949 Assembly saw the first attempt to replace the Commission by a one man mission. My first conversations with the Secretary General and his immediate colleagues convinced me that this idea lay at the root of his plans for the future action of the United Nations in Palestine. The effects of the contrast between the brilliant atmosphere of activity and efficiency surrounding the figure of the Mediator who, in the persons of Count Bernadotte and Ralph Bunche, had succeeded in barely a year in imposing the truces and concerting the armistices, and the restrained, placid and slightly phlegmatic Conciliation Commission, which after a year of patient and tenacious effort appeared before the Assembly confessing its failure with sober and simple dignity, were already beginning to be felt. For the moment, no one thought of inquiring whether, and in what measure, this contrast had its origin in the essential and profound difference between the imposition of a truce and the concerting of armistices in which all the political, economic and legal questions outstanding between the parties were expressly left unsolved, and the negotiation of a real peace treaty between them, which implied the solution of all these questions. And everyone seemed to have

7. *Vide* Chapter XII.

forgotten that "conciliation" figured largely in the mandate conferred on the Mediator by the Assembly, that in this direction Count Bernadotte had been able to accomplish absolutely nothing, had admitted this to be so, and had recommended the Assembly to appoint a new body, whose mission it would be to attempt it.

The United States government also harbored this idea of replacing the Conciliation Commission by a one man mission, but in a different form from that which was inspiring the various draft resolutions the Secretariat was preparing. The project which the State Department communicated towards the middle of October, not to the French and Turkish members of the Commission, but to the respective embassies in Washington, would have left the Commission as a supervisory body, but the negotiations with the parties were to be placed in the hands of a single person, appointed by the Commission and responsible to it.

In the end, nothing came of all this. During the long interview which the Commission had on November 3, 1949, with Mr. McGhee, Assistant Secretary of State dealing with Middle Eastern affairs, followed by a courtesy visit to the Secretary of State, not the slightest allusion was made to the draft resolution which had been communicated to the French and Turkish Embassies a few days previously, and the plans for the Commission's future activities which were discussed and, to a certain extent, agreed upon during the interview were based on the continuation of the Commission without any change in its organization or its attributes. As far as the draft resolutions prepared by the Secretariat were concerned, no further mention was made of them, and in neither of the two resolutions which the Assembly adopted on Palestine, one relating to Jerusalem and the other to the refugees, was there a single word introducing any change either in the organization, or in the competence, or in the methods of the Conciliation Commission.

*   *   *   *

Before bringing its meetings in New York to a close, the Commission had decided to continue its negotiations with the parties in Geneva. The idea was that the Geneva meetings should begin where the Lausanne meetings of the previous summer left off; but in reality they took on a very different character, mostly because the governments concerned were tired of supporting the expense of large delegations, for long periods of time, without any hope of reaching positive results. The delegations which the Arab states, with the exception of Egypt, sent to Geneva were markedly inferior, both in the number and the rank of their members, to those which they had sent the previous year to Lausanne. And the State of Israel seized the opportunity to emphasize, by an outward and visible sign, the scant favor with which it had always regarded the Commission by refraining from sending a special delegation to Geneva, and maintaining liaison with the Commission by means of the permanent Israeli delegate to the European Office of the United Nations.

In New York the Commission had already examined the possibility of—according to the well-worn formula—passing from conciliation to mediation. This formula was intended to express the idea (I do not guarantee its accuracy) that the Commission, instead of confining itself to serving as a friendly and neutral intermediary, interchanging the proposals and suggestions of the parties, should assume a more active rôle by preparing and submitting to the parties its own formulas of compromise. This idea gained new strength in Geneva, where the vacuum created around the Commission made it more patently urgent every day to revise the hitherto exclusively passive and conciliatory procedures and methods which the Commission had been applying. The Arab delegations immediately displayed great enthusiasm for this new form of intervention on the Commission's part; the Israeli delegation showed its displeasure and opposition from the outset, even attempting to prove—an attempt as vain as it was illfounded—that the Commission lacked the right to formulate and submit to the parties its own compromise proposals. On top of all this, there was the growing difficulty of continuing to cope with the Arab delegations' persistent refusal to countenance anything that might entail contacts or discussions with the Israeli delegation.

All these anxieties led to the most important and spectacular step taken by the Commission in the whole of its existence, with the sole exception of the Paris Conference which was convened fourteen months later, and the proposals submitted to the parties there. I refer to the proposal to appoint mixed committees, that is, committees composed of Arab and Jewish delegates who, under the chairmanship of a representative of the Commission, would study the compromise formulas submitted to them. The idea was to combine mediation, which the Arabs favored, with direct negotiations, which the Jews regarded as the panacea for all difficulties. Admittedly, the formula did not favor both sides equally; Israel's interest in negotiating directly with the Arabs was greater than the interest of the Arabs mediation. Above all, the Arab governments' aversion for direct negotiations with the Israeli government was incomparably more profound than Israel's dislike for mediation. In spite of everything, the formula afforded both Arabs and Jews an opportunity to make a gesture of good will and to rescue the negotiations from the morass in which they had been struck since their initiation a year ago. The formula was, more than anything, a touchstone for proving the existence of that good will.

A first draft of the proposal was submitted to the Commission by its secretariat during the early days of March. With slight modifications of form, the draft was immediately accepted by the representatives of France and Turkey. The United States delegate thought it necessary to submit it to the State Department, whose approval was received at Geneva on March 28. On the following day, the 29th, the proposal was officially communicated to the Arab and Israeli delegations in the course of two consecutive meetings specially convened for this purpose. The next thing was that the Commission decided that M. de Boisanger, its Chairman, accompanied by the Principal Secretary, should go to the Middle East to explain the proposal to the governments concerned and discuss with them any objections they might have before they were bound by an official reply.

In accordance with this plan we left Geneva on April 4, and, after spending the night at Athens, reached Jerusalem on the following day, where we made the first contacts with the governments of Israel and Jordan. We all thought that these two governments would show a special interest in the proposal for mixed committees, as a raft they could cling to in the sea of insuperable difficulties in which they were overwhelmed as the result of the famous direct negotiations secretly begun under the personal pressure of King 'Abdallāh. By accepting the Commission's proposal, these secret and shamefaced negotiations would have been instantly legitimized and could have continued in a regular form under the auspices and guarantee of the Commission.

The Israeli government's reaction was not unfavorable, although in the interview between the Chairman of the Commission and the Minister for Foreign Affairs, the latter could not resist the temptation of giving us a fresh demonstration of his acuteness of intellect by producing a critical analysis of the proposal in which all its deficiencies and lacunae were underlined with logical force. Once again excessive cleverness proved to be the bane of politics; excellent arguments, brilliantly expounded, frustrated a political purpose which could have been achieved with a little intuition and good sense. For what good sense dictated at that juncture was a plain unadorned acceptance of the proposal, without straining every nerve to bring into the light of day deficiencies and lacunae which we ourselves knew better than anyone.

The reserved and vacillating attitude of the government of Jordan and of King 'Abdallāh himself proved to us that our illusions were vain. After many conversations and consultations in which, as usual, the King spoke a different language from that of his ministers, everything finally reduced itself to this—that the first thing was to secure the acceptance of the Egyptian government; in other words, Jordan was aligning herself with the other Arab states and accepting the leadership of the Arab League.

During our visit King 'Abdallāh, as was his usual custom, gave an official luncheon in honor of the Chairman of the Commission, and I once again had occasion to admire the subtlety of his mind in the remarks he addressed to me about his recent visit to Madrid, knowing as he did my unyielding opposition to the Franco régime. After luncheon he had the two horses which Franco had presented to him as a souvenir of his visit brought to the great square in front of the principal entrance of the palace; two magnificent Arabs, one white and the other chestnut, which would no doubt have attracted attention in Madrid, but which were not much different from any of the horses of a squadron of the Arab Legion or of the mounted police in Cairo. I thought to myself that to present King 'Abdallāh with a couple of Arab horses was rather as if King 'Abdallāh had presented Franco with a couple of La Mancha mules!

The visits to Damascus and Beirut were little more than a formality; the Ministers for Foreign Affairs and their chief assistants were at Cairo taking part in a meeting of the Arab League, and the only conversations of interest were those held by the Chairman of the Commission with the Minister of his own country, the British Minister and the United States Minister in the two capitals. All had received somewhat vague instructions to recommend the respective governments to accept the Commission's proposals, but how they were expected to carry out their instructions when, as we found to our astonishment, they did not know what the proposals were, history does not relate. I especially remember our conversation with the United States Minister in Damascus, who confessed to us bitterly that his recommendations would have just the opposite effect to what was intended, because the Syrian government systematically regarded all recommendations by the American government as inspired by the desire and the intention to favor the State of Israel.

The round of visits ended with our visit to the Egyptian Government on April 13 and 14. A meeting of the Arab League was taking place in Cairo at the same time to decide, among other things, the terms of the reply to the Commission's proposals. Our first visit was to the United States Ambassador and the interview was revealing for the light it threw on the support, or rather the lack of support, the Commission was receiving from its members. The ambassador told us that two or three days previously he had gone to see the Minister for Foreign Affairs in order to urge acceptance of the Commission's proposals, and the minister had replied that there would be no difficulty at all over this. When we expressed surprise, he summoned Philip Ireland, who was considered to be one of the best experts on Eastern questions in the American diplomatic service and who was then counsellor at the Embassy in Cairo, and asked him if he had any information on the subject. Ireland explained that the acceptance of the Arab states was conditional upon the acceptance by Israel of the principle of the return of the refugees to their homes. But what was a revelation to us was that the ambassador contented himself with shrugging his shoulders and saying: "No doubt someone went to see the minister after his talk with me and convinced him that they ought not to accept." And that was all. As it was now nearly two o'clock, the hour when he invariably stopped work, he took leave of us and we did not see him again. Is it likely that if it had been a matter that vitally concerned the American government, the ambassador would have reacted to the minister's *volte face* with equal calm?

The following day we had an official interview with the Egyptian Minister for Foreign Affairs, at which 'Azzām Pasha, the Secretary General of the Arab League, and two representatives of the Lebanese and Syrian governments, respectively, were present. The object of the meeting, which was invested with some solemnity, was to communicate to the Chairman of the Commission the joint reply of the Arab states, as agreed upon at the recent meeting of the League, to the Commission's proposal for the appointment of mixed committees. The reply, set out in a long declaration which was recited rather than read by the minister, coincided, in substance, with what Mr. Ireland had told us during our visit the previous day to the American Ambassador: the Arab states were prepared to accept the Commission's proposal and to collaborate in the mixed committees on condition that Israel first accepted the principle of the return of the refugees to their homes, which had been laid down in the Assembly's resolution of December 14, 1948, and that the task of the mixed committees should be to discuss and regulate its practical application.

We returned that same night to Geneva and the Commission spent the next few days carefully examining the situation created by Israel's acceptance and the conditional acceptance of the Arab states. The Commission could have admitted the Arab states' conditional acceptance and communicated it officially to the Israeli government, asking the latter whether it was prepared to fulfill the required condition. But this manner of proceeding was judged to be incorrect and the Commission decided to regard the conditional acceptance of the Arab states as a refusal. Things would have been altogether different if the Israeli government had spontaneously taken the initiative and accepted in principle the return of the refugees to their homes, reserving the right to discuss the practical application in the mixed committees. I think, as I always thought, that this step would have borne fruit. The Israeli government would have cut the ground from under the feet of the Arab states, making it impossible for them to persist in their obstinate and increasingly unjustifiable refusal to enter into direct negotiations, without running any risk of finding themselves obliged to open their frontiers to large masses of refugees. As was well known, the obstacles to the return of the refugees were rooted, not in principle, but in practical considerations; and the terms of the resolution of December 14, 1948, laid down requirements and conditions which would have made it possible for the Israeli government to bar the way, or impose restrictions on practical grounds, with as much or greater facility than on grounds of principle.

The Commission's last efforts to rescue its proposals from the failure to which they were being condemned by the conditions exacted by the Arab states, in return for their acceptance, took up the two remaining months of its stay at Geneva. On June 15, realizing with some depression of spirits that the vicious circle in which the negotiations were moving could not be broken, the Commission decided to try a different tack and moved to Jerusalem, its official seat, intending to pursue its work of conciliation in direct contact with the governments. But, as could have been foreseen, these contacts, in which, as usual, official interviews were interspersed with private conversations, produced no results either. It was becoming more and more obvious that without the decided and resolute support of the governments composing the Commission, in particular the American government, there was no chance of surmounting the obstacles which blocked the path. And it was equally becoming more and more obvious that this support was not, nor was it ever likely to be, forthcoming. This was clear from conversations with the diplomatic representatives of the three governments accredited to the Arab states and the State of Israel, who, with rare and honorable exceptions, revealed a complete ignorance of everything touching the activities of the Commission, and what was worse, complete indifference, if not (as in the case of the United States Ambassador in Tel Aviv) open and marked hostility.[8]

From Jerusalem, the Commission paid an official visit to the Turkish government, as it had done to the French government from Geneva and to the United States government from New York. We travelled in a United Nations airplane, in bad weather and with a heavy load, so that the take-off from Kalandia was difficult and caused great alarm to those who were seeing us off; fortunately all went well in the end. From a tourist's point of view, the visit was very interesting and would have been more so had the weather been better; rain, wind and fog are not the most propitious elements for admiring the marvels of Santa Sophia, still less the enchantments of the Golden Horn or the Bosphorus. Politically, the visit had no real value, except to show, once again, the ignorance and indifference reigning in official and diplomatic circles at Ankara in regard to the Commission's activities.

*   *   *   *

The Commission resumed its meetings at the beginning of October in New York, where it remained until the early days of December. The 1950 Assembly devoted a great part of its time and attention to the Palestine question, but in conditions very different from those surrounding its examination in the Assembly

8. The best evidence of this state of mind can be found in his book, *My Mission to Israel*, by J. MacDonald.

of the previous year. The first thing worth noting is that, this year, there were none of the underground movements of the previous year, either in the Secretariat or in the American government, threatening the Commission with violent death or general paralysis. Not only this, but for the first time the delegations showed a certain interest in the Commission's periodic reports on its activities. No doubt this was partly due to the fact that the Commission, breaking what had been its constant practice of sending to the Secretary General of the United Nations purely objective reports containing little more than the bare and unvarnished narrative of its activities, submitted to the Assembly in October, 1950, a report in which it expressed opinions and judgments on the profound causes of the conflict.[9]

The Commission's report was criticized in some quarters and praised in others. The Chairman (who was at that time Mr. Palmer, United States) expounded the Commission's point of view to the Political Committee of the Assembly, and all this culminated in an attack by the Arab bloc, led by the Egyptian delegation, on the failure to implement the directive in the resolution of December 14, 1948, relating to the return of the refugees to their homes, and a proposal by the same delegation that the Assembly should appoint a body with the specific duty of taking the necessary measures to ensure the immediate implementation of the said directive. This proposal, with others aimed at introducing changes in the composition of the Commission, was submitted to the usual process of elaboration, in which discussions in committees and sub-committees mingled and combined with all kinds of private talks and consultations, the final result being a resolution which the Assembly adopted on December 14, 1950, directing the Commission to appoint a body similar to that proposed by the Egyptian delegation.

*   *   *   *

From New York, the Commission went directly to the Middle East and, at a meeting held in Beirut on January 25, 1951, complied with the instructions it had received from the Assembly by creating what was known as the Conciliation Commission's Refugee Office, shortly afterwards appointing as its Director the Danish diplomat, Mr. Holger Andersen. The Refugee Office carried out, during the summer of 1951, an intensive work of docu-

9. This report was published as an Assembly document A/1367/Add I on October 24, 1950.

mentation and research on all the aspects of the refugee question, the results of which were communicated to the Commission in a voluminous and informative report. Except for the section which dealt with compensation, the report suffered from the fact that it did not sufficiently take into account the practical spirit which, in accordance with the terms of the Assembly's resolution of December 14, 1950, should have informed the labors of the new Office. But this does not detract from the merits of the report, and the section relating to compensation will be an invaluable starting-point on the day when circumstances make it possible for this aspect of the refugee question to be dealt with in a practical and realistic manner.

The six months of the Commission's stay in Jerusalem, from the middle of January to the middle of July, 1951, were beyond doubt the most lamentable in its history. All negotiation between the Commission as such, *in corpore,* and the parties was suspended. In contrast, private conversations and contacts between each member of the Commission and official or unofficial personalities, both Arab and Jewish, flourished and multiplied as never before and problems were discussed in an atmosphere ill-suited to their gravity and delicacy. The result of all this was that the Commission itself lost a good deal of prestige and its future possibilities of action as an organ of the United Nations were seriously jeopardized. The truth is that the Commission had become an instrument that neither the governments composing it nor the United Nations knew how to use; it seemed to me that the French and Turkish members openly waited for their American colleague to take the initiative and, that, as the latter was without instructions or directives from his government and was unsuited by temperament and professional habit to take the initiative or to accept responsibility on his own, the Commission fell into a state of what can without exaggeration be called atrophy.

The theme which predominated in these negotiations, which were conducted not so much by the Commission as by its individual members, was the payment of compensation to the refugees for their property abandoned in Israel, together with the settlement of the refugees in the Arab countries. The discussions revealed the first signs of a favorable disposition on the part of the Arab governments to the permanent settlement of refugees in their territories. This led to friction with UNRWA,[10] the or-

10. United Nations Relief and Works Agency.

ganization which was especially responsible for everything affecting the relief and resettlement of the refugees, thus making it necessary to arrive at a kind of *modus vivendi* between the two organizations, according to which the settlement of refugees in the Arab countries was to be the concern of UNRWA, while the Conciliation Commission was to continue to deal with their repatriation and the payment of compensation for their property abandoned in Israel.

*   *   *   *

This period in the life of the Commission cannot be reviewed without a reference to the assassination of King 'Abdallāh in Jerusalem. This occurred on July 20, when he was entering the Aksa Mosque in the Old City. Whether the assassin, a youth of twenty-one, was in contact or not with the Muftī of Jerusalem (then in exile in Egypt) and his organization among the Palestinian Arabs, is something that has never been cleared up. What appears to be beyond dispute is that King 'Abdallāh was the victim of the wave of hostility which he provoked among the Arab population of Palestine, first by annexing to the Kingdom of Jordan the part of Palestine which was not occupied by Israel, and secondly by his policy in favor of negotiations for a separate peace with Israel. The brutality of the measures taken by the Arab Legion against the Palestinian Arabs and particularly against the population of Jerusalem confirms this interpretation. For a week the Old City of Jerusalem was practically occupied by the Arab Legion, under a real reign of terror. The sole topic of conversation was the brutal reprisals taken by the Legion against the defenseless inhabitants of the Old City. The day following the assassination, I wanted to find out for myself whether the rumors of fire and destruction in the Old City were true and I went through it with two of my colleagues from the Commission's secretariat. No doubt there had been some exaggeration about the havoc caused, but I have never had such an impression of collective terror; not a shop, not a door, not a window was open and the streets were deserted and completely silent, a silence broken only by the tramp of the Legion's patrols. There was not the slightest doubt that the assassination of the King had been fully avenged on the Arab population of Jerusalem. How many victims the reprisals claimed is difficult to ascertain. The judicial proceedings ended with the execution of several of the accused, among them our friend Dr. Mūsā Ḥusaynī; but the general opinion in Jerusalem was that the trial was conducted with so many irregularities and with such violence and cruelty that it lacked any value as evidence of the guilt of the accused. In reality, it was a political trial, that is to say, its object was not so much to dispense justice as to produce a political effect, in this case the intimidation of the Arab population of Palestine.

The tension in the days immediately following the outrage was great and the feeling that an incident of some sort might provoke a real catastrophe created an atmosphere of unrest and constant alarm. At that time we were living in the American Colony, in the Arab part of the city, but outside the walls of the Old City; and to go to Government House where we had our offices meant crossing the line of demarcation between the two zones of the city and passing through the Jewish zone to reach the entrance of the neutral zone of Government House. On the day of the assassination I returned a little earlier than usual because we had invited some people to lunch. During luncheon we were continually hearing rumors that something had happened in the Old City, but the official news of the assassination only reached us as we were rising from the table, just as we had noticed that the Arab Legion were setting up machine-gun posts at the gate of the American Colony and at nearby corners. Some of the consuls who had been lunching with us and whose consulates and residences were in the Jewish part of the city wanted to return immediately, but the Legion had already blocked the road over the line of demarcation so thoroughly and with such lack of good sense that the French, Belgian and Swiss Consuls had to wait until ten o'clock in the evening, that is, more than eight hours, until the order came authorizing them to pass so that they could return to their consulates—a typical example of the arbitrary and capricious manner of exercising authority and of the measure in which the tragic event had caused the Arab authorities in Jerusalem to lose their heads.

*　　*　　*　　*

It was at this stage in the life of the Commission that the first clear signs appeared of its organic disintegration and of the inevitable consequence—incoherence and lack of unity in its work. We have already seen how the tendency to replace the action of the Commission *in corpore* by the individual activities of its members almost reached the point of nullifying the contacts between the Commission and the parties. Another manifestation of the same phenomenon was the exaggerated reliance the Commission placed in the brand new Refugee Office, as if it were Providence itself. Attributing heaven knows what miracle-working propensities to its Director, Mr. Andersen, the members of the Commission (especially the American) expected that in a few weeks he would have overcome the obstacles which had held up the work of the Commission for two years. Their disillusionment was swift, for a few months later they learned from reading the report submitted by Mr. Andersen that not only had the obstacles not been overcome, but that the Refugee Office had not made the slightest effort to overcome them. In this atmosphere of confidence in the Refugee Office as the panacea for all ills, the Commission decided on June 1, as soon as the Refugee Office had been constituted and its terms of reference fixed more or less precisely, to suspend its own sessions in order to leave the way clear for the latter to work the expected miracle.

The atrophy of the Commission during those early months of 1951 spurred its secretariat into concentrating its efforts on analyzing the causes of and suggesting remedies for the malady. Thus it was that the Commission's secretariat itself began to lay the groundwork of a plan to review not only the terms of reference and organization of the Commission, but the United Nations action in Palestine as a whole. In our opinion, the root of the evil lay in the existence in Palestine of three distinct organizations, namely, UNRWA, TSO[11] and the Conciliation Commission, with ill-defined terms of reference and functioning not only absolutely independently of one another, but with all kinds of mutual suspicions and animosities.

UNRWA was responsible for the resettlement of the refugees, while the Conciliation Commission continued to be responsible for their repatriation and the payment of compensation for property abandoned in Israel. The bond between these two questions was so close, their interdependence so indissoluble, that it is hard to conceive how they could be treated efficiently by separate organizations, even if the most intimate and cordial collaboration had reigned between them. But the fact is that no collaboration of any sort ever existed between the Conciliation Commission and UNRWA, much less cordial collaboration. In the interests of truth it must be admitted that the Commission was always animated by a spirit of loyal and sincere cooperation towards UNRWA; but, in return, it never met with anything but distrust, indiffer-

11. Truce Supervision Organization.

ence and coldness, if not open and declared hostility. One of the most painful memories of my service with the Conciliation Commission is that of the meetings between the Commission and the Director of UNRWA and his consultative committee. The meetings were in themselves absurd, because they brought face to face, frequently maintaining opposite points of view in relation to the same question, the representatives of the American, French and Turkish governments, respectively, on the Conciliation Commission and the consultative committee of UNRWA. The British government was represented only on the consultative committee of UNRWA and thus escaped this curious experience in international relations. But this would not have mattered if important questions had been discussed at the meetings and joint resolutions adopted leading to some practical and positive result. I do not believe this happened once. The meetings dragged on painfully in an atmosphere of boredom, if not of distrust, and more than once I noticed that distinguished and eminent members of the UNRWA delegation did not scruple to show their indifference by indulging in a refreshing nap or by "doodling" with youthful zest.

Nor were the relations between the Commission and the TSO ever so close and cordial as could have been desired. Although the Security Council had expressly directed that the Chief of Staff of the United Nations in Palestine, the official head of the TSO, should keep the Commission regularly informed of anything in his sphere of action that might be of interest to it, this was never done save in a desultory and sporadic manner and with very bad grace. The crisis which occurred in March, 1951, on the occasion of the works begun by Israel in the demilitarized zone of Lake Hulé in the upper valley of the Jordan, showed how far the rivalries and suspicions that animated the TSO in its relations with the Commission were a challenge to good sense and the most elementary prudence. And, as in the case of UNRWA, it is fair to say that the origin of this deplorable situation must be sought in the attitude of reserve and even hostility which the Chief of Staff of the United Nations in Palestine, General W. Riley, adopted from the outset towards the Conciliation Commission. The incidents at Lake Hulé degenerated rapidly, as were continually pointed out in official notes and press commentaries, into a real political crisis between Israel and Syria, undoubtedly the most serious since the signing of the armistices. This crisis, besides constituting a danger, afforded a unique opportunity to initiate contacts and negotiations between the two states and to break the vicious circle in which all the Commission's attempts to establish direct contact between Arab and Jewish representatives had been caught. It would have been natural for the United Nations to have intervened at such an important juncture through the medium of the organization with the greatest political authority on the spot, namely, the Conciliation Commission. But, incredible though it may seem, the negotiations relating to this crisis, which took place, as was natural given the eminently political character which the affair assumed from the outset, not between the military leaders of Israel and Syria, but between the governments represented by their Ministers for Foreign Affairs, were entrusted to the Chief of Staff of the United Nations, an office that, as General Riley was on sick leave in the United States, was being discharged at the moment by one of his aides, Colonel de Ridder of the Belgian Army. The Conciliation Commission, with its three members present in Jerusalem or Beirut during the whole of the crisis and with its secretariat well equipped with political, legal, economic and other advisers, was deliberately prevented from intervening, directly or indirectly, in the affair. The Chairman had to ask the Chief of Staff to keep the Commission informed about what was going on before he would consent to meet the members of the Commission on June 3, after a dinner to which we were all invited by Mr. Palmer at one of the most luxurious hotels near Beirut in the mountains of Lebanon. But all was in vain; the isolation of the Commission continued to be complete and absolute and the situation did not improve when, in the middle of May, General Riley, restored to good health, returned to the Middle East. True, this time it was he who suggested a meeting with the Commission, which was duly held at Jerusalem on May 19; but things went on as before, the only difference being that a copy of the quarterly reports from the Chief of Staff to the Secretary General of the United Nations was sent to the Commission—documents that were out of date before they reached the Commission.

At bottom, the most serious thing was not the attitude of the Chief of Staff in excluding the Commission from the negotiations, but the fact that the Secretary General, the Security Council and the governments composing the Commission seemed to agree in approving this attitude. During the discussions in the Security Council about the incidents at Lake Hulé, not the slightest allusion was made to the Commission. As it was not very likely that everyone had suddenly been stricken by loss of memory where the members of the Commission were concerned, the only possible explanation of this silence is that the Conciliation Commission was deliberately excluded from the negotiations relating to one of the most acute crises between Israel and an Arab state that occurred during its existence.

The affair of the New Gate in the Old City of Jerusalem was another example of the difficulties arising out of the absence of cooperation between the Commission and the TSO and the fact that their respective spheres of authority had never been properly defined. The New Gate gives access to the Christian quarter of the Old City and its closing obliged the population of that quarter, including the Latin and Greek Orthodox Patriarchates and their dependencies, to make a long detour on foot through the steep cobbled alleys of the Old City in order to reach, through the Damascus Gate, either the Arab districts outside the walls or, what was equally if not more important, the Arab part of Palestine and Jordan by the Nablus and Jericho main roads, respectively. It can be readily understood, therefore, that the opening of the New Gate was the subject of vehement demand by the Christian population (both Catholic and Greek Orthodox) of Jerusalem, vigorously supported by the two Patriarchates whenever the occasion presented itself. In principle, there was nothing to prevent the Conciliation Commission from dealing with the matter and embarking on the necessary negotiations with the two governments of Israel and Jordan, had it not been that, for the opening of the Gate to serve any useful purpose, it would have had to be accompanied by a revision of the demarcation line between the two zones, which would have permitted access from the New Gate to the Arab zone outside the walls; and anything that affected the lines of demarcation was the preserve of the TSO and jealously guarded by the Chief of Staff. I spoke to the latter several times on the subject, always as the result of pressing requests I was constantly receiving from influential elements among the Christian population or the Patriarchates; but I was never able to obtain more than the usual evasive answer with which the TSO received any suggestions emanating from the Commission or its secretariat. In view of this attitude, I decided in the spring of 1951 to risk a personal approach to the two governors, Arab and Jewish respectively, of Jerusalem. The two came to tea at my office in Government House; Hamilton Fisher, the Commission's principal political adviser, was present too, and we discussed for more than two hours the various possibilities of establishing communication between the New Gate and the rest of the Arab zone outside the walls of the Old City. The interview convinced me that there was no obstacle, in principle, to an agreement which, within its modest limits, would have had considerable symbolic value, besides alleviating the hardships of a large section of the population of Jerusalem. However, I did not think it prudent to pursue the matter for fear of stirring up the latent discord between the Commission and the TSO. And, in any case, the assassination of King 'Abdallāh, which occurred a few days after the interview with the two governors at Government House, made it impossible for the moment to continue any measures of this sort.

In view of all this, logic and justice demanded that the action of the United Nations in Palestine should be subject to a general review; and it was with this end in mind that the Commission's secretariat began to prepare the ground. But neither logic nor justice have ever played a major part in the activities of the United Nations in Palestine and, as we shall see, the result was not a general review of United Nations action in Palestine, but, purely and simply, the elimination of the Conciliation Commission, as if it, and it alone, was responsible for the prevailing disorder.

As I have said, the Commission's secretariat devoted much of its time and attention during those months to sketching out plans to serve as a basis for the comprehensive review which we all thought necessary if the United Nations action in Palestine was to be efficient and recover prestige and moral authority. What we were aiming at was the orderly allocation of spheres of authority and the coordination of the various United Nations bodies in Palestine. On June 19, as the result of our discussions, I sent to Mr. Cordier, Executive Assistant to the Secretary General, a draft plan for reorganizing the United Nations in Palestine. All these ideas and suggestions were discussed with Mr. Lie when he paid a visit to Jerusalem, accompanied by Mrs. Lie, towards the end of April, 1951. Both the Secretary General and the high officials who accompanied him seemed to us receptive and in agreement with the general lines of our suggestions, but when the time came in the Assembly to incorporate these suggestions in a draft resolution and to prepare the ground for its adoption, the Secretary General retained nothing of the general plan but one solitary idea—the elimination of the Conciliation Commission. All the rest became a dead letter and simply passed into oblivion.

In the early days of August, 1951, the Commission held a series of meetings at Geneva to decide on its future activities. In reality, it had to discuss the method of putting into practice the instructions which Mr. Palmer, the American delegate on the Commission, had received in a letter from the Secretary of State himself, Mr. Acheson. The Secretary of State proposed that the Commission should immediately convene a conference of the Arab states and the State of Israel to examine and discuss concrete proposals which the Commission was to prepare on the various outstanding questions. The letter indicated the general lines which these proposals might take and suggested Istanbul as the meeting place of the conference. The Commission naturally accepted the American proposals *en bloc,* with the single exception of the last point; as the United Nations Assembly was meeting in Paris at the beginning of October, it was considered preferable to hold the conference also in Paris.

The conference began on September 13 at the Hotel de Crillon in an atmosphere of skepticism and with a conflict already brewing between the French delegation (this time vigorously supported by its government) and the American delegation over the proposals which the American government had sent to the Commission for submission to the parties at one of the first meetings of the conference. The French delegation's objections were not justified and the truth is that though officially the draft proposals were communicated to the Commission by the American delegate, the substance of the text had been drawn up by the Commission's secretariat (actually by Hamilton Fisher, its principal political adviser). Moreover, the immediate submission of these proposals to the parties, as the American delegation suggested, was the only effective way of giving a concrete and definite character to the negotiations from the outset. My impression was that the attitude taken up by the French government and its new delegate on the Commission, M. Marchal, was mainly an expression of resentment at the growing dictatorship which the American government was seeking to exert on the conduct of the negotiations. This first obstacle was overcome by the time-honored procedure of a slight alteration in the text which, without changing the sense at all, had the merit of making its acceptance possible without diminishing anyone's prestige.

The Commission was now ready to establish contact with the parties and begin discussing its proposals with them. But at this juncture an American suggestion, deceptively innocent in appearance, became a reef so perilous that it finally succeeded in wrecking the Commission's proposals and with them, the entire conference. The suggestion was to get the Arab and Israeli delegations to accept a kind of common declaration of pacific intentions, which was to be by way of a preamble to the proposals the Commission would immediately submit for their consideration. The Commission prepared a draft consisting almost exclusively of phrases contained in the first articles of the armistice agreements, thinking that this was the easiest way of getting them accepted by both sides. But we had not reckoned with the inexhaustible capacity of Arabs and Jews to raise doubts and objections about the interpretation of the clearest and most crystalline texts; above all, we had not taken into account the substantial difference between the armistice agreement with Egypt and the agreements with the other three Arab states bordering on Israel.[12] While the armistice agreement with Egypt prohibited, solely, acts of hostility committed by the land, sea and air forces, the other three contained in addition a clause prohibiting acts of hostility in general. Hence, if the declaration of pacific intentions was to conform with the terms of the armistice agreement with Egypt, its effect would be to restrict the undertakings accepted by the three other Arab states in their respective armistice agreements in relation to the prohibition of hostile acts—a state of affairs the Israeli government could hardly be expected to relish. But if, on the other hand, the declaration of pacific intentions was to reproduce the terms of the clause prohibiting hostile acts *in general* contained in the armistice agreements with Lebanon, Jordan and Syria, but not in the agreement with Egypt, the result would be to add to the obligations accepted by Egypt in relation to the prohibition of hostile acts. This addition the Egyptian government would in no wise be prepared to accept, especially if we recall the thesis it had maintained, and still maintains, before the Security Council, that the measures preventing the passage of cargoes for Israel through the Suez Canal were not contrary to the armistice agreement, precisely because the latter merely prohibits hostile acts committed by land, sea and air forces, and not hostile acts in general.

Little or nothing was said about all this in the innumerable private conversations and official meetings to which these difficulties gave rise; but I am convinced that here lay the real cause of the first check to the conference. When, after weeks of efforts as exhausting as they were sterile, the Commission became convinced of the impossibility of finding a way out of the labyrinth,

12. *Vide* Chapter IX.

it decided to cut the Gordian knot by stating that the formulas proposed by the parties, though they did not coincide with the Commission's formula, "constituted a basis for the consideration of its comprehensive pattern of proposals" and without more ado, communicated these proposals to the parties and asked them to submit their observations at the earliest possible moment.

These proposals were, in my opinion, the most serious, balanced and reasonable attempt that had been made during the whole history of the Palestine conflict to open a path to negotiations capable of leading to the establishment of normal relations between the Arab states and the State of Israel. The Commission's proposals formed an organic whole, which was presented in two parts. The first section provided for immediate agreements on war damage, repatriation of refugees, payment of compensation to those not repatriated for property abandoned in Israel and unfreezing of blocked accounts standing in Arab names in Israeli banks; the second provided for an agreement for a meeting of a new conference under the auspices of the United Nations in order to consider a revision of the armistice agreements in connection with a series of concrete points, among them the following: territorial adjustments, demilitarized zones, utilization of the waters of the Jordan and Yarmuk rivers, disposition of the Gaza strip, creation of an international port at Haifa, etc.

The observations which the parties submitted to the Commission were a veritable exercise in the critical spirit. Between the two of them, there was not a single clause in the proposals, among the many which lent themselves to criticism, which they failed, with naïve pedantry, to point out. Everything in them was negative. But neither Arabs nor Jews were clever enough to perceive that the Commission had prepared and submitted to them its proposals, not as the subject for a thesis, but as the touchstone of their desire to negotiate on a reasonable, practical and objective basis. And the result was conclusive; the parties' observations contained not the slightest sign of a desire to enter upon the road of true conciliation. The Commission drew the obvious conclusions and on November 19 informed the parties of its intention to bring the Paris conference to a close.

*   *   *   *

There was only one more thing for the Commission to do: to draw up its report and communicate it to the Assembly which was then meeting in Paris.[13] The report contains a detailed exposé of the Paris negotiations, followed by some brief conclusions in which the Commission sets forth very frankly the result of its three years' experience and the consequences which, in the light of that experience, might be expected to follow. The final paragraphs are as follows:

This final effort at the Paris conference was no more successful than the prior attempts by the Commission during the past three years. Despite that lack of progress, the Commission recognizes that both sides have expressed their desire to cooperate with the United Nations towards the achievement of stability in Palestine; but the Commission believes that neither side is now ready to seek that aim through full implementation of the General Assembly resolutions under which the Commission is operating.

In particular, the Government of Israel is not prepared to implement the part of paragraph 11 of the General Assembly resolution of 11 December 1948 which resolves that the refugees wishing to return to their homes and live at peace with their neighbors should be permitted to do so at the earliest practicable date.

The Arab Governments, on the other hand, are not prepared fully to implement paragraph 5 of the said resolution, which calls for the final settlement of all questions outstanding between them and Israel. The Arab Governments in their contacts with the Commission have evinced no readiness to arrive at such a peace settlement with the Government of Israel.

The Commission considers that further efforts towards settling the Palestine question could yet be usefully based on the principles underlying the comprehensive pattern of proposals which the Commission submitted to the parties at the Paris Conference. The Commission continues to believe that, if and when the parties are ready to accept these principles, general agreement or partial agreement could be sought through direct negotiations with United Nations assistance or mediation.

The Commission is of the opinion, however, that the present unwillingness of the parties fully to implement the General Assembly resolutions under which the Commission is operating, as well as the changes which have occurred in Palestine during the past three years, have made it impos-

13. The Commission's report was published as Supplement 18 to the Official Records of the Sixth Session of the Assembly (A/1985).

sible for the Commission to carry out its mandate, and this fact should be taken into consideration in any further approach to the Palestine problem.

Finally, in view of its firm conviction that the aspects of the Palestine problem are interrelated, the Commission is of the opinion that in any further approach to the problem it is desirable that consideration be given to the need for coordinating all United Nations efforts aimed at the promotion of stability, security and peace in Palestine.

The discussion on the Palestine question in the Sixth Assembly was, as was now customary, the scene of mutual diatribes and arguments between the Arab delegations and the delegation of Israel, interspersed with the ridiculous rhetorical flights of certain delegates who were unable to restrain their eloquence when confronted with a theme which gave them the opportunity of dragging into the discussion Moses and the prophets, Jesus Christ and the Apostles, and even the charger Burāq on which Muḥammad ascended into heaven from the rock which is venerated in the great mosque at Jerusalem. But what characterized the discussion this time was, on the one hand, its result as contained in an ambiguous and equivocal resolution and, on the other, the intensity of the underground campaign to deal the Commission its death blow. The terms of the resolution which the Assembly adopted on January 26, 1952, could be interpreted to mean either that the Commission would continue, for another year, its efforts at mediation between the parties on the basis of the Paris conference proposals, or that it would disappear as a body acting on its own initiative and become a merely passive instrument awaiting total oblivion. In my opinion, the first alternative was undoubtedly the one that induced the Arab delegations to accept the resolution. In all their interventions during the plenary session of January 26, they took for granted that the Commission would continue to function as heretofore and it was not without difficulty that the United States delegation persuaded them to postpone for a year their proposal to increase the number of members of the Commission, in the expectation that the latter would achieve positive results before the next Assembly. Conversely, it is not fanciful to presume that the Israeli delegation would throw all its weight into the scales in favor of the second interpretation. The government of Israel had always considered that the Commission offered the Arab states a kind of justification for their refusal to negotiate directly with Israel; consequently, it had never concealed its dislike of the Commission, even when the latter confined itself to the rôle of a passive and inoffensive conciliator. The active rôle of real mediator which the Commission had adopted at the Paris conference caused great alarm and anxiety at Tel Aviv, and, since it was not possible to eliminate the Commission directly in the text of the resolution itself, it was necessary at all costs to destroy its power to act by making the alternative interpretation prevail.

The Secretary General, without even waiting until the Commission itself had interpreted the Assembly's resolution, and in agreement, no doubt, with the American delegation, confronted the Commission with a *fait accompli* in favor of the second alternative by practically dissolving the Commission's secretariat and abolishing the post of its Principal Secretary. When the Commission met in New York in April, 1952, it confined itself to bowing to the *fait accompli* and confirming the interpretation adopted by the Secretary General. According to this, the Commission was to stay in New York "at the disposal of the parties" and the states composing it, instead of being represented on it by specially appointed delegates, were to be represented by members of their permanent delegations to the United Nations.

In justice to the Commission itself and its secretariat, it must be acknowledged that, with the loyalty that always inspired its proceedings, it greatly facilitated the success of the intrigue which led to its undoing. For many months previously it had been more or less openly admitted by everyone in the Commission and its secretariat that for it to continue with its present organization and attributes was not desirable. And this was said and repeated as often in private conversations as in official and public documents. It is significant in this respect that the last paragraph of the conclusions of its report to the Sixth Assembly refers expressly to the need for a general reorganization of the United Nations activities in order to ensure better coordination of all its efforts to promote stability, security and peace in Palestine. This was the constructive and revivifying idea; and it would have mattered little if, within the framework of that general reorganization, the Conciliation Commission had been reformed, or even abolished. But all our efforts were in vain and everything was reduced to a base intrigue in which political egoisms, coupled with animosities, suspicions and personal ambition, had the deplorable result of removing from the Palestine scene the only organization which was capable of, and equipped for dealing with political questions, leaving the Palestine question as a whole, with all its psychological, political, economic and social complexities, in the hands of two eminent American citizens—a marine general and a dynamic and irascible businessman.

CHAPTER XII

The Issues

1. *Jerusalem*

THE IDEA of removing the city of Jerusalem and its environs from the sovereignty of a given state had already been clearly expressed in the reports of two of the Commissions of Enquiry sent out to Palestine by the British government during the mandate—the report submitted on June 22, 1937, by the Royal Commission on Palestine, presided over by Lord Peel, and the report of the Palestine Partition Commission, under Sir John Woodhead, published on October 19, 1938. What these reports proposed for Jerusalem was not internationalization properly so-called; Jerusalem and its environs were to form one of the zones, excluded from partition, which were to remain under an international mandate. The idea of internationalization appears in clear and unmistakable terms in the report of the United Nations Special Committee on Palestine (UNSCOP). This report, like the previous British ones, recommends that Jerusalem should be excluded from partition and should become a zone endowed with a permanent international statute, drawn up and guaranteed by the United Nations. Following the recommendations of this report, the resolution which the United Nations Assembly adopted on November 27, 1947, contains a detailed international statute for the city of Jerusalem and its environs, in which the little city of Bethlehem is included. The statute is based on the idea of the *corpus separatus*, making of the Jerusalem area an entity not only independent of the two states, respectively Arab and Jewish, into which the same resolution divided Palestine, but scrupulously protected against the danger of interference in its affairs or threats against its independence.

In principle, internationalization is a formula which would have corresponded well with the peculiar circumstances of Jerusalem. Its application would not have been founded, as was the case in the two most notable precedents, Tangier and Danzig, on political, strategic or economic reasons, but on considerations of a spiritual nature. This should have been enough to prevent the supposed failures of internationalization in Tangier and Danzig from acting as a brake on Jerusalem's progress towards the same goal. Besides, if we study the subject closely, it is obviously an error to regard the international régime of Tangier as a failure; while in the case of Danzig, internationalization failed, not as a result of its own defects, but in the general shipwreck of the whole international organization, provoked by Fascism. Without allowing myself to be influenced either by the supposed failure of Tangier and Danzig, or by the blind alley into which the internationalization of Jerusalem has stumbled, or by the immense difficulties which the establishment of an international régime in Trieste had run up against, I still believe that the formula of internationalization contains the seeds of success and is destined to play a most important rôle in future international organization.

The truth is that there never has been a real opportunity to introduce into Jerusalem a genuine and authentic international régime such as, for example, that approved by the Assembly in its resolution of November 27, 1947, for the simple reason that, when the British mandate expired, the partition of Jerusalem, like that of the rest of Palestine, was already an accomplished fact. From that moment it was necessary, if internationalization was to become effective, to overcome the resistance of the two states which, a few days after the evacuation of Jerusalem by the British authorities and troops, had divided up the city between themselves—namely, Israel and Jordan.

Jordan's opposition would not have been an insuperable obstacle, since the other Arab states were in favor of internationalization and Jordan could not, therefore, have persisted in her attitude without breaking the unity of the Arab bloc with respect to one of the most important elements of the Palestine question. Moreover, British support for internationalization would have sufficed to neutralize any serious attempt at opposition on Jordan's part.

Israel's opposition was more serious and, as events have shown, ended by becoming an obstacle against which all attempts to achieve the complete or partial internationalization of Jerusalem have shattered. Israel's success in preventing, by her antagonism, the enforcement of the international statute approved by the Assembly's resolution of November 27, 1947, is due to two main causes. In the first place, Israel succeeded, in this as in other things, thanks to the political strength the Jews in the United States were able to muster, in arresting the impetus of American support for the idea of internationalization. In the second place, the implacable antagonism of the State of Israel set such difficulties in the way of introducing an international statute and making it function that no one had any confidence in the ability of the United Nations to overcome them, particularly if the determined and wholehearted support of the United States could not be relied upon.

The Conciliation Commission realized immediately the practical impossibility of setting up a genuine and integral international régime in Jerusalem, which would be based on the idea of the *corpus separatus* and, conforming scrupulously with the terms of the United Nations Assembly resolution of November 27, 1947, would convert the Jerusalem area into a political entity wholly independent of the two neighboring states. Availing itself of the freedom of interpretation allowed by the flexibility of its terms of reference regarding Jerusalem, the Conciliation Commission, from the outset, directed its labors towards the elaboration of a limited and modified international statute, which would be compatible with the *fait accompli* of the partition of Jerusalem between Israel and Jordan.

The preparatory work on the statute began, shortly after the arrival of the Commission in Jerusalem in February, 1949, with the appointment of a special committee composed of three advisers of the members of the Commission. This committee set about its task immediately and spent six months on a detailed study of all aspects of the question, keeping in constant and close touch with the most authoritative and representative elements, both civil and religious, of the Arab and Jewish populations of Jerusalem. As a result of these labors, the committee submitted to the Commission a draft statute which, having been approved by the latter, was communicated to the Assembly on September 1, 1949.

We have already seen[1] what kind of a reception the Conciliation Commission's draft met with in the Assembly, both from the delegations and the Secretariat. Despite the auguries of the Palestine experts, the draft was pigeon-holed without even being accorded the honor of a debate, as a result of the pressure of a group of delegations representing such diverse countries as the Soviet Union and its "satellites," the Arab states (except Jordan),

1. *Vide* Chapter XI.

and Australia together with a good number of Latin-American countries, which under the Vatican's pressure, were not prepared to agree to anything less than integral and complete internationalization as defined in the resolution of November 27, 1947. The Israeli delegation, for entirely different reasons, was equally antagonistic to the Commission's draft, and to complete the picture, the rest of the Assembly, including the three delegations of the states members of the Commission, watched the shipwreck of the draft statute with supreme indifference, without making the slightest effort to prevent it.

Here I must call attention to the deplorable inconsistency the United Nations has shown in dealing with this important aspect of the Palestine question. In 1948, the Extraordinary Assembly, consigning to the scrap-heap the statute contained in its own resolution of November 27, 1947, directed the Trusteeship Council to draw up a new statute similar in character to the one embodied in the said resolution. Full of zeal, the Trusteeship Council prepared a new statute, which it submitted to the Extraordinary Assembly on April 21, 1948. During the months that followed, until the truces put an end to hostilities, there was no question of enforcing any kind of régime, either international or national, in Jerusalem, which had by then become a veritable battlefield. But the curious thing is that when, in December of the same year, the Assembly considered the moment had come to revert to the question of Jerusalem, it suffered a new attack of amnesia and, forgetting that it was already in possession, since April, of a draft statute prepared by the Trusteeship Council, directed the Conciliation Commission to draw up yet another, the third within the space of a year. And to crown all, with a fidelity to its own inconsistency worthy of a better cause, the Assembly, when it received the Conciliation Commission's draft in 1949, ignored it with the same supreme indifference with which it had ignored the Trusteeship Council's draft a year ago and, turning again to the Trusteeship Council, instructed it to refurbish and produce its draft of the previous year. The Trusteeship Council devoted innumerable meetings to the question and the same arguments of Arabs, Jews, Catholics, Orthodox and Protestant churches, were repeated once more, with the same negative results as before. On April 4, 1950 the Trusteeship Council approved at Geneva a new statute—the fourth—and recommended its Chairman, M. Garreau, to communicate it personally to the governments of Jordan and Israel. But when the government of Jordan greeted the announcement of his visit with silence, the Chairman of the Trusteeship Council gave up the idea and returned from Rome to Paris. It would be unfair not to mention the personal suggestions which the Chairman of the Trusteeship Council submitted to his colleagues with the object of facilitating the mission entrusted to the Council by the Assembly. These suggestions, which when published were described in the press as the "Garreau Plan," reflected more credit on the inventiveness and imagination of their author than on his sense of realism or knowledge of the actual situation in Jerusalem.

It is hard to imagine what more the United Nations Assembly could have done to assist a process which has ended by destroying the last possibility of establishing a régime in Jerusalem deserving the name international. Faced with such inconsistency and—not to put too fine a point on it—levity on the part of the Assembly, who can be surprised that the two occupying states felt morally entitled to consolidate their positions in Jerusalem? As far as Israel was concerned, this consolidation took a form that was of undeniable importance to the future of the city. The drive and determination with which the government of Israel has carried out its plan to make Jerusalem the capital of the state, in defiance of the letter and spirit of various Assembly resolutions, in the teeth of Arab opposition and, what is more surprising, in the face of the opposition of the Catholic world, deserves a tribute of admiration. And without letting one's judgment be colored by the fact that King David had already made Jerusalem the capital of Israel, it is just to recognize that the temptation to establish the capital of the new state at Jerusalem was too strong to be resisted without provoking serious political difficulties within the state, while the latter was still in process of being constituted. But once all this has been acknowledged, it must be admitted that the establishment of Israel's capital at Jerusalem has been one of the chief causes of the fears and suspicions harbored not only by the Arab countries but by a considerable body of international public opinion concerned with the spiritual significance of the city of Jerusalem, as to Israel's future intentions with regard to her frontiers. All these elements fail to understand how half a city, divided by an international frontier cutting across its streets and squares, can be regarded as an appropriate place for the capital of Israel; and it is not surprising if they see in this decision, and in the zeal with which it has been executed, an alarming sign of possible plans of terri-

torial expansion. In their eyes, the establishment of the capital
in the half of the city actually occupied by the Jews is ridiculous
and inexplicable. On the other hand, Jerusalem in its entirety
is not only the natural, but, as it were, the compulsory site of
the capital of a state whose frontiers coincide with those of Palestine properly so-called; that is, the Palestine which was the subject of the mandate entrusted to England after the First World
War, before the first partition took place with the creation by
the British of the emirate (afterwards the kingdom) of Transjordan. This, more than anything, is what surrounds the question
of Jerusalem with an atmosphere of fear and suspicion which
makes any attempt at settlement so difficult.

In the situation created by this conjunction of circumstances,
the only method of preserving a limited system of internationalization in Jerusalem is the conclusion of an agreement between
Jordan and Israel, negotiated under the auspices of the United
Nations and with its guarantee. Apart from slight adjustments in
the line of demarcation between the Arab and Jewish districts of
Jerusalem, the essential aim of this agreement should be the progressive restoration of normal communications between the two
zones. The ground could be prepared by comparatively unimportant arrangements and agreements, bearing always in mind, however, that the task is one which demands great care and infinite
perseverance and patience if it is to succeed. The demarcation
line should lose its military character and become an ordinary
frontier, which the inhabitants of the two zones could cross with
a minimum of formality. In this respect it may be pointed out
that, in frontier problems, however important it may be to ensure
that the actual line of demarcation is fairly and wisely drawn,
what finally determines the possibility of arriving at a satisfactory
solution is the state of relations between the two neighboring
states. When these relations are cordial, the most absurd frontiers become, in practice, compatible with the establishment of
normal communications between the populations in the border
zones. When the relations between the states are governed by distrust and hostility, no demarcation of the frontier will result in
the establishment of normal communications. Hence, any advance along the road to an improvement in the present situation
in Jerusalem will depend, in the last analysis, on the progress
realized in promoting peaceful relations between the State of
Israel and the Arab states and, in particular, the kingdom of
Jordan.

More important, perhaps, than the restoration of communications between the two zones of Jerusalem would be the consolidation of the neutrality at present enjoyed, under the guarantee of the United Nations, of Government House and Mount Scopus. This neutrality was established, under United Nations auspices, by the truces and the armistice between Israel and Jordan; its consolidation, therefore, would not imply any marked change in the actual situation. But it would be of immense assistance in dissipating the animosities and suspicions with which the atmosphere of Jerusalem is poisoned, thus contributing to the maintenance of peace in the divided city. Even the least military-minded among us can grasp the fact that once these positions fall into the hands of either of the occupying powers, the peace of Jerusalem will be broken or gravely threatened.

Since Government House was taken over by the United Nations in circumstances that I have described elsewhere[2] it has become the headquarters of the Chief of Staff of the United Nations in Palestine and the official seat of the Conciliation Commission. Its continued use as the seat of whatever institutions the United Nations thinks fit to establish in Palestine is of the greatest importance for the preservation of peace in Jerusalem. No better way of discouraging a policy of *coups de main* and *faits accomplis* can be found than the physical presence in Government House of United Nations organizations with political and technical missions, and the personalities directing them.

The case of Mount Scopus is in an altogether different category, for linked to its military and strategic importance is the cultural significance conferred on it by the magnificent buildings of the Hebrew University, with its priceless library, and Hadassah Hospital, rising from its summit. The neutral zone of Mount Scopus, where these institutions are, forms an enclave in Arab territory under the protection of the United Nations, whose flag waves over the hospital and university. A symbolic guard of eighty Jewish police and a reduced staff of employees and workmen protect the buildings and struggle valiantly against their progressive deterioration. Food supplies and a change of guard are brought up once a fortnight by a military convoy under the escort of the Truce Observers.

Nothing in Jerusalem is so depressing as to visit Mount Scopus and see how, barely a mile and a half from the city, that magnificent group of buildings—the hospital, the library, and the various

2. *Vide* Chapter X.

MISSION IN PALESTINE 1948-1952

scientific institutes forming the university, all endowed with the most modern installations—is falling victim to the slow but inexorable process of deterioration which is the inevitable result of its abandonment. The damage caused to the buildings by the fighting has not been great and, to my mind, the immense benefit that would accrue if that great cultural and humanitarian center could return to life would far outweigh the cost of necessary repairs. But the longer the buildings are allowed to lie empty, the greater that cost will be; until one day it will reach an astronomical figure and the institutions on Mount Scopus will have to be finally written off as a dead loss to the cultural and scientific progress of the Middle East. It is with this consideration in mind that the cultural and scientific center on Mount Scopus ought to be revived. The United Nations ought to make such arrangements as are necessary with the Israeli government and with the various bodies to which the grounds and buildings legally belong taking as its point of departure the existing institutions, and organize on Mount Scopus, through UNESCO, a great international cultural foundation to serve both Arabs and Jews, the two great Semitic peoples of the Middle East. The Arab states and the State of Israel, their national cultural and scientific institutions, similar institutions belonging to other countries, great international figures in the world of science, literature and the arts, should take part in the administration of the Mount Scopus International Foundation. Nothing, in my opinion, would do more to calm the turbulence and restlessness that afflicts the whole of life in this part of the world than the creation, in Jerusalem, of a great focus of spiritual life, potent and fecund, in which Arabs and Jews, within an ample framework of world importance, could jointly bring as a salve to the common unrest the immense treasure of their cultures and civilizations.

2. The Refugees

For years the Palestine Arab refugees have occupied a foremost place on the international stage and have been the chief topic of the disputes and discussions between Arabs and Jews on the Palestine question. This mass of refugees, the number of whom, at the time of writing,* must amount to approximately 750,000 individuals or some 150,000 families, is formed of Palestine Arabs who, for motives which, though varied, are always connected with the establishment of the State of Israel, decided to leave their

---

* It will be remembered that the time of writings was 1952. *Ed.*

homes, their lands, their businesses, their professions, and take refuge either in the bordering Arab states or in part of the Palestine which remained under the dominion and authority of the Arabs.

As to the reason which impelled this part of the Arab population of Palestine to take so drastic a decision, and one that was so full of tragic consequences, there exist, as might be expected, two opposing schools of thought, the Arab and the Jewish, respectively. According to the Arab thesis, what determined the exodus of the Arab population from the territories occupied by the State of Israel was, apart from the struggle itself (which rarely caused permanent displacements of the population affected), the weapon of terror deliberately employed by the Jewish authorities against the Arab population, with the object of provoking their flight, thus eliminating, or reducing to a minimum, the dead weight of a large Arab minority which would have been very burdensome to the new state. The Jewish thesis is that the abandonment of their homes by the great majority of the Arab population of the territories occupied by Israel was the result of the propaganda campaign launched by the Arab political leaders in Palestine (in particular, by the Muftī of Jerusalem and his agents), inciting them to abandon their villages, houses and lands rather than fall under the power and domination of the Jews; with the added threat (to ensure that the campaign took effect) that those who accepted Jewish authority would be branded as traitors, and the assurance that the Jewish occupation would last only a few days— until the liberating armies of the Arab states had exterminated all the Jews in Palestine.

As usually happens in these cases, the two theses contain a measure of truth, but neither contains the whole truth. It is undeniable that the Jewish authorities, especially during the first months, applied to the Arab population a policy of terror varying in intensity, and that the atmosphere thereby created contributed, to an extent that is hard to determine, to the exodus of the said population. But it is equally certain that the campaign launched by the Arab political leaders in Palestine was a powerful factor in the abandonment *en masse* by the Arab population of their villages, homes and lands. It is to be hoped that, in the interests of the refugees themselves, this sterile and demoralizing controversy will cease at once. Both sides should stop looking for a scapegoat and join forces to liquidate this problem of the Palestine Arab refugees which not only constitutes a danger, but prejudices the reputation of all the peoples of the Middle East for efficiency and humanity.

* * * *

The problem of the Arab refugees was already one of Count Bernadotte's chief anxieties at the outset of his mission as United Nations Mediator. At his instigation, and with the dynamism and vigor that characterized all his actions, a team of supposed specialists was improvised in the early days of August, 1948. This team undertook, with feverish energy and in a somewhat disjointed and chaotic manner, the task of providing the refugees with bare essentials in the way of food and shelter. The appeal made by Count Bernadotte himself to some thirty countries to send gifts in kind for the Arab refugees did not meet with the enthusiastic response that was expected. The impossibility of co-ordinating efforts, in the midst of all that frantic haste, resulted in rather paradoxical situations, like that created by the accumulation of canned food, which the refugees refused to eat (and which appeared within twenty-four hours on the black market of Beirut or Damascus), while the wheat and oil which are the basic elements of the Arab peasant's diet were lacking. Whether or not all that activity resulted in effective aid to the refugees, it is fair to recognize that, in that initial stage, two ideas which have subsequently served as a basis for all international action regarding the Palestine refugees were clearly defined and consecrated as dogmas. The first was that their maintenance and sustenance, together with their economic and social rehabilitation, was a responsibility and obligation devolving upon the whole international community. The second was that, in the discharge of this obligation, the international community ought to begin by solemnly proclaiming the right of the refugees to return to their homes and to receive adequate compensation for their abandoned or destroyed properties. These two ideas can be found clearly expressed in the Report of the Mediator to the United Nations Assembly which met at Paris in the autumn of 1949; and this report is the true origin of the positive measures adopted by the Assembly which met at Paris in the autumn of 1949; and this to, and rehabilitation of, the refugees by means of international organizations and confirming their right to return to their homes and to receive appropriate compensation.

These two principles, and in particular the one relating to the right of the refugees to return to their homes, have become, in practice, the great reef on which any serious attempt to solve the problem of the Arab refugees in a constructive manner has been wrecked. Count Bernadotte himself had sufficient judgment to realize that this principle, whatever its theoretical value, was inapplicable in practice. Its solemn proclamation by the Assembly and its incorporation in the text of the resolution of December 14, 1948, have had three results. In the first place, a platform has been provided, of inestimable value to all those Arab political elements who are more interested in keeping alive the political struggle against the State of Israel than in putting an end, by means of a practical and reasonable compromise formula, to the tragic situation of the refugees. The truth is that since the resolution of December 14, 1948, proclaimed the right of the refugees to return to their homes, the Arab states, whenever the question arose, have done nothing but attack Israel for its refusal to implement the Assembly's resolution and demand that implementation as the prior condition for all other negotiation. It is fair to recognize that, once the principle had been proclaimed by the United Nations Assembly, it was almost impossible for Arab statesmen to refrain from using it in what they considered then, not without reason, as the supreme interest of the state, namely, the political and economic struggle against the State of Israel. The second result of the proclamation of the right of the refugees to return to their homes has been complementary to the first—to paralyze any possible initiative on the part of those who would have preferred to give priority, not to the struggle against Israel, but to the solution of the refugee problem by means of a reasonable and constructive compromise formula. Finally, the proclamation of the principle and the propaganda surrounding it have created a state of mind among the refugees, based on the vain hope of returning to their homes, which has immobilized their cooperation, a cooperation which is an indispensable condition if a way is to be opened to a solution at once practical and constructive of their distressing problem. These circumstances, taken as a whole, have been the principal cause why, after years of effort, the sole achievement has been to feed and shelter the refugees in some sort of fashion, without taking a single step along the road to their economic and social rehabilitation.

* * * *

During this initial stage, which started with the Mediator's action and very soon became stabilized in the form of an organization, through which the three great international humanitarian institutions—the International Committee of the Red Cross, the League of Red Cross Societies and the Society of Friends (Quakers)—undertook, respectively, the relief of the refugees in the zones of Arab Palestine, the Arab states and the Gaza sector, the chief, if not the only, preoccupation lay in assuring to the refugees food, shelter and a minimum of medical and cultural aid. To the Economic Survey Mission, appointed by the Conciliation Commission under the chairmanship of Mr. Gordon R. Clapp and sent to the Middle East in the autumn of 1949, belongs the credit for having first pointed out in a direct and decisive manner the need to transfer the center of gravity of international action from the mere lending of humanitarian relief to the economic and social rehabilitation of the refugees. Its interim report, devoted especially to the refugees, expresses in terms which are admirable in clarity and persuasive force the two basic ideas of a practical and immediate solution of the problem, namely, the progressive abolition of relief with all its demoralizing effects, and the initiation of a plan of public works which would provide employment for the refugees and thus enable them to earn their livelihood. Viewing the situation in a way that was at once penetrating and realistic, the Economic Survey Mission did not hesitate to recommend to the Assembly that relief should be reduced to a third, as of January 1, 1950. In its resolution of December 8, 1949, the United Nations Assembly accepted the suggestion contained in the Economic Mission's interim report to the effect that relief should be rapidly replaced by a plan of public works which would provide employment for the refugees and enable them to normalize their economic life. But unhappily it did not accept the report's more radical proposal to cut down relief to one third from the first of the year. Mr. Clapp and his colleagues, more astute than the Assembly, realized that as long as relief continued, the refugees would continue too, and the most powerful lever to ensure the rapid implementation of the public works program was, precisely, the abolition of relief. The Assembly appointed a new body, the Relief and Works Agency for Palestine Refugees in the Near East, with the twofold mission of replacing the International Committee of the Red Cross, the League of Red Cross Societies and the Quakers in the administration of relief, and of carrying

out the works program recommended by the Economic Survey
Mission, a program which had already been admirably expounded
and analyzed in its final report and technical supplement.

The new organization was to have a Director appointed by the
Secretary General of the United Nations. After some difficulty, a
suitable candidate was finally selected in the person of a distinguished Canadian, General Kennedy. On June 30, 1950, when
his term of office expired, General Kennedy was succeeded by
Mr. J. B. Blandford, an American administrator who had been
drawn into the diplomatic service. But the truly original feature
of the new organization was the appointment of an *advisory* commission, composed of representatives of the American, British,
French and Turkish governments. In itself, this organization was
absurd, for it was not clear how the opinion of the four governments could have a purely advisory value for the Director;
but in actual practice, all this was unimportant, for what dominated—and still dominates—the functioning of UNRWA is
the origin of the funds placed at its disposal both for relief and
works, and, as everybody knows, the overwhelming majority of
those funds comes from the American government—the result
of which has been, and continues to be, that the American representative on the advisory commission has the last word in all
matters of importance. So long as General Kennedy was Director, the key to the functioning of UNRWA was his acceptance of
the directives of the American member of the advisory commission. The appointment of Mr. Blandford as Director made the
situation perfectly clear: Mr. Blandford, who, during the period
when General Kennedy was Director, had been the United States
representative on the advisory commission, saw to it that American influence was, openly and unconditionally, predominant in
the direction and administration of UNRWA. The members of
the advisory commission, including the American, have been reduced, in practice, to the rôle of mere observers.

UNRWA promptly declared that the plan recommended by
the Economic Survey Mission to the Assembly, which it had been
appointed to implement, was incapable of being applied. It may
well be that this was due to the irregularity with which the funds
intended for its implementation were being received, as Mr.
Blandford indicated in his report to the 1951 Assembly; but if
this had been the true cause of the abandonment of the Economic
Mission's plan, the logical thing would have been to replace it
by another, cheaper plan and not, as was done, by a formula

which, as events have proved, has multiplied in almost astronomical terms the cost which the mission allowed for the execution of its own plan. Other factors have contributed to the abandonment of the plan and among these, the two following seem to me of particular interest. In the first place is the fact that, as we have already seen, the Assembly adopted only that part of the Economic Mission's recommendations relating to the execution of public works to provide the refugees with a livelihood, but rejected the mainspring of the plan, the immediate and progressive abolition of relief—a measure which, though ostensibly cruel and inhuman, was in reality the only one which would open the path of redemption to the refugee and was, therefore, the essential condition for the success of any policy aimed at his reintegration into a normal economic life. In the second place is the congenital hypertrophy from which United Nations organizations suffer and, as the inevitable consequence of this, a marked tendency to megalomania. A body which numbered within a few weeks nearly two hundred international functionaries (those recruited locally exceeded a thousand), among whom could be, and still can be, reckoned a great number of specialists eminent in the most diverse branches of science, could not reconcile itself to being the mere executant of a plan already established and approved by the Assembly of the United Nations. The result of all this was that the plan recommended by the Economic Survey Mission to the 1949 Assembly, and approved by the latter, was rejected as unserviceable, though there had been barely time to put its merits or demerits to the proof, and replaced, not by another more or less studied and elaborate plan, but by a simple declaration, according to which

> the reintegration of the refugees into the economic life of the Near East, either by repatriation or resettlement, is essential in preparation for the time when international assistance is no longer available and for the realization of conditions of peace and stability in the area.[3]

The Economic Survey Mission's plan would have made it possible to offer the refugees, within a reasonable space of time, opportunities for work and obligated them to take full advantage of those opportunities by abolishing relief on a given date: an unambitious formula, but one that was practical and might have, above all, lead to the liquidation of the refugee problem within a limited period of time. For a whole generation to lapse into the

3. Resolution adopted by the Assembly on December 2, 1950.

condition of refugees is a catastrophe which cannot be wholly remedied; and it is a thousand times preferable to concentrate on a rapid though partial remedy than to prolong the situation, with the inevitable demoralization it entails, in the hope of a better solution.

UNRWA's plan, reverting to the original idea of the American government, as explained to the Conciliation Commission by Mr. Porter on his arrival in Lausanne in July, 1949, placed the solution of the refugee problem within the framework of the comprehensive plan for the economic reconstruction of the Middle East, through the idea of reintegrating the refugees into the regional economy—an idea which the Director of UNRWA himself has interpreted with his famous formula: "A job and a home for every refugee." It is indeed an excellent formula, which might well be extended not only to the Palestine refugees and the millions of refugees in other parts of the world, but to all the citizens of countries that are better organized politically, economically and socially. If this formula is to prevail, it will be well for the refugees, the victims of all these improvisations and fantasies, to arm themselves with patience and abandon hope of seeing an early end to their miseries.

The fundamental difference between the formula recommended by the Economic Survey Mission and that adopted by UNRWA is that while the former envisages the problem as one affecting the whole mass of refugees regarded as a social phenomenon which must be dealt with by measures of a general character, the latter aims at solving the individual problem of each refugee by assuring to every family "a job and a home." The most efficient and best organized administration of a state in the full tide of prosperity might hesitate before taking on a task of economic super-planning such as the provision of permanent employment and homes for a population of some 150,000 families. Nevertheless, UNRWA, with enviable optimism, considers that the still somewhat rudimentary administrations of the Arab states functioning in a political and social atmosphere which is characterized neither by discipline nor stability, can bring the task to a successful conclusion before the last refugee has died of misery and desperation or, weary of waiting for UNRWA's "job and home," has decided to solve the problem of his existence in his own way as best he can.

There is a final aspect of the question which merits attention, and that is the aspect which refers to the individual liberty of the refugee. The super-planning implied by the formula "a job and a home for every refugee," apart from its technical and physical difficulties, does not reveal in its authors much confidence in the virtue of liberal principles. The refugees are human beings, not pawns to be moved to the plains of Jezireh in Syria, or to the valley of the Jordan, according to the exigencies of the game which the Director of UNRWA and his advisers are directing from their offices in Beirut. As human beings they have the right to demand that their opinion not be ignored in deciding the new course that is being mapped out for them. It is significant to find the Americans, the apostles and standard-bearers of free enterprise and private initiative as the bases of economic life, brushing aside these principles and indulging in the most unbridled planning as soon as it is a question of an emergency—especially if the emergency arises some thousands of miles away from the United States.

*   *   *   *

The solution to the problem of the Palestine Arab refugees must be sought by following the tradition which has been established, unhappily, by numerous precedents, on the basis of two principles. Viewing the problem from its individual aspect, it must be recognized that every refugee is concerned with rebuilding his life and the lives of his family in the most favorable circumstances permitted by his aptitudes, his resources and his good or evil star. External aid, whether international or national, after its initial humanitarian stage (which should be as short as possible in order to avoid the demoralization of the refugee himself) should be directed towards placing the refugee in conditions similar to those enjoyed by the citizens of the state where he settles.

In the concrete case of the Palestine Arab refugees the application of these principles would have meant negotiating agreements with the Arab states whereby the United Nations would lend them the necessary technical and financial assistance for the rapid execution of a certain number of public works (and the Economic Survey Mission included in its final report a veritable catalogue of about seventy which might be initiated or continued immediately, with very detailed preliminary technical surveys); and the Arab states would each take a certain number of refugees, granting them full citizenship or, at least, a status which would enable them not only to work, but to move freely about in search of work. This formula, far from representing a sacrifice on the part of the Arab states, would have bestowed on them a dual benefit: that accruing from the execution of the public works and the indirect, but no less positive benefit, of the incorporation into their own populations of some hundreds of thousands of new citizens who, spurred on by necessity, would have acted as a leaven to accelerate economic and social advance.

This is how the countries of Latin America understood it when, with a clear vision of their true interests, they welcomed hundreds of thousands of Spaniards at the end of the civil war in Spain, affording them all kinds of facilities to rebuild the lives which had been destroyed by Franco's victory. There was nothing to prevent the Arab states from doing as much for the Palestine Arab refugees, instead of wasting precious years in a sterile political struggle to force their return to Israel.

3. *The Frontiers*

From a practical and concrete point of view, the territorial aspect of the Palestine question consists in the delimitation of the frontiers between the new State of Israel and its four Arab neighbors, namely, Egypt in the south, Jordan and Syria in the east and Lebanon in the north.

The frontiers between the two states, Arab and Jewish, established by the plan of partition approved by the United Nations Assembly in its resolution of November 29, 1947, remained, like the rest of the plan, a dead letter, as a result of the "crusade" against the partition of Palestine launched by the Arab states. The famous Lausanne Protocol[4] momentarily rescued these frontiers from oblivion by getting the parties to agree to regard them as the point of departure for future negotiations. This move by the Conciliation Commission, despite the complications and tergiversations to which it gave rise, had the merit of helping to define the attitudes adopted, respectively, by the Arab states and the State of Israel in regard to this territorial aspect of the Palestine question. In effect, after the adoption of the Lausanne Protocol, the Arab states, however paradoxical this may appear, stabilized their attitude by demanding the boundaries laid down in the partition plan of November 29, 1947 (against which they had launched their "crusade") as their definitive frontiers with the State of Israel. And it will surprise no one that Israel roundly re-

4. *Vide* Chapter XI.

fuses to agree that no account should be taken, in the delimitation of her frontiers, of the military results of this same "crusade," which the Arab states launched with the avowed intention of wiping the State of Israel off the map almost before it had had time to put in an appearance there. For those results, as embodied in the lines of demarcation established by the armistice agreements, have placed under Israel's authority a territory larger than the one consigned to her by the November 29 plan.

It is enough to state these two attitudes to be able to predict which will prevail in the end. The attitude of the Arab states suffers from the weakness inherent in its inconsistency; for the frontiers they are now claiming are precisely those which they waged, and lost, a war to destroy. Israel's attitude has the immense advantage of being able to count on the irresistible tendency of all *de facto* situations to become, with the mere lapse of time, converted into *de jure* situations—a transformation that takes place all the more readily if, as has happened in this case, it receives a political and moral reinforcement as powerful as that represented by the guarantee conferred in 1951 by the United States, France and England on the demarcation lines established by the armistices.

These borders, taken as a whole, are neither better nor worse than any others would be. It might be argued that it would be more reasonable to fix the frontier between Israel and Syria at the *thalweg* of the Jordan, instead of the present delimitation of the armistice line which leaves the two banks of the river in Israeli territory. Something will have to be decided about the Gaza area, now occupied by Egypt, once the reasons of prestige that determine that occupation disappear. Again, it would not be unreasonable for Israel to insist on a rectification of the demarcation line with Jordan in the region of Tulkram, where Israeli territory forms, between the frontier and the sea, a corridor less than nine miles in breadth. No doubt, the line of demarcation that crosses the city of Jerusalem ought to be subject to rectifications and adjustments in harmony with the final and permanent status of the city and with what is decided in respect to Government House and Mount Scopus. But the truth is that these and other modifications which it may be necessary to introduce into the present demarcation lines in order to convert them into real frontiers present no serious difficulties once the discussion of them can take place in an atmosphere of mutual understanding and good will. And, unlike what might happen in other cases, none of these rectifications is of sufficient gravity and importance to constitute the obstacle which is impeding the creation of that atmosphere. It is not by moving a frontier backwards or forwards a few miles here and there that the animosity and distrust that characterizes Arab reactions to Israel, or the self-confidence and driving force of the Jewish attitude to Arab claims, can be dispersed. But time, good counsel and friendly pressure, the impossibility of prolonging beyond certain limits a situation which daily becomes more remote from reality and its needs, will do their work in the end and, little by little, the tension will lessen until the moment comes when the frontiers can be discussed with the calm and serenity that are essential if the work of delimitation is to satisfy both the demands of justice and the dictates of good sense.

4. *Economic Relations*

It is generally realized that the establishment of economic relations between the Arab states and the State of Israel would constitute one of the most effective aids to the restoration of a balanced and normal political life in the Middle East. Nevertheless, not only have economic questions not been the subject of negotiations properly so-called between the Arab states and Israel but, with the sole exception of Jordan (or rather, of King 'Abdallāh), no Arab state seems to show the slightest interest in the establishment of economic relations with its new Jewish neighbor. This is readily understandable. Neither Syria nor Lebanon, and still less Egypt (as far as Iraq and Saudi Arabia are concerned, the question has not even arisen), can hope for substantial benefits from the establishment of economic relations with Israel. On the other hand, they are perfectly aware that the opening of the road to economic and commercial relations would sap the very foundations of their attitude of uncompromising opposition and negation to anything implying, directly or indirectly, political recognition of the State of Israel. Jordan's case is different. Commercial relations with Israel would lead to a considerable improvement in its fragile and precarious economy, an advantage that, in King 'Abdallāh's opinion, would have offset any disadvantages caused by leaving the road open to the political and economic consolidation of Israel. But whatever the rôle played by economic questions in the official and secret negotiations between the agents of Israel and Jordan, the fact is that Jor-

dan aligned herself with the other Arab states in applying to Israel the rigorous economic blockade which has been, since the
creation of that state, the keystone of Arab policy in economic
matters as far as the Palestine problem is concerned.

It can, therefore, be readily understood why the Conciliation
Commission never had the opportunity of fulfilling the concrete
mission entrusted to it by the Assembly in economic affairs,
namely: "to seek arrangements among the Governments and authorities concerned which will facilitate the economic development of the area, including arrangements for access to ports and
airfields and the use of transportation and communication facilities."[5] Its only substantial contribution to the study and solution
of the economic problems posed by the Palestine situation has
been the creation of the Economic Survey Mission, whose mandate, as approved by the Conciliation Commission, was to "examine the economic situation in the countries affected by the recent hostilities and to make recommendations to the Commission
for an integrated program: a) to enable the Governments concerned to further such measures and developments as are required to overcome economic dislocations created by the hostilities; . . . . . . c) to promote economic conditions conductive to
the maintenance of peace and stability in the area."[6]

The Economic Survey Mission devoted its final report to this
general part of its mandate. I shall not venture to give an opinion on the intrinsic merits of this document from a technical
point of view, but the basic idea expressed in the first of its conclusions that "peace and stability cannot be achieved in the Middle East until the masses of its peoples are able to enjoy a higher
standard of living than at present," seems to me to contain a
profound truth. This idea ought to be the guiding principle for
all action aimed at ensuring the economic reconstruction and political stability of the Middle East. So long as that action continues to be dominated by strategic considerations or, what is
worse, by the anxiety to preserve privileged economic positions,
we cannot nourish the hope that it will prove effective in bringing about the political and economic transformation of the Middle
East. Once more the so-called Western democracies, this time in
the guise of American capitalism, are about to defraud the vehement desires of those "masses" to which the Economic Sur-

5. Resolution of the United Nations Assembly of December 11, 1948, art. 10.

6. (b) refers to the specific problem of the refugees, which is the subject of the
Economic Survey Mission's interim report; *Vide* Chapter XI.

vey Mission refers for reform and progress—that reform and progress which are the only road to peace and stability in the Middle East. And the Middle East is not an exception in this respect; the same could be said with equal reason of any other region of the world.

CHAPTER XIII

Looking Forward

IN 1919, President Wilson, with his famous Fourteen Points,
implanted in the universal conscience the idea of national self-
determination; and this in spite of the falsifications and tergiversations due to the manner in which these Fourteen Points (and,
in particular, the one relating to national self-determination)
were interpreted in the peace treaties that put an end to the First
World War. The solemn pronouncement of this principle fired
the Arab world, touching off the explosion that, to judge by the
signs, is about to enter upon its active period; for in the political and social field explosions are not instantaneous, as they are
in the physical world, but are prolonged for years and sometimes
for centuries.

The victors of the First World War—in actual fact, France and
England—succeeded, immediately after their triumph, in restraining the initial force of the explosion. By a clever conjuring
trick, they effectively disposed of the liberation of the Arab
peoples at the end of Turkish rule, substituting for the latter
their own rule, thinly disguised under the formula of international mandates: a French mandate over Syria and Lebanon; a
British mandate over Iraq and "Greater" Palestine.[1] But though
the force of the explosion could be momentarily curbed, there
was no likelihood of its being permanently suppressed. The pressure went on increasing until it finally created such a state of
violence that the mandatory powers themselves were forced to
bring the mandates to an end and grant independence to the
Arab peoples under their rule. But they did it only after much
haggling and ill-will, and in most cases after periods of repres-
sion that were not only fruitless, but provoked counter-measures.

1. Palestine, as subject to the British mandate, comprised the present Kingdom
of Jordan. Egypt was already a British protectorate. Saudi Arabia was ignored;
King Ibn Saud had not yet consolidated his state—and the rich oil deposits under
the sands of his immense deserts had not yet been discovered.

Today the Arab peoples are independent, at least in name; they are recognized as sovereign states, they are members of the United Nations, they send and receive diplomatic envoys. But their independence suffers from the congenital weakness inherent in their disunion and internal struggles. Had the Arabs been capable of overcoming their own idiosyncrasy by re-creating a great political unit, such as they created in the seventh century, their independence would be real and effective. But as long as this independence consists of the existence of several small states not only disunited (in spite of the Arab League) but engaged in the dangerous game of internal struggles and rivalries, they cannot prevent the Great Powers from trying, with all the means at their disposal, to interfere in Arab affairs, especially since the discovery of a considerable part of the world's oil reserves in the subsoil of Arabian territories. All this, combined with the circumstances in which they won their independence, the consciousness (or subconsciousness) of their congenital weakness, the feeling of being surrounded by threats and traps, has given the Arabs at once an inferiority complex and a persecution mania which make every attempt at intervention from abroad, even if inspired by the purest and most disinterested motives, a highly delicate diplomatic and psychological problem.

Against this background, it is not surprising that the creation of the State of Israel should have made so profound an impression on all the Arab peoples. In the first place, as I have said elsewhere, the Arabs regard Palestine as an Arab country and, judging by the historical and chronological criteria on which the titles of each nation to given regions of the earth's surface are based, it seems clear that this claim is justified. In the second place, they are convinced that what they regard as an unjustifiable attack on their territorial patrimony has taken place at the instigation, and with the persistent complicity, of England and the United States. England has succeeded to a great extent, during the period of her mandate over Iraq and Palestine, and thanks to a policy of good administration sympathetic to the Arabs, in pacifying their initial anger and hostility. But the United States, regarded by the Arabs as not only the creator of the State of Israel, but as the leading partner in the enterprise which makes its existence possible and keeps open the road to its consolidation, continues to be the target of the most undisguised and uncompromising hostility and, what is worse, absolute and complete distrust.

To all this we must add the ferment of social reform that accompanies or closely follows every nationalist movement. The small minority which, thanks to a feudal economy, keeps in its hands the domination and government of the Arab communities, has mobilized the masses in order to give vigour and consistency to its national claims. But once the dike is breached that keeps the popular masses shut off from every manifestation of public life, it is impossible to prevent them from turning their attention from national claims to what affects and concerns them more directly—economic and social claims; all the more so as, in this case, the masses live in conditions of hardly imaginable poverty and neglect.*

From this economic and social point of view, the State of Israel, which forms a kind of Jewish incrustation on the Arab population of the Middle East, might have found an opening for winning the approval of the young and progressive Arab elements which realize the urgent need for radical reforms in the economic and social structure of their countries. It is hard to say whether the advantages, from this point of view, of having as a neighbor a state like Israel, modern and progressive in its economic and social conceptions and endowed with considerable resources and admirable technical, personal and material elements, can one day succeed in overcoming the profound emotional reaction caused by the establishment of the State of Israel in the Arab land of Palestine. But what can be said with certainty is that the more Israel orientates her policy towards a strengthening of her political and economic ties with the United States, the less likelihood there is of her being able to fulfill the rôle of instigator and guide in the great enterprise of the political, economic and social transformation of the Arab populations in the Middle East.

This transformation is on the march. The internal and external ferments which are going to maintain and, possibly, accelerate its rhythm during the next few years are too powerful for any foreign influence to entertain the hope of holding back its course. Within its vast sweep, the establishment of normal relations between the Arab countries and their new neighbor, the State of Israel, will find a place, as one of its component parts. In this great enterprise, East and West confront one another in Baghdad, in Damascus, in Cairo, in Jerusalem. Time will show

---

* Cf. First paragraph of Epilogue.

which of the powers have best understood how to harmonize their intervention with genuine and sincere respect for, and support of, the profound aspirations of the Arab peoples for complete national independence and a radical transformation of their economic and social organization.

Epilogue 1965

THIRTEEN YEARS have passed since I put the final touches to my book on Palestine. Nevertheless, the book is published now as it was then drafted, without making any changes or modifications in the text. This is perfectly explainable and natural if one bears in mind that, when I wrote it, nothing was further from my intention than the attempt to give the reader a comprehensive study of the exceedingly complex social, economic and political situation leading to the birth of the State of Israel. The book's purpose is much more modest and consists of setting down a record of the author's personal experiences during the four years in which he had the privilege of collaborating on various United Nations activities relating to the Palestine question. That is, in reality, it is a book of an historical nature; its sole merit consists in bearing direct and personal witness to much of what happened in Palestine, or related thereto, during this four-year period between February 1948 and March 1952. In reality, there would be no sense in revising the text in order to "bring it up to date."

On the other hand, while it is true that during the past thirteen years events of greatest importance have taken place in the Middle East which in many aspects have changed profoundly and substantially the social, economic and political situation of the Arab states, and to a lesser degree that of the State of Israel, it is also true that these changes have left intact, at least basically, the conflict which the State of Israel, since its creation, represents to the Arab world.

Of the six Arab states, three (Egypt, Syria and Iraq) have experienced changes so profound in their political, social and economic structure as well as in their general politics that they could well be considered revolutionary; in the other three (Lebanon, Jordan and Saudi Arabia) as well as in Israel the changes, though not as radical as those experienced in Egypt or in Iraq, are no less substantial and profound. It would be vain, for example, to close one's eyes to the difference which separates the Israel of Weizmann, Ben Gurion and Shertok, which had to struggle daily for its existence, from that of present-day Israel.

Now then, throughout these changes and transformations, there is one thing that has remained unalterable: the relationship between the Arab states and the State of Israel. Today, as they did fifteen years ago, the Arab states keep ignoring the existence of the State of Israel and, as a consequence, refusing to maintain any kind of relations with it. And, for its part, Israel, although well disposed toward negotiating with the Arab states, still refuses to accept the return of the Arab refugees to their homes— a preliminary condition imposed by the Arab states for establishing any kind of relations with it.

Nevertheless, I believe it timely to submit a few brief suggestions concerning the recent evolution and present situation as related to three fundamental aspects which the so-called Palestine question raises: supervision of the armistice and borders, normalization of relations between the Arab states and Israel and, finally, everything pertaining to the Arab refugee situation.

The system set up by the armistice for supervising the borders has been operating regularly and effectively. And in this respect there is worth pointing out an innovation of great significance, not only on the local level of Palestine but in the character of United Nations intervention in general in cases of armed conflict. I am referring to the establishment of a neutral zone between the demarcation lines of Egypt and Israel, in the Gaza region, and its occupation by an international force recruited, commanded and maintained by the United Nations ("blue helmets").

The origin of this important innovation is found, as everyone knows, in the deplorable episode of the Franco-English invasion of the Suez Canal zone, as a consequence of its nationalization by the Egyptian government, and followed up with an advance by the Israeli army in the Negev. Energetic diplomatic intervention by the United States and the Soviet Union, together with United Nations action, ended this senseless adventure within a short time, and among the means employed for this purpose was the sending of a United Nations military force to be stationed between the rival armies. Since that time this force has been occupying a neutral zone established between the Egyptian and Israeli lines in the Gaza region.[1]

1. See, above all, the extensive report and study submitted by the Secretary General to the 1958 Assembly (A/3899 and A/3943).

As was foreseen, the experience of the past thirteen years since the Conciliation Commission's headquarters were moved from Jerusalem to New York[2] has confirmed that in practice its strictly political activities have been interrupted, and the Commission, in its own words, "has continued to direct its efforts to the solution of concrete problems which might be of direct interest to a great number of refugees and to which progress could be made independently of the readiness of the parties to reach over-all agreements."[3]

It was evident that the political activity of conciliation, leading toward a normalization of relations between the Arab states and the State of Israel, needed the Commission's presence in the area. Only in Jerusalem, and through direct and uninterrupted contacts of an official as well as a personal character with the governments concerned, could this mission of real and authentic mediation be carried out, which the Assembly assigned to the Conciliation Commission in its resolution of December 14, 1948.

It was thus understood not only by the Assembly itself but by Count Bernadotte, whose last report as United Nations Mediator in Palestine served as a basis for the above resolution when Jerusalem was expressly named as the official headquarters of the Conciliation Commission. As a consequence, the confession of the inability to carry out this mission and the decision to devote itself to the question of the Arab refugees, contained in the Commission's report to the 1958 Assembly, could not have come as a surprise to anyone.[4]

But this abandonment of its own political activities had, as was expected, a very unfavorable repercussion on this same Arab

2. See pp. 178-9.

3. See its report to the 1958 Assembly (A/3835).

4. The truth is that since the Conciliation Commission's headquarters were moved to New York the conciliation work proper has remained as fragmentary and sporadic as the negotiations imply, rather than providing the means for improving the situation of the refugees and the frequent border incidents between Israel and its Arab neighbors. And in this regard it is necessary to mention the valuable and commendable work being quietly carried out by Mr. Henri Vigier as political advisor to the various generals who, during this period, have held the office of United Nations Chief of Staff in Palestine. It is as difficult to calculate the progress which would have been made in normalizing relations between the Arab states and the State of Israel if the Conciliation Commission had still been operating in Jerusalem as it would be to imagine its deterioration had the organization for supervising the armistice and borders not been able to count on the exceptionally valuable collaboration of Mr. Vigier.

refugee question toward which the Commission had decided to direct its efforts.

And concerning this extreme, that is, concerning the interdependence between progress in normalizing relations between the Arab states and the State of Israel on the one hand and progress in solving the concrete problems relative to the refugees on the other, we may rely upon an opinion of exceptional authority which must be mentioned here. In fact, in the summer of 1961 the Conciliation Commission had the excellent idea of naming the present President of the Carnegie Endowment for International Peace, Mr. Joseph E. Johnson, as its special representative "to undertake a visit to the Middle East to explore with the host governments and with Israel practical means to seeking progress on the Palestine Arab refugee problem, pursuant to resolution 1604 (XV) of the United Nations Assembly." After his visit, which took place in September, 1961, Mr. Johnson submitted to the Commission an extensive report which, in my opinion, is one of the most valuable documents yet written on the Palestine question.[5]

In his conclusions appear the two following paragraphs, which deserve special attention:

52) It is clear that as matters now stand there is no prospect of an early resolution of the Palestine question as a whole and, as can be seen from the precedents [sic] sections, there are many indications that no progress can be made on the Palestine Arab refugee question apart from, or in advance of, an over-all settlement.

53) However, the willingness that the parties expressed to me to consider the possibility of a step-by-step process without prejudice (to) the position on the other related questions leads me to believe that it is worth while continuing the effort that the Commission has now begun. Whether progress will be possible no one can now say for certain, but, to state the matter in the most negative way, the signs that progress is impossible are not so conclusive as to justify a decision not to try.

Regarding that which refers particularly to the question of the Arab refugees, and aside from the results obtained by the United Nations Works and Relief Agency (UNWRA) as related above all to their living conditions, I believe that what is of major interest is the realization of a program for identifying and evaluating the real property abandoned by the refugees in ter-

5. Doc. A/4921 / Add. 1.

ritory which presently forms part of Israel and the freeing of their accounts in banks located in this same territory. Prior to the transfer of its headquarters from Jerusalem to New York, the Conciliation Commission, through its Refugee Office,[6] had already carried out studies on these two items (on the first in particular). Annex A of its report to the 1951-52 Assembly, which met in Paris, is an extensive document prepared by its Refugee Office, setting forth the status of its work in this respect.[7]

Since being moved to New York the Conciliation Commission has reexamined this concrete matter not by means of its Refugee Office, which was disestablished when the Commission's headquarters were transferred to New York, but through a new agency whose special task was the identification and evaluation of real property abandoned by the refugees. In its report No. 22 (relative to the period from September 1963 to April 1964) the Commission could announce that this task had been completed.[8] In fact, as an annex to this report there appears a working paper prepared by the Commission's expert on real property questions in which the method used for identifying property and the techniques employed in the evaluation thereof are set forth.[9] According to this document, the essential difference between the way property was evaluated by the Refugee Office in 1951 and the technique used by the Commission's expert in 1964 is that the first study tried to obtain "a broad estimate of over-all value based on the knowledge of the existing use of broad categories of land," while in 1964 the second one "led in terms of a consistent method, to an opinion of value of each individual parcel having regard to its individual market value on 29 November 1947." It should be noted that this document is limited to an explanation of the methods and techniques used and does not contain any evaluation figures.

One last observation à propos of this activity of the Concilia-

6. See p. 272.

7. Doc. A/1985, Annex A. In this document appear the following evaluations of real property abandoned in Israel by the Arab refugees:

Rural Lands .... £69,500,000 Sterling
Urban Lands .... 21,600,000 "
Jerusalem .... 9,250,000 "

8. Doc. A/5700. This document should have been examined by the 1964 Assembly, but, as is known and for reasons that need not be specified here, the Assembly found it impossible to examine, discuss or agree on matters whose prior unanimity could not be counted on.

9. A/AC. 25/W.84.

tion Commission regarding the Arab refugees. In its resolutions of the past few years the Assembly, at the same time as it approves the Commission's course of action in concentrating its attention in a practical way on the identification and evaluation of the refugees' real estate and the freeing of their accounts, urges the Commission to continue its efforts toward solving the refugee problem in accordance with Paragraph 11 of the Assembly's third resolution adopted December 14, 1948. Now then, in this paragraph the Assembly confers on the Conciliation Commission the threefold task regarding the refugees, namely: their repatriation, their resettlement and economic and social rehabilitation and, finally, payment of compensation. For my part, I believe it would be a matter for congratulation if this attitude of the Assembly could be interpreted as meaning that the United Nations has abandoned repatriation, if not explicitly at least implicitly, as one means of solving the Arab refugee problem, confining itself to achieving their resettlement and economic and social rehabilitation and, above all, the payment of compensation—two reasonable and viable means comprising part of the total plan for reintegrating the refugees into the Arab countries, the only road which can lead to a complete and definitive settlement of this deplorable matter which, after fifteen years, has become one of the principal obstacles to arriving at a solution to the Palestine problem.

One must say, without cavil, by judging the results of the discussion of the Palestine Question in the General Assembly of the UN in its 1965 session, that progress toward solution of the Arab refugee problem has been as dilatory as that concerning conciliation between the Arab states and Israel. In fact, after a long and sterile discussion in the Special Political Commitee, all that the Assembly was able to do was to prolong the mandate of UNRWA until June 1969; not without having noted "with regret that repatriation or compensation of the refugees has not been effected, that no substantial progress has been made in the program for the reintegration of refugees either by repatriation or resettlement" and once more "called upon the United Nations Conciliation Commission to intensify its efforts for the implementation of par. 11 of the Resolution 194 (III) and to report thereon as appropriate and not later than October 1966."[10]

Geneva, December 1965

10. Resolution 2053 (xx), adopted by the 20th Regular Session of the Assembly, December 15, 1965.

Dave BURRELL CSC
TANTUR. Israel